MW00803614

INFINITE
DREAMS

INFINITE DREAMS

THE LIFE OF ALAN VEGA

Laura Davis-Chanin
and Liz Lamere

Foreword by Bruce Springsteen

Backbeat
Books

ESSEX, CONNECTICUT

Backbeat Books

An imprint of Globe Pequot, the trade division of
The Rowman & Littlefield Publishing Group, Inc.
4501 Forbes Blvd., Ste. 200
Lanham, MD 20706
www.rowman.com

Distributed by NATIONAL BOOK NETWORK

British Library Cataloguing in Publication Information available.

Library of Congress Cataloging-in-Publication Data

Names: Davis-Chanin, Laura, author. | Lamere, Liz, author.
Title: Infinite Dreams : the life of Alan Vega / Laura Davis-Chanin and Liz Lamere.
Description: Essex, Connecticut : Backbeat, 2024. | Includes bibliographical references and index.
Identifiers: LCCN 2023050224 (print) | LCCN 2023050225 (ebook) | ISBN 9781493072484 (cloth) | ISBN 9781493072491 (epub)
Subjects: LCSH: Vega, Alan, 1938-2016. | Singers—United States—Biography. | Punk rock musicians—United States—Biography. | LCGFT: Biographies.
Classification: LCC ML420.V3254 D38 2024 (print) | LCC ML420.V3254 (ebook) | DDC 782.42166092 [B]--dc23/eng/20231101
LC record available at https://lccn.loc.gov/2023050224
LC ebook record available at https://lccn.loc.gov/2023050225

Dedicated to All the Frankies

There was simply no one else remotely like him.
—Bruce Springsteen

CONTENTS

PART THREE: ". . . [THE] ELEGANCE OF HE WHO DEFINITIVELY
EMBODIED THE FLIPSIDE OF ROCK 'N' ROLL"

FOREWORD

ALAN AND I WERE IN THE SAME STUDIO—the Hit Factory. He was there working with Ric Ocasek. Alan was coming from the outside but I'd heard of his group and I'd heard some of their music and it entranced me—his courage and his aesthetic was something that deeply appealed to me. He was just incredible. So that was kind of when we actually met and struck up a small conversation.

His level of integrity and the way he approached his work was inspiring—quite inspiring. And that's the way I always found him to be, and he was also very sweet—in the time that we spent, he was always a sweetheart of a guy. Of course, I loved his music and did that recut of "Dream Baby Dream," which people really loved. It's the classic American hymn. It's just really beautiful. And I had an idea that if Roy Orbison had lived, this was a song he should have cut. So, my own approach to performing the song was if Roy Orbison had sung this song, he would sing it something like this.

And "Frankie Teardrop"—that was incredible. That might be his greatest piece of work right there—certainly his scariest. It had a terror-filled ambience that people weren't expressing in rock music at the time, and it was totally unique. The sound of his voice was: "Whoa, this is—!" It was something I really related to. And definitely inspired the way I wrote "State Trooper" and a few other things on *Nebraska*. Very, very influential.

I liked the idea that he approached his work as mainstream. He would say, "Hey, why shouldn't everybody be getting this?" Well, it wasn't quite that and obviously if you get on the wrong bill, you're going to have a problem. I opened up for Chicago for thirteen shows and dodged Frisbees for a good part of it. But it was nothing like what Alan had to suffer. And I know that he and Marty really went through a lot and it took real courage; they were brave. In the end though, Alan will last forever . . . his music will be here forever.

—Bruce Springsteen
2023

PREFACE

I KNEW ALAN VEGA WAS A UNIQUE, REMARKABLE, ABERRANT, and often shocking presence onstage. I was very aware of him because my band, the Student Teachers, opened for Suicide several times in the late '70s. I was but an unseasoned, youthful fifteen-year-old drummer at the time and my first memory of seeing Suicide was—"Are you kidding me? This isn't rock 'n' roll!"

How wrong—and right—I was. Of course, youth is a keen deceiver.

During the writing of this book, I learned about a man who struggled with many demons—the Vietnam War, the oppression of the disenfranchised, the confusion with his born religion—many issues. He weathered life in fierce and volcanic tones and wrote, performed, and sculpted this experience.

And he needed to share all of it. It was important. We are enriched when we are shown the threads of darkness in our world—it inspires us to create more light.

He disclosed to us what we needed to know to become better human beings.

I am honored to have had the opportunity to write this book and learn about the man I sciously misunderstood. Alan has taught me so much and I am very grateful.

And I thank my agent Lee Sobel for arranging this project for me and introducing me to a remarkable woman—Alan's wife, Liz Lamere, who made Alan's life so grand, so special, so complete with love.

We are all Frankies.

—Laura Davis-Chanin

WRITING ABOUT THE LIFE OF ALAN VEGA is akin to capturing lightning in a bottle. One of my dreams is that this book conveys Vega's electric energy to fuel inspiration. Inspiring others was likely one of his greatest achievements. My hope is that this biography will give a deeper understanding of a human being who was often misunderstood and never wavered in his commitment to pure artistry: fearlessly seeking new ground. Alan Vega lived his life through the lens of creation: tapping into the full spectrum of human emotion, deeply exploring the human condition and the duality of beauty and despair while never losing sight of hope. Many have heard the legends of the intense stage persona; far fewer have a deeper knowledge of the full spectrum of creative pursuits and sphere of influence of the man himself.

I'm filled with gratitude for the thirty-one years we had together, the invaluable creative lessons and unconditional love and truth imparted from one of the most genuinely sincere, authentic, empathetic, and loving persons to walk this planet.

Writing Alan's biography wasn't something I had planned to do. It was sure to be a daunting experience and I thank literary agent Lee Sobel for knowing it needed to be written, setting the challenge, and connecting me with my steadfast and wonderfully creative cowriter Laura Davis-Chanin. She couldn't have anticipated what a complex trip it would be and took the ride with abandon.

I'm humbled by the generosity of spirit and sentiment of those whose interviews and quotes about Alan are contained herein and of the great photographers who contributed their amazing images. This was truly a mission of love. To all of you and everyone who seeks to discover more about Alan Vega, I'm deeply grateful.

Special thanks to Toots Melgard, Dante Vega Lamere, Amie, Beth, Sue and Mariette Bermowitz, Dr. Marty Levitt, Mel Auston, Ric Ocasek, Peter Crowley, Marty Thau, Perkin Barnes, Howard Thompson, Kevin Patrick, Michael Zilkha, Roy Trakin, Hegg, Michael Alago, Kate Hyman, Claire O'Connor, Henry Rollins, Larry Hardy, Caleb Braaten, Paul Smith, Susan Stenger, Jesse Malin, Bruce Springsteen, Billy Idol, Phil Hawk, Kid Congo Powers, Elvis Costello, Ben Vaughn, Mika Vainio and Ilpo Väisänen, Mark Kuchinsky, James Murphy, Gregg Foreman, Bob Gruen, Ivan Karp, Barbara Gladstone, Jeffrey Deitch, Mathieu Copeland, Thierry Raspail, Laurent Godin, Ben Tischer, Marc Hurtado, Lydia Lunch, Marie Losier, Jared Artaud, Michael Handis, Martin Rev, and every human being who touched Alan's life and whose life Alan touched. Love forever!

—Liz Lamere

PART ONE

"MEMORIES ARE NOISE"*

---

* Alan Vega Notebook, courtesy of Saturn Strip, Ltd.

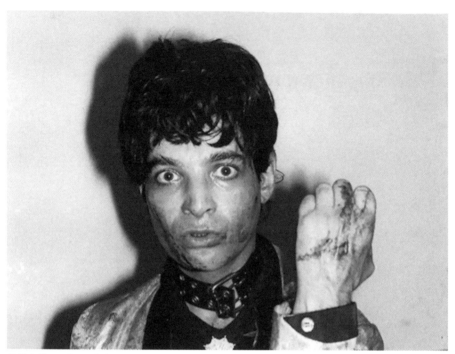

1 America Is Killin' Its Youth*

1969

> Hey, Hey LBJ, How many kids did you kill today?[†]
> —Protest Chant, 1967

New Year's Eve
#6 Subway

The graffiti sang. He sat in the weaving and banging subway car, bouncing back and forth to its commands. As the tunnel sped by, he stared at the blood-orange, savage-red screams laced across the train walls: "CoCo 144," "Hurt 168," "Kill," "Stank." Pure art, he thought to himself. The entire subway car was ablaze with them. New York subways in the seventies were steel canvases pleading for a voice.

The torment of the spray-painted words dragged him inside their agony. He had ridden this train from home in Ocean Parkway to the Bowery in Lower Manhattan every weekend for the last year. But this was the first time he was so deeply pulled into that world unfolding around him.

It was 1969 and thirty-one-year old Alan Bermowitz was seeing life differently. He squeezed the suitcase between his thighs.

---

* "Ghost Rider" by Alan Vega and Martin Rev.
† See https://www.cfr.org/blog/vietnam-war-forty-quotes.

I have to walk down to the river . . . a steady, flowing, crawling
and impulsive surge, a welling flood that would come on
forever and knew no limit to the invasion of its power.*
—Alan

One Week Earlier

Dancing Bensonhurst holiday lights swarmed around them as Mariette and Alan walked slowly down Nineteenth Avenue. Holiday shadows blinked and flickered in the brick building windows as the season slowly shifted to a close. The season had ended for Alan and Mariette two weeks ago when she lit the last candle on the menorah. Mariette had been alone at that moment. Alan wasn't there. He hadn't been home much for a long time.

They reached the corner of Nineteenth Avenue and Eighty-Fourth Street and crossed over approaching Alan's parent's building. A short time after he was born in 1938, the family lived on the Lower East Side of Manhattan, until they moved here—to Bensonhurst. They settled into a small, one-bedroom apartment where Alan followed and adored his mother—Tillie—and where he spent years meeting up with his cousins to play baseball and wager on the Dodgers. It was also where he and his brother Robbie laughed and wrestled on the living room floor—and where he needed to walk away from—forever.

Mariette watched as Alan opened the lobby door. Petite, with tender, curled brown hair, tight caramel eyes, and a distinct European presence, Mariette's world had become stained inside a damaged reality with her husband of nine years. She didn't recognize him anymore.

He had let his hair grow and was wearing tormented black clothes. He was burning plastics and piling junk up every day in the apartment for his artwork, then recording unrecognizable, agonizing sounds, vibrations, and echoes every night.

***

"What's happened to you?"

"What are you talking about, Pop?"

Alan took a deep swallow of Chablis and lit an unfiltered Lucky Strike at the looming oak table in his parents' dining room. It was Friday night. Dinner with the parents. The Brooklyn Dodgers could be heard on the RCA TV in the next room.

"Look at you . . . you're a disgrace."

Louis rubbed his head as he finished his coffee.

Not that tall, but with rich, wavy black hair and a striking Cary Grant demeanor, Louis had worked tirelessly that day—like every day. He was fatigued and stressed. Dealing with his son was the last thing he had energy for, but Tillie

---

* Letter from Alan Bermowitz to Mariette Bermowitz, 1961.

had begged him and his culture, his tradition, the times—all dictated his son should stop acting crazy and go to graduate school.

"You had it, son. You were in astrophysics at Brooklyn college. You had it," Louis groaned, and turned his chair away.

Alan got up and walked around to his father. The ladies had cleaned off the Friday night fare and disappeared into the kitchen for girl-chat. Despite the screaming baseball-crazed fans from the living room, Louis was unmoved.

"Why have you grown your hair like that?" he posed, staring at his son. "And why do you dress like a depraved demon?" Louis didn't blink.

Alan stabbed an uncompromising look back at his father then turned and walked out of the house.

Louis shook his head. He called after him, "Look at your brother! He's a meteorologist—and your cousin, he's a dentist!"

2 Days Later

Mariette had come home early. She was worn out. It had been a trying day. Teaching French was usually more than fulfilling but lately her students had become apathetic—being high school seniors, they had the more pressing demand of New Year's Eve parties on their minds.

When she opened the front door of the narrow Ocean Parkway apartment she shared with Alan, where there was a small bedroom, a cornered kitchen, and small bits of sunlight slipping through the living room window, she found Alan sitting with one of his new friends. He was someone she didn't really know and felt uncomfortable around. They were recording sounds on Alan's Revox tape recorder. Unusual sounds. Abnormal sounds. She'd heard them before. They bothered her.

Alan barely noticed her standing there.

Over the last year, Alan had become obsessed with creating music. But he wasn't a musician or a songwriter or a singer. He was an artist—or that's what Mariette thought—a painter, a sketch artist. That's the degree he graduated with from Brooklyn college—Art.

A few months back, he had his first gallery show in Park Slope—even though Mariette was the only one to purchase any of his work.

Which she never told him.

She looked at Alan and his friend quizzically. Alan closed his eyes to the reverberating echoes of distortions and disfiguring sounds. He looked at peace to her. She realized they were living on planets far from one another.

***

And then there was Vietnam.

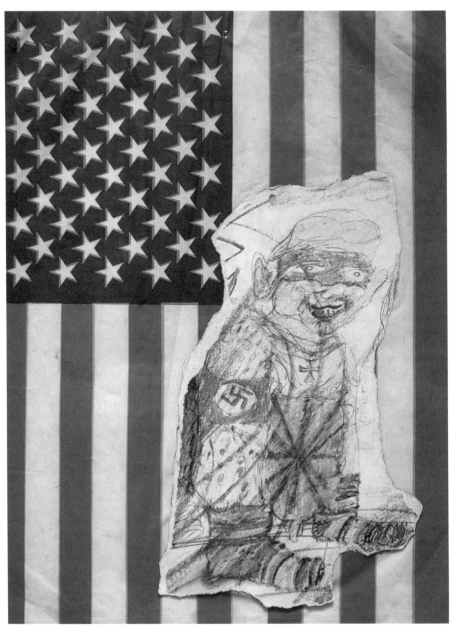

"Untitled," 1969. *Photo by Mel Auston*

Alan's disenchantment with his old job, his outrage at the local New York city government, and America's never-ending murder of young men in Southeast Asia—was only the beginning. The war, the oppression of the poor, the lack of care for the common man—were causing a torrent of fury within him. He had become obsessed with the "splintering of America's soul."*

Something had changed.

> I so wanted truth, whatever the truth meant to me.†
> —Alan

Mariette watched Alan and his friend as the sounds howled. After a moment, she turned away and went into the bedroom to change and take a shower.

1976

The lights dim. A pulsing, oscillating noise drones. A single spotlight focuses on Alan as he stares out at the audience. The sound gets louder and louder. The electronic tones are asynchronous, unusual, brutal. The audience is confused. Where's the drummer? Where's the guitar?

The modulating synth textures carry on as Alan oscillates between soft groans and clipped shrieks. He stares at the audience—delivering his lyrics with an intensity the audience finds menacing. They boo and chant their loathing. Alan's eyes spear back harder with his pounding incantations. They scream at him to get off the stage. He balks. He bangs the mic stand on the stage, then he strikes himself with the mic—hitting his leg, his chest, his face. The sounds from Martin Rev's synthesizer rip across the club. Alan chants:

> Hey, baby, baby, baby, he's a-screamin' the truth
> America, America is killin' its youth
> America, America is killin' its youth‡

The crowd's angst blows up. Alan pulls out a bicycle chain and thrashes it around the stage, above his head—swooning in staccato starts:

> America, America is killin' its youth!
> Hey, baby, baby, baby!§

---

* Mariette Bermowitz, *Mindele's Journey: Memoir of a Hidden Child of the Holocaust* (self-pub., CreateSpace, 2012), 209, Kindle.
† Paul Tschinkel, Inner-Tube Video LLC.
‡ "Ghost Rider" by Alan Vega and Martin Rev, *Suicide*, 1977.
§ Ibid.

"Get off the stage!" the crowd howls.

Alan hits himself with the chain. He barks as he slams it. The audience's boo-ing deafens the club. He whacks it into his leg—and his chest, then tightens it around his waist—clenching, straining. He pulls harder. The distorted wall of tremolo from Marty's amplified keyboard and drum machine goes on and on . . . and on. . . .

1969

New Year's Eve

The subway pushed to a heaving halt. The wheels grated against the rails. Passengers fell to the side of their seats as the car came to a full stop. The train doors quickly opened. Alan looked at the exit. He stood up, grabbed his suitcase, went out and up the stairs to the street.

As he emerged from the subway station, the New Year's Eve moon shone stark into his eyes. He looked around him.

His heart pounded. He peered across the broken Lower East Side streets laden with polluted garbage, black potholes, and the homeless coiled on every street corner. He remembered what he had told Mariette once: "This is going to be the story of my life. I will be a failure."*

He shook himself and lit a cigarette. That was a long time ago, he thought. He didn't feel like that anymore. He picked up his suitcase and marched ahead—as a profound smile unfurled across his face.

> I made the biggest trip of all . . . Brooklyn to Manhattan.
> It's . . . a longer trip than going from Manhattan to Europe.
> It's not about miles.
> It's about mentality.†
> —Alan

---

* Letter from Alan Bermowitz to Mariette Bermowitz, 1961.
† Paul Tschinkel, Inner-Tube Video LLC.

2 The Candy Store

THIRTY-ONE YEARS EARLIER

> I got all my boyhood in vanilla winter waves around the kitchen stove.*
> —Jack Kerouac

On June 23, 1938, Alan Vega was born. And that was a secret he held onto close to the day he died.

His birth name was Alan Bermowitz. The name Bermowitz was a distortion of his family's true name, "Bednowitz." In 1918, when his father and his grandparents arrived at Ellis Island, Isadore Bednowitz was instructed by the immigration officials to make his "name more American."†

Alan was the first child of Tillie and Louis Bermowitz.

Tillie was born in New York in 1912 and Louis had immigrated with his family from Poland when he was seven years old.

They were both raised in the cold, broken world of poverty and overcrowding in the dusky, beaten-down shades of Manhattan's Lower East Side. Thousands of German, Italian, and Jewish immigrants built their futures there as they escaped the despots destroying their home worlds. Crammed with 400,000 hardworking, determined settlers with horse-drawn wagons, dripping clothes hanging from every window and fire escape, cracked cobbled streets and endless boxes of stored-up food, the Lower East Side in the 1920s was the beginning of a new life for millions.

As it was for Louis Bermowitz and Tillie Lipstein.

---

* Jack Kerouac, *Doctor Sax* (New York: Grove Press, 1987), Book I, 19.
† Mathieu Copeland, *Alan Suicide Vega, Infinite Mercy* (Museé d'art Contemporain de Lyon, 2009), 43.

Alan with his mother, Tillie, 1941. *Courtesy Jack and Riva Levitt Estate*

Alan with his father, Louis, 1941. *Courtesy Jack and Riva Levitt Estate*

Louis grew up with his family amid those bustling streets. His father, Isadore, worked as a presser of men's apparel in a local tailor shop and Bertha, his mother, stayed home.

As he grew, Louis became strikingly handsome—dark hair with a finely proportioned face and pin-sharp black eyes. He was raised to become a diamond setter. He ended up working fifty hours a week on Canal Street at "Seltzer and Bermowitz" and was a rising success in the dense Orthodox Jewish diamond-cutting district. Every day, he hurried to work on the subway to Canal Street in Manhattan, where he sawed, blocked, bruted, and polished the rocks in his care with precision and tenacity. Louis loved his work.

But not more than he loved his nightly poker game. Playing cards at the local club with mafia dons and their lieutenants gave Louis immeasurable satisfaction—nearly existential legitimacy. After marrying Tillie, his obsession with his cards found him out of the house constantly—withdrawn from her and the family—every night after work.

Tillie Lipstein's mother, Fannie, and her father, Isadore, arrived in the city from Russia in 1906.

They ran a news and candy stand on Henry Street and lived in a cramped one-bedroom basement apartment just behind it.

Tillie and her four sisters and brother matured, assimilated, and blossomed in that basement apartment. They were raised Orthodox Jews and often had to shower at the Educational Alliance down the street.

Alan's Grandparents—Isadore and Fannie Lipstein, 1906. *Courtesy Sue Bermowitz*

Sadly, Fannie's husband, Isadore, died not long after their son, Charles, was born in 1918. Fannie was left to raise their six children by herself. Her own family would be entirely exterminated in the Holocaust—a bitter reality well known to everyone—but which no one was allowed to bring up—ever.

Fannie ran the news/candy stand on bustling Henry Street with the help of her daughters, and she was known locally for creating the finest egg creams in the city.

Though most of the girls went to high school, the educational focus was more on her son, Charles. The girls were needed to work. They attended high school but no further.

When Tillie was on the job, she made sure to read the newspapers—absorb it all, learn and understand everything. In late 1929, the *New York Daily News* headline splayed across Fannie's newsstand screamed: "WALL STREET PANIC." Tillie read it with confused seventeen-year-old concern while she stirred the egg creams.

The world was becoming a darker, more backbreaking, undependable place. Tillie wanted to make the days better and between egg creams and newspapers, she attended Seward Park High school and became a bookkeeper. She had worked briefly in that position when she met Louis Bermowitz in the early 1930s.

They married in 1934.

Louis and Tillie. *Courtesy Sue Bermowitz*

They lived in Fannie's apartment as husband and wife and Tillie kept up her job as a bookkeeper. Everything seemed to be going well until one day when Louis sat her down and told her the working had to stop.

"No wife of mine," he insisted.

His traditional values dictated he should be the sole breadwinner. But Tillie couldn't bear the thought of not working, of not calculating, of not using her mind.

Meanwhile, the stress of the tiny apartment they were living in with Tillie's family and the exploding number of people on the Lower East Side was becoming impossible to manage. After years of suffering under the weight of oppressive overpopulation, rampant destitution, and struggles between ethnic groups, the neighborhood became warehouses of exhaustion and despair. Residents tried to live productive lives as crushed sardines inside a tin can.

While the decade moved on, Tillie and Louis decided, as many Jewish families did then, to move to Brooklyn. Added to their concern for a better life was the recent birth of their first child—Alan.

They found a one-bedroom apartment at 1901 Eighty-Fourth Street in Bensonhurst, Brooklyn.

Alan slept in the bedroom with his parents. Tillie worked endlessly to make the apartment a warm, comforting home. She was highly energetic and a near perfectionist. While Louis was at work, she cleaned the house from top to bottom at least three times daily, punctuated by endless vacuuming.

Alan was wildly curious, digging into everything around him, yet never completely satiated—always searching. It found Tillie on edge—adoring him but balancing her perplexity as to how to measure up and be everything her son needed. And his father, Louis—work and the world behind it kept him emotionally distant.

Alan, two years old. *Courtesy Jack and Riva Levitt Estate*

Tillie with Alan in front of the Newsstand, Henry Street, 1940. *Courtesy Jack and Riva Levitt Estate*

Alan, Robbie, and their father, 1942.
Courtesy Estate of Tillie Bermowitz

In January 1941, Tillie gave birth to her second son, Robert. Alan now had a brother, and he was thrilled. The boys shared the bedroom while Louis and Tillie slept on the sofa bed in the living room.

Money was tight. Tillie suspected it was because Louis gambled any minor excess which could be used for their home or the boys—at his nightly poker game. That may have been true. But Louis still didn't want Tillie to work. So, she vacuumed and vacuumed and vacuumed. . . .

As Alan grew, more of his extended family joined them in Bensonhurst.

His grandmother, Fannie, moved in with her daughter, Riva Levitt, and her sons on Nineteenth Avenue—only a

Alan and Marty, 1940. *Courtesy Jack and Riva Levitt Estate*

Alan and his Aunt Becky, 1941. *Courtesy Jack and Riva Levitt Estate*

Robbie and Alan, Catskills, 1947. *Courtesy Sue Bermowitz*

few blocks away. She lived there until she died in 1959. Tillie's other sisters, Sarah Hilsenroth and Anna Krause, moved nearby with their families as well. Her sister, Rose Halpern, moved to Prospect Park and her brother, Charlie, moved upstate. Despite his distance, Uncle Charlie was very close with the family. During WWII Charlie served as an intelligence officer translating German. Alan adored him.

It was a widening, a deepening of the apartment on Henry Street stretching its arms out around the city—more than in name, more than in history—but by a physical connection within the world—and as a fortress against it.

The family went to the Catskills during the summer months and Louis dropped them off at the Borscht Belt haven, then turned around and went back to Brooklyn. Yet, he would return on the weekends for family time and film the boys playing with their cousins and their moms chatting happily nearby. This reality was fine with Louis—there and not there. Like many fathers of his generation, he was somewhere else the majority of the time.

***

The cousins—Alan, Robbie, Marty, Herb, Carl, Irvin, Miltie, and Irving—essentially grew up together.

When they started attending grade school, they walked to school together every day. Alan and Robbie went to PS 200 and their cousins went to PS 128.

Alan didn't feel super comfortable getting to know other kids. He was very shy. He mostly hung out and cavorted with his brother and his cousins.

Of greatest importance was his passion for sports. And he shared this spirited obsession with them—basketball, football, and—of highest priority—baseball. Baseball ruled his thoughts and his fantasies—and the Brooklyn Dodgers were his holy grail.

Three of Alan's cousins and his Uncle Sam. From left: Sam, Miltie, Alan, Irvin, and Marty, 1940. *Courtesy Jack and Riva Levitt Estate*

Alan playing stickball, 1947. *Author's collection*

He played stickball in the street constantly.

When Alan was older and "Bensonhurst Park" opened with a baseball field and a basketball court, he raced over there with his cousins to realize his dreams.

***

The sun is lowering over the Bensonhurst Park baseball field and the air is crisping up. Alan, his brother, Robbie, and his cousins, Marty, Miltie, and Carl are poised on the field.

Alan is at bat ready to hit it out of the park.

Carl winds up and pitches.

Alan's eyes are fiercely focused as he connects and the ball sails up and up and up . . . until . . .

"Foul!" Marty cries from the outfield.

Alan is completely thrown.

"That was not foul!" he shouts. "It was just inside the pole!"

Alan throws his bat over his shoulder and marches over to Miltie for what he saw.

"Did you see that? Was it a foul?" he asks him.

Miltie looks uneasily at the outfield fence. "I don't know," he shakes his head. "It was super close."

"No way! It was over there!" he says. He points inside the baseline, in fair territory. He marches back to the plate and prepares to hit again.

"Let's do it again!"

But Marty runs up and tosses his glove to Alan.

"I gotta get home. I'm supposed to help Grandma with the shopping." He jogs toward the park exit. Carl follows him, waving back to Alan. Robbie and Miltie head over to Alan, who is still waiting to hit.

"Let's go," Robbie suggests, grabbing Alan's bat and throwing it onto his shoulder.

"Thinking about it now, you know," says Miltie as they head home, "it was fair. The ball was fair." He pats Alan on the back. Alan tries to smile as they walk out of the park.

***

Alan's connection with the game was so dedicated that while he was in high school, he was scouted by the Philadelphia Phillies. However, one day when he was playing stickball and running to catch a fly ball, he smashed into a parked car and suffered an injury—a damaged shoulder joint. As such, the scouting went nowhere.

But it was not a loss. Playing the game, knowing everything about it, fed him on a daily basis. He became a tower of information—tracking everything about all the teams, especially the Brooklyn Dodgers, and eventually the Mets—their

Tillie cooking dinner. *Courtesy Jack and Riva Levitt Estate*

lineups, their stats, following each and every player's background and prospects—it fueled his fascination.

Despite the reality of very little money and living in a minimally sized apartment with his parents sleeping in the living room, Alan had little sense of deprivation. Tillie was very dedicated to making life for her family comfortable, clean, and enjoyable. She never conveyed a sense of lacking or of being in need.

Between racing to the neighborhood baseball field with his cousins after school, then heading home for an afternoon snack with his mom, Alan had the good life. It was all there in Brooklyn for him.

However, despite his passion for sports and everything energetic and dynamic, Alan was often ill when he was a child and found himself at home a lot. He spent those lost days in bed reading about WWII and drawing.

He loved sketching out his favorite comic characters:

He also sketched famous figures who he was learning about in school, such as President John Adams.

Drawing was an existential release, which he wasn't quite aware of as a child but which he realized as he grew up.

> With drawing . . . I'll sit down, out of my mind and at peace.*
>
> —Alan

---

* Mathieu Copeland, *Alan Suicide Vega, Infinite Mercy* (Museé d'art Contemporain de Lyon, 2009), 43.

Bugs Bunny, 1948. *Photo by Mel Auston*

Porky Pig, 1948. *Photo by Mel Auston*

He also read obsessively about the Nazis, their patterns, their loyalties, the blindness within their cruelty. The Third Reich's brutalization of the world and the horror of their savagery pulled him in deep.

There was a project assigned in Alan's sixth-grade class where each student was to research, write, and draw illustrations of different countries in Europe. Two of the countries Alan focused on were Albania and Norway. He wrote up a short essay about them and made note of the "war" pictures he had seen of the country.

He signed it off noting the amount of time between his birth and the start of WWII:

John Adams, 1948. *Photo by Mel Auston*

> I was born on June 23, 1938,
> one year before WWII. Right now I attend PS 200.*
> —Alan

---

* Ibid.

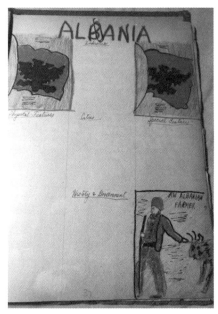 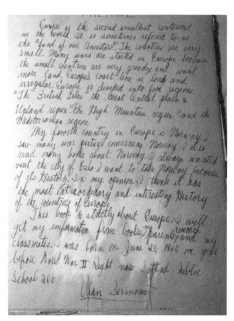

Sixth-grade essay—Albania, 1949. *Courtesy Mariette Bermowitz*

Even at a young age, Alan connected himself intrinsically with war. The aching humanitarian conflict inherent in it existed somewhere inside him. His tethering of his birth date to the birth of WWII presaged the future internal outrage he experienced at the realities inside the Vietnam War in the '70s—which ripped him up. In many important ways, war fueled portions of the art he created due to the emotions it hammered within him.

War was his muse.

> The Nazis, it was the uniforms, the atrocities,
> the concentration camps.
> It was partly fascination, partly horror.*
> —Alan

***

Bensonhurst had become a sanctuary for Jewish families in the beginning of the nineteenth century and as time moved on, more and more Italians also settled in Bensonhurst. Many of them were escaping sulfur mine work in Sicily and other degradations forced on them by their oppressive government.

Both groups were influential in the area and had large cultural effects on the Bensonhurst community. Though close with his cousins, Alan had a number of Italian friends, and as he got older he spent the majority of his time with them.

---

* Mathieu Copeland, *Alan Suicide Vega, Infinite Mercy* (Museé d'art Contemporain de Lyon, 2009), 39.

He felt his Italian buddies were tough, and even more so, he came to appreciate the Catholic church. Not only were there a lot of stories about all the saints and their teachings, but there were also statues, paintings, and Christian iconography inside the church. Alan found it all very interesting and beautiful.

He had become disheartened by the Jewish religion he was forced to follow. Although Louis and Tillie weren't Orthodox, they were observant. They recognized the major Jewish holidays as well as the Sabbath every Saturday and they expected and planned on their sons to engage in the Jewish coming-of-age ritual—the Bar Mitzvah.

***

The room feels barren. The pews are dark wood. The walls are white and vacant. At the front is the Ark where the Torah is housed.

As Alan's nerves start to stiffen, he is pulled out of his seat and his father leads him to the front of the synagogue—to the Bimah. The Rabbi drapes the Tallit over Alan's back and shoulders. He opens the Torah and starts to turn Alan toward it. But that simple move becomes a struggle as Alan seems to be resisting. Louis steps over and tightens a grip around his son's arm. Alan turns to the Torah after giving the Rabbi a look. He looks down and slowly recites:

> *"Ba-ruch a-tah A-do-nai Eh-lo-hay-nu meh-lech ha-o lahm,*
> *a-sher ba-char ba-nu mi-kol ha-a-meem, v'na-I la-nu et Torah-toh.*
> *Ba-ruch a-tah A-do-nai, no-tayn ha-Torah."**

Then the Rabbi takes Alan's arm and turns him back toward him. Alan starts to overheat. He looks around the synagogue. The austere ceremony overwhelms and disturbs him. Where are the statues and the paintings, the stained glass, the gothic windows?

> Kid, you're told "You are a Jew!" And you grow up with it,
> you understand that there is a tradition before you which you
> mustn't veer from. But I am not a Jew, strictly speaking, I am not
> Catholic, I'm nothing like that. I am what I decided to be.†
> —Alan

The Rabbi steps up and starts reading the Torah, then turns to bless Alan.

But Alan can't take it anymore. He kicks the rabbi in the shin. The Rabbi doubles over. Louis races around, grabs Alan with an infuriated grip of his arm and drags him, shaking, out of the synagogue.

---

* *The Aliyah, Step by Step*, https://www.chabad.org/library/article_cdo/aid/1933255/jewish/The-Aliyah-Step-by-Step.htm, Chabad.org.
† Alexandre Breton, *Alan Vega: Conversation with an Indian* (Le Texte Vivant, 2017), Kindle.

> You know, Jew is something that comes from history, you can't
> escape it. . . . Try as I might, I can't help it, I will always be a Jew.*
> —Alan

***

The following year, Alan, Robbie, and their cousins started at New Utrecht High School and Lafayette High School. They all performed well. It was expected they achieve. Success was an unspoken, fundamental understanding within their tradition and cultural structure. Young Jewish men could not fail. And they were to shift whatever focus roaming inside their young minds and hearts to the sciences and preferably put a medical degree on their docket when they started college.

Alan didn't fight this expectation. He won a science fair award for building his own telescope. He was fascinated by astronomy and loved seeing the stars from his bedroom window. Achieving excellent grades was an unconscious process for him. Second nature.

What was more important, though, were the Dodgers, playing ball, and the beating heart of sports. Academia was a toy to be squeezed.

Between baseball outings, Alan worked as a lifeguard at Coney Island Beach during the summer months. He had also started discovering rock 'n' roll, and Elvis Presley was his first hero:

> For me it was first seeing Elvis. He has one of the greatest voices
> of all time. I couldn't go to school unless I put on an Elvis record
> like "Blue Suede Shoes" to give me the will to get there.†
> —Alan

He listened to Fats Domino and Chuck Berry and Little Richard around the clock. He was sensing a new and mysterious world. He also found himself mesmerized by creating strange sounds.

> I used to scratch records and play them over and over to
> make a crazier sound. I had a two-track recorder that I used
> to fool around with, because I loved listening to static.‡
> —Alan

***

---

* Ibid.
† Kris Needs, *Dream Baby Dream: Suicide: A New York City Story* (Omnibus Press, 2017), 19, Kindle.
‡ Luke Turner, "Suicide's Alan Vega in His Own Words," *Dazed*, July 16, 2016, https://www.dazeddigital
.com/music/article/25895/1/suicide-s-alan-vega-in-his-own-words.

Throughout high school Alan remained shy and introverted. He spent much of his time with his cousins, particularly Miltie.

Alan was very close with Miltie, who was one year older, very attractive in the classic young Brooklyn teen look of the time. He was also brighter than most of his friends. He was particularly popular with girls. They were always after him, but he didn't pass it off as some egocentric reality. He was cool.*

Alan and Miltie spent a lot of time together because they were both highly active and skilled baseball players. It was one of the closest friendships he had as he entered junior year at New Utrecht.

***

Friday evening was one of his favorite times of the week. It was when he could watch baseball on WPIX and boxing on NBC—the Gillette Cavalcade of Sports broadcasting from Madison Square Garden.

> I've loved boxing since I was five years old . . . [s]moke-filled boxing rings, men smoking cigars, the whole family there in Brooklyn. Then my father in front of his TV screen. We'd watch the boxing every Friday.[†]
> —Alan

Captured by Rocky Marciano and Sugar Ray Robinson, Alan developed a love and fascination with the sport. The danger—the broken bones, blood, and swollen faces—he was captivated by the risk these men were willing to take on. As he got older, his intrigue with boxing continued unabated. But his grasp of what was really going on during those matches, of why these men continued to stand up to endless violence—hardened—with a tinge of deep concern.

> Kids wanting to be rich, ending up brain-dead.[‡]
> —Alan

The other reason Friday evenings were enticing to him was he would be with his father—watching it all.

If his father stayed home.

***

"Dad where are you going?" asks Alan.

"What is it, Alan?" Louis gently combs his hair in the hallway mirror.

Alan dashes to the TV and turns it on. He falls back onto the sofa.

---

* Interview with Dr. Marty Levitt, 2021.
† Kris Needs, *Dream Baby Dream: Suicide: A New York City Story* (Omnibus Press, 2017), 15–16, Kindle.
‡ Mathieu Copeland, *Alan Suicide Vega, Infinite Mercy* (Museé d'art Contemporain de Lyon, 2009), 40.

"The Dodgers are coming on, Dad! They're playing the Yankees! And Sugar Ray is in the ring later!"

Alan sits forward and beelines the TV screen. The Dodgers are walking out onto the field.

"Look Dad—it's Jackie Robinson!"

"Next time, son."

Suddenly, the sound of a door shutting shakes the room.

Alan stands up and turns. He eyes the closed front door.

He sits back down and starts mouthing the batting stats for each player as they enter the field: .211, .220, .216, .245. . . .

***

Alan and his cousins, including his buddy, Miltie, graduated from high school early and started attendance at Brooklyn College.

Miltie had been short-listed for a basketball scholarship as he was "the most valuable player in the 16–18-year-old competitive basketball league"[*] in Brooklyn at that time. However, he was unable to accept it.

Near his eighteenth birthday, Miltie became very ill with "Bright's Disease"— known today as nephritis or kidney disease. After some treatment during a long hospital stay, he went into remission. He returned to Brooklyn College to resume his studies. However, his remission was short-lived and Miltie died as he was about to turn nineteen.

> Ah, ah, Ah
> Come on, get up
> We're all Frankies
> We're all lying in hell
> Come on, get up, come on
> Ah, ah, ah[†]

Alan's other cousins—including Marty and Carl—noticed a whirlwind change in Alan from that point on. Alan had always looked up to his big cousin Miltie. Whatever twinkle he had in his eye—whatever calm, peace, ease with life—transformed. They rarely saw him smile again.[‡]

***

---

[*] Interview with Dr. Marty Levitt, October 2021.
[†] "Frankie Teardrop" by Alan Vega and Martin Rev, *Suicide*, 1977.
[‡] Interview with Dr. Marty Levitt, October 2021.

They had both been sentenced to death. But one of them was to be released. He was amazed himself at their choice. As they were freeing him from his chains, he had seen the other man between the soldiers disappear through the archway, with the cross already on his back.[*]

—Barabbas

---

[*] Pär Lagerkvist, *Barabbas* (New York: Vintage Books, 1951), 7.

Courtesy Mariette Bermowitz

3 Stranger

1956

Nobody realizes that some people expend
tremendous energy merely to be normal.*
—Albert Camus

Nicknamed "the poor man's Harvard," Brooklyn College was a short walk from Alan's home on Eighteenth Avenue. All his friends were going to the "neighborhood" school, which turned out major achievers from Nobel prize winners to US senators.

Tying himself into the routine of college—highly expected by his family—placed him in a safe and predictable place—a place which had been threatened by the recent death of Miltie.

He majored in astrophysics as contemplated by his parents. Alan was OK with that blueprint. Being emotionally deactivated at the time, he was comforted by the ease and predictability the walls of physics gave him to lean on. And he was really good at it.

School assignments in the science department and required lab work were a breeze. He didn't have to do any heavy lifting to pass his physics classes. And he was becoming comfortable talking with and hanging out with girls, entertaining them with his quick wit.

The days became more serene than they had been in a long while.

Yet . . . there was a restless tapping inside him.

His mother had become worried about her son. She had noticed changes in him—changes which not only confused her, but presaged realities she feared were far from acceptable to the family—mostly to his father.

---

* Albert Camus, quoting Blanche Balain, *Notebooks 1942–1951* (New York: Alfred A. Knopf, 1943).

She knew he wasn't having problems with the demands of academics, and he was still as passionate about sports as ever. But he had been reading books that weren't for school and were by authors she didn't recognize—Sartre, Kerouac, Camus. He spent hours in his room drawing images that couldn't have been for school. She didn't know what to think when she saw them. Fear wrapped itself around her and she often sat down for her afternoon tea to sip through her unease.

Many times through the years, Alan initiated that very afternoon tea with his mom to ease himself, as well. Alan was concerned she never stopped cleaning. He often urged her to stop and sit down for "coffee and chocolate cake." This ritual was a regular dance for Alan and his mother—he thought she was just beautiful and brilliant and yet, wasting away stuck in the house. And now she was as concerned for her son.

***

It's a bracing, brisk day early in Alan's second semester at Brooklyn College. He had settled at a table in the cafeteria with a strong coffee and a roll and was sketching intently. He was waiting for his General Physics Lab to start—the next class on the schedule.

The lunchroom was abuzz, but Alan heard none of it. He was entranced as he drew figures across the pages of his Italian textbook.

Suddenly, he felt a tap on his shoulder. He turned and looked up. It was Morris Dorsky, the head of the Art Department. Alan groaned, assuming he was about to get a talk down. He had missed his art class with Professor Seligmann that morning, having slept past the alarm clock's demand.

> That first year at college, I excelled in math and science.
> My lowest grade ever was art.*
> —Alan

Dorsky, a renowned art historian, "was very interested in the younger generation . . . and was a marvelous teacher."†

That afternoon he was searching for something to eat when he came across Alan and noticed his sketches.

***

"Quite impressive," Dorsky remarks, as his eyes linger over the images.

Alan nods and thanks him.

"What's your name?

---

* Kris Needs, *Dream Baby Dream: Suicide: A New York City Story* (Omnibus Press, 2017), 17, Kindle.
† Michael Boyle, "The Man Who Turned Down a Rothko, from Mark Rothko—Remembering Morris Dorsky," *Michael L. Boyle's Art Log*, March 3, 2009, https://mikeboyle494.typepad.com/blog/morris-dorsky/.

"Alan Bermowitz."

"You're in Seligmann's class, right?

"Yes, sir," Alan confirms.

Dorsky scans Alan, then turns back to the drawing.

"This is remarkable," he observes.

Alan can't believe what he's hearing.

"Are you an art major? I haven't seen you around the department much."

"No, sir. I'm majoring in astrophysics," Alan replies.

Dorsky looks at the drawing again. He is gripped. After a moment, he turns to Alan.

"You need to change that—seriously."

"Sir?"

Dorsky looks across the lunchroom, then turns back.

"I'm going to speak to Professor Seligmann. He'll put you on the right path."

Dorsky walks over to the coffee machine. Alan doesn't know what to think. He looks at his drawing, then back at Professor Dorsky.

He's having feelings he doesn't recognize. He had been dissuaded by his mother whenever she saw him drawing and now he was feeling the positive sensation of affirmation. Confirmation that he had a gift he should develop.

***

Kurt Seligmann was a renowned and influential Swiss abstract painter and engraver. Considered one of the first great surrealist painters, he and his wife escaped to New York after the Germans invaded Poland in 1939. After he relocated, he helped other artists escape the German purge and established himself as one of the most celebrated artists in the United States. He started teaching at Brooklyn College in 1953.

> A characteristic Seligmann painting depicts a kind of dance macabre
> in which anthropomorphic figures . . . cavort in unknown rituals
> in darkly cavernous, yet undetermined, space. This distinctively
> Seligmann scene, with its haunting and expressive beauty, its dark
> pessimism, its cruel and angular shapes, was his own invention.*

That afternoon, Professor Seligmann contacted Alan and they sat in his office where Seligmann assisted Alan in changing his major to art. He then invited Alan out for an early dinner where they discussed the art world and, to Alan's surprise—life.

---

* Stephen Robeson Miller, "Kurt Seligmann," *Orange County Citizens Foundation*, June 1995, https://web
.archive.org/web/20070421140209/http://www.occf-ny.org/Seligmann.htm.

Kurt Seligmann, "Vanity of Ancestors." © *2023 Vision Hudson Valley/Artists Rights Society* (ARS), *New York*

They met in a small restaurant down the street from the college. The professor bought his mentee dinner and they talked for hours. Alan learned from Seligmann the way parables and fables we tell ourselves live within our minds and are depicted on the canvas by him.

While discussing the oscillating sphere behind his art, Seligmann took a sip of cabernet and asked Alan:

"Are you sure this switch in your major is something you want?"

Alan's eyes widened.

"Although you may argue physics is not far from art on one level," Seligmann added, "on a practical, academic level—it's another universe."

"No, no—" Alan shook and turned his head. He took a moment then came back. "I really want this. I didn't realize it, but I do—I really want it."

Seligmann took another sip of wine and nodded his head in pleased agreement. He looked at Alan.

"How will your parents feel about the change in your academic pursuit?"

***

Plates of buttered potatoes and a thick roast beef barely warm the icy discord weaving across the oak dinner table.

Suddenly, Louis bangs his fist on the table. Alan gulps down his potatoes. Tillie turns and looks at her son.

"Why do you want to do this? It will affect your entire life, dear," she said.

"Professor Seligmann, my art professor, says I'm good." Alan replies.

"Yes, dear," she says. "But—"

"Really good," Alan continues.

Louis bangs his fist on the table again. Reluctantly, he turns to his son and looks him directly in the face.

"Who do you think you are?!"

Alan pauses the spoon of green beans heading toward his mouth and looks up at his father.

Louis questions him again: "Who do you think you are?

Alan remains silent. He looks over at Robbie. Alan has no answer for his father, or no answer he would accept.

Tillie rises and goes into the kitchen. Robbie quietly returns to his roast beef.

Louis stands. He turns toward the wall and slams his fist into it—a small gash in the plaster cracks open.

Alan and Robbie stop eating.

Louis walks out of the room. A moment later, Alan hears the front door slam shut.

***

Kurt Seligmann had a profound effect on Alan at this time. His medieval illustrations and paintings were inspirational. Alan had always been enthralled by medieval art. It spoke to him. He felt intrinsically connected to it.

> My parents didn't want me to become an artist,
> no sane parent would. I wouldn't want anyone
> to go through what I went through.*
> —Alan

Seligmann's poignant interest in Alan, his desire to know the young man more and engage him in discussions about art, philosophy, and purpose, helped Alan evolve. He took real satisfaction in working with and guiding Alan. Seligmann never had children and it is said that a father-son connection grew between them.

Then a remarkable moment happened. Alan was chosen by another professor in the Art Department—Ad Reinhardt—to be part of a select group of students

---

* Mathieu Copeland, *Alan Suicide Vega, Infinite Mercy* (Museé d'art Contemporain de Lyon, 2009), 42.

to study under him. This development essentially created the ethos of minimalism that Alan Vega, as we knew him, would live by.

Ad Reinhardt had started teaching at Brooklyn College in 1947 and continued there until his death in 1967. He was an abstract expressionist and was instrumental in the development of the Abstract Expressionist movement. He was renowned for his "black" paintings which reflected his approach to art.

> As an artist I would like to eliminate the symbolic pretty much, for black is interesting not as a color but as a non-color and as the absence of color.*
> —Ad Reinhardt

Ad Reinhardt, "Abstract Painting No. 5," 1962. © 2023 Anna Reinhardt/Artists Rights Society (ARS), New York

---

* "Ad Reinhardt," *The Art Story*, 2022, https://www.theartstory.org/artist/reinhardt-ad/.

Reinhardt had a co.pletely differen approach than Seligmann and other professors in the department. His work was very minimal and conceptual, and it resonated deeply with Alan.

> The impersonality and exactitude of his works
> presaged those of the Minimalist painters.[*]

As well known as Reinhardt was for his paintings, his perspective and dogma on the meaning of art and its place, or non-place, in the world was even more enticing to Alan.

Reinhardt's philosophy of "Non color," "non-existent"—the essence of the "non" acutely affected Alan. It helped him see his purpose and opened up complex feelings about the role art—and eventually, music—have in the world.

> [A] pure, abstract, non-objective, timeless, spaceless, changeless,
> relationless, disinterested painting—an object that is self-conscious (no
> unconsciousness), ideal, transcendent, aware of no thing but art.[†]
> —Ad Reinhardt

***

As Alan continued his studies, he maintained his stellar science grades while now achieving accolades in the Art Department. He started to feel more welcome as he received more support for his work. He actually had a small show through the Art Department which gave him a stronger sense of viability and acceptance and he began making new and different friends.

***

On a lazy day at the end of the semester when Alan was hanging out with his friend Evelyn and her boyfriend, he met a woman named Mariette. She was Evelyn's friend from her French class. Alan was strangely nervous the moment they entered the same head space. Strikingly beautiful, with dark curly hair, brown eyes, and a lovely figure, she was getting her degree in French Literature. She had come to the United States from Belgium, escaping the Holocaust with her father after she lost her mother and her siblings at Auschwitz.

Alan didn't know any of this. He was enchanted and asked if she wanted to go out sometime. And she did.

***

Before Alan graduated, Professor Reinhardt asked him to substitute teach his freshman art class for a few weeks. Alan was surprised—he never thought of

---

* "Ad Reinhardt," https://www.britannica.com/biography/Ad-Reinhardt.
† MOMA, "Ad Reinhardt," 2022, https://www.moma.org/collection/works/78976.

himself as a teacher as his focus had always been on learning. Then he realized maybe he could share some things he had learned about the creative process and his evolving philosophy on art. He told the professor he'd like to teach a class on drawing.

One day in class, after a brief instruction on the value and dynamics of self-portraiture, the students engaged in a lively discussion with Alan. He thought of how full of hope and eager to impress the teacher they seemed. At the end of class, he instructed the students to go home and draw a self-portrait and bring it in for the next class.

When the next class arrived, Alan asked everyone to pull out their self-portraits and hold them up. After the class complied, Alan said to them:

"Now, take your drawing and rip it up."

***

"I just won't sleep," I decided. There were so
many other interesting things to do.*
—Jack Kerouac

---

* Jack Kerouac, *On the Road: The Original Scroll* (New York: Penguin Classics, 2008, originally pub. 1957).

4 Old Wives' Tales

1960 . . . 1963 . . . 1968

> The evil in the world comes almost always from ignorance,
> and goodwill can cause as much damage.*
> –Albert Camus

It was in 1961, after Alan and Mariette had graduated from college, when they got married. They had started dating within days of first meeting and never stopped.

> Our meeting was like a rocket ship going off.†
> —Mariette

Mariette was as taken with Alan as he was with her.

> [with] curly black hair and hazel-gray eyes . . . [he] was slender
> and almost ethereal looking with skin as white as porcelain. He
> claimed it was the only fragile aspect of his being, something he
> inherited from his delicate mother. . . . He was just gorgeous.‡
> —Mariette

Not long after graduation, Alan and Mariette also got jobs. Mariette taught French at a local high school and Alan went to work for the NYC Welfare department—a job he despised, except when he could help a client directly with hands-on-care.

---

* Albert Camus, *The Plague* (London: Hamish Hamilton, 1948).
† Interview with Mariette Bermowitz, September 2021.
‡ Mariette Bermowitz, *Mindele's Journey: Memoir of a Hidden Child of the Holocaust* (self-pub., CreateSpace, 2012), 209, Kindle.

Alan and Mariette. *Courtesy Sue Bermowitz*

However, that was not what he was hired to do. Rather, he spent his days typing up the proper forms to get welfare funds dispersed to the correct clients.

***

A few months before they married, Mariette went to Belgium to visit "les tantes"—local nuns in Belgium who had hidden Mariette in a convent from the Nazis. They cared for and consoled Mariette while her father desperately coordinated their future.

Mariette and her father ended up emigrating to the United States. Mariette was twelve years old at the time and she remained forever faithful to her loving tantes. Those women, who had saved her life, meant everything to her. They wrote letters constantly, and when she was old enough, she returned to visit as often as possible.

While Mariette was in Belgium, she received daily posts from Alan—a deluge of love letters expressing his perpetual, undying adoration. They reflected a heart-rending struggle being away from her. He had become attached to Mariette in a way that gave him a sense of value and devotion he hadn't experienced before in his life—except for moments with his mother.

The letters also went on at great length about other confusing and disturbing worries Alan possessed. Adding to his enormous rage against America's role in the Vietnam War—like many other young men Alan's age—he dreaded being drafted. In his letters to Mariette, he expressed these concerns and what she should do if he was drafted before she returned.

In addition, throughout much of his stated disquiet, he reveals a deep, boiling sense of uselessness.

***

THE LETTERS

In one, he writes about a female client of his at the Welfare Department:

> A half hour later I went downstairs. I went to see Jenny . . . this woman has a lot of faith in me, she trusts me . . . [t]his time Jenny looked different. Her eyes were bleary and red. Her lips were swollen, her breasts looked to have been swollen as though they were infected. Miss Jenny could not talk with ease. Her child could not stop crying even as I put my arm around her. . . . Jenny . . . told me she was having labor pains . . . [she] had not eaten for twelve hours. Her child had not eaten. Even though I was threatened that I would lose my job if I left the Welfare center . . . I went out immediately to get Jenny a sandwich . . . [then I] . . . got an ambulance. But you know how long it takes for an ambulance to come. Jenny knew that she was to become a mother for the second time, and no one was going to harm her child ready to surge out of the vagina into the sun filled room.*
> Jenny had become Mary and the infant Jesus was to be born.*
> —Alan

A key theme for Alan—Jesus. He had become sharply interested in the Christian figure—who he was, what had happened to him, and why. One of his favorite books at this time—*Barabbas* by Pär Lagerkvist—is based on the New Testament story of a prisoner who was chosen by the crowd to be released by Pontius Pilate

---

* Letter from Alan Bermowitz to Mariette Bermowitz, 1961.

over Jesus and pardoned. Jesus is then nailed to the cross and crucified. The story haunted Alan.

Themes of Jesus and his suffering appear in much of Alan's work—most poignantly, in his eventual sculptures of the crucifix. He wrote about him not always in name but in experienced suffering.

> Mariette, I did a great painting on that large canvas that is in your apartment. . . . One of the figures was a portrait of a man in his late forties, with a round head sallow in color but charged with red in various places. It was a man who had a rather thin body, a sunken chest, thin legs, his hands rough and wrinkled, long fingers with yellow nails more yellow on the nails where he holds his cigarettes. The head appeared extremely large but that was because his head was round contrasting the thin body. This was a man who was once healthy, but no longer is.*
>
> —Alan

He often brought up work he had created before.

> Do you remember the first painting that I gave you, when we first started to date, the portrait of a man done on cardboard?†
>
> —Alan

Yet, as he described the works he had created and continued to create—his self-deprecation dripped over them.

> I have partially completed the large canvas. It is an abstract painting. . . . However, much more work is needed. The painting itself looks like a vast battleground . . . a battleground of all my energies, brought to consummation in one large work. It was like Jacob wrestling with the angel. It was Alan wrestling with his conscience.‡
>
> —Alan

> The realism that I try to grasp gets lost in the whirlwind of romanticism. I am faced with the reality of life every day yet I cannot face it. I want to face it, one part of me tells me to do so and yet the other drives me away.§
>
> —Alan

---

* Ibid.
† Ibid.
‡ Ibid.
§ Ibid.

Photo by Mariette Bermowitz

> If anything, the painting or rather the act of painting tired me physically
> and mentally. As a matter of fact the painting looks as if done by a
> "tired" artist, a washed out artist. How else can I describe myself.*
> —Alan

Alan looked forward with great anticipation in composing these letters and wrote them with fervor and dedication. But laced throughout them, within the thin ink of the typeface, was a cry of self-deficiency.

> If one were to give an opinion of my abilities,
> I believe "washed out" would be most appropriate.†
> —Alan

---

* Ibid.
† Ibid.

***

Mariette returned in early September of 1961. Alan met her at LaGuardia Airport with flowers and excitement at her finally being home—back with him. Mariette initially proposed marriage to Alan before she left, and he was now very tuned into following through and tying the knot. He had become concerned she may not get home before he was drafted into the army.

> He couldn't understand why I went away for two months when he loved me so much, when he was so worried about being drafted. Didn't I care to be with him, by his side one last time before he went off to the army?
> "You still want to marry me, don't you?" he said.
> "Of course," I assured him, holding his hand tightly.*

When the military finally came knocking, Alan consumed gallons of salted water, causing his body to go into a hypertensive fit. He ended up being hospitalized and the army decided they didn't want him.

Alan and Mariette married the next month—October. The ceremony was very simple and pleasant. It was held in Alan's parent's apartment with family, a few select friends, and a rabbi. Tillie had created a sweeping buffet of mouthwatering dishes and a towering wedding cake.

After the ceremony was finished, Alan started drinking, with a more than healthy zeal. He became quite drunk, put on strange clothing, and turned into someone Mariette felt he shouldn't have been—at her wedding.

> Alan's rebellious streak showed up immediately after the ceremony when he got drunk and insisted on being photographed wearing a hat like Modigliani, a cigarette dangling from his mouth. He delighted in the effect he was creating, and we all laughed. But inwardly I was expecting a different beginning to married life.†
> —Mariette

***

The first four years of their marriage were easy-going and good-humored. They both enjoyed each other's intellectual curiosities, visiting galleries and museums together, and Alan joined Mariette on one of her visits to les tantes in Europe.

Every Friday evening, they had dinner with Alan's parents. Mariette had become very close with Tillie—to the point where she considered Tillie her mother. She

---

* Mariette Bermowitz, *Mindele's Journey: Memoir of a Hidden Child of the Holocaust* (self-pub., CreateSpace, 2012), Kindle.
† Ibid., 188.

Table at Alan and Mariette's wedding. *Author's collection*

Mariette, Alan, Robbie and his wife, Sue, Bermowitz Wedding, 1961. *Courtesy Sue Bermowitz*

was a seamstress and often made beautiful dresses for Mariette. Tillie was also a passionate cook and showed Mariette how to cook some of her finest dishes.

And on those nights, Mariette and Tillie would talk for hours during dinner—their connection was a great comfort to Alan, whose mother meant everything to him—and now, so did his wife.

Yet Friday nights were as distant a world for Louis as ever. He was generally separate, sitting in front of the TV with a perpetually lit cigarette. Alan would join him to watch the Mets when they were on, and they commingled their betting on the home team—tradition.

***

After a couple of years of marriage, Mariette got the idea to purchase a town house in Park Slope. She had been able to find one for $21,000 with a winding staircase and a garden in the back. She was enchanted.

Alan wouldn't even discuss it. His only remark was "owning a house is too bourgeois."*

Not much later, Alan quit his job at the Welfare Department. His inability to truly and humanely help his clients had become unbearable. Every day he witnessed their endless struggle—unable to get enough food, get a home, care for their children—he felt inadequate, powerless.

At the same time, his passion for painting and drawing took on a greater self-defining role. He would now devote his time entirely on creating art and not return to that soul-crushing workforce. Mariette didn't have a problem with being the only breadwinner. She actually felt quite charmed she was able to contribute to her husband's passion for creating art. And she loved the smell of oil paint on the canvases when she got home from work.

At first.

During this time, Alan had a show in Park Slope of his drawings. He titled the show "Opus Anus."

> He was a very deep, deep thinker . . .
> he scared me because he was so intense . . .
> I didn't know if I could keep up with that man.†
> —Mariette

The drawings in pen and ink in the show were largely compositions of fury—at Lyndon Johnson, the Tet Offensive in the Vietnam War which destroyed American support, at the oppression he witnessed in the city—and so much more. His wrath at the government's killings of American soldiers exploded.

---

* Ibid.
† Interview with Mariette Bermowitz, September 2021.

Opus Anus: "America Home of the Ugly and Dead," Pen and Ink, 1968. *Photo by Candice Herman*

> He was driven by anger and frustration and morbid ideas of destruction
> and apocalypse he got from the news on TV of the war in Vietnam.*
> —Mariette

The show was fairly well attended. Mariette, though, had a rough time with the depictions in the drawings.

> There was no hope in his drawings.
> His expert draftsmanship made them all the more difficult to look at.
> In fact, the whole thing was deeply troubling to me.†
> —Mariette

Two of the drawings in the show were purchased. However, despite Mariette's expectation that the art collectors she invited to the show would purchase a piece, they said they found the work "impressive . . . [b]ut too difficult to look at."‡ Mariette then snuck some money from her own bank account, purchased the drawings and hid them in the back of her closet.

After the show, Alan's obsession with his work grew into a pillar of conviction. He created drawings and paintings every minute of the day. With no clock

---

* Mariette Bermowitz, *Mindele's Journey: Memoir of a Hidden Child of the Holocaust* (self-pub., CreateSpace, 2012), 206, Kindle.
† Ibid., 207.
‡ Ibid.

Opus Anus: "Untitled," Pen and Ink, 1968. *Photo by Candice Herman*

to punch, he had limitless time to create a universe for his imagination and his vision.

Their cramped apartment was overwhelmed with canvases, open cans of paint, wet brushes, and scratched images everywhere—you could barely move without tripping into an unfinished painting spattered with images of his creative ideations.

Art became life.

Mariette started to have real trouble with the noxious odor permeating the house—the paint all over the floors, the "burned-out wires and rancid oil"*—but more consequential—the rampant turpentine everywhere. That odor—and Alan's credo—caked the house.

---

* Ibid., 204.

Opus Anus: "Laurel and Hardy," Pen and Ink, 1968. *Photo by Candice Herman*

[H]e thought that Evil would never go away . . . he saw it through
the hypocrisy of government. . . . I don't know where that
anger really came from. . . . [A]ll artists reflect—the pain and the
beauty around them, and sometimes it's the same thing.*
—Mariette

Mariette couldn't smell the food she cooked in the kitchen—her oasis. The intense smells accosted her every day when she got home from work. She started

* Interview with Mariette Bermowitz, September 2021.

tutoring students in the evenings as a way to stay out of the house, away from the mess, the chaos . . . away. . . .

Reality in their home was fast rebuilding itself. Alan was gripped by his need to create. He was singularly focused and his interest in Mariette—fading.

***

I believe that life is a huge concentration camp.*

—Alan

---

* Alexandre Breton, *Alan Vega: Conversation with an Indian* (Le Texte Vivant, 2017), Kindle.

5 Dust Devil

1969 . . . 1970 . . .

> Life is like riding a bicycle.
> To keep your balance you must keep moving.*
> —Albert Einstein

It was at the gallery show in Park Slope when Alan met Mel Auston. Alan rarely socialized. He preferred to never leave his apartment unless he was going to his studio. But when he made a friend, it was usually for life. Mel became one of those lifers.

Mel had been walking through the Park Slope neighborhood near his home when he came across the gallery opening. He wandered in and looked at the artwork. He found it remarkable. He saw the artist speaking with a group of visitors at the show. He walked over. As the visitors dispersed, Mel approached Alan.

Within minutes they made plans to meet later. They became fast friends, connecting on a nearly unexplainable level.

Mel was a performer on Broadway in the show, *Oh! Calcutta!* It was an exciting and new world for Alan. Not only did he go and watch Mel perform but he and Mel were together constantly. They were Brooklyn boys joined on a life level as well as a spiritual one.

> [T]he beauty of my relationship with Alan was whenever either
> one of us was kind of in the dumps about anything the other
> was not . . . [he] could reach into my soul and pull me out.†
> —Mel

---

* Walter Isaacson, *Einstein: His Life and Universe* (New York: Simon & Schuster, 2007), Location 13, Kindle.
† Interview with Mel Auston, October 2022.

Photo by Mel Auston

Mel hung out at Alan's apartment a lot—a regular, conspicuous presence. He was very attractive and usually brought his girlfriend with him, who was a dancer in the show with Mel. Mariette felt disconnected from these new friends and the confusing, very different lifestyle Alan seemed to be living.

I felt so dull and plain next to this glamorous theatrical couple.*
— Mariette

During the time of their friendship, Mel introduced a universe to Alan which he hadn't been seriously acquainted with before—or at least not as profoundly. That world was late 1968 when Mel gave Alan his first hit of LSD.

The cosmos transformed.

Alan started growing his hair, spending most of his time with Mel and people Mariette didn't know or understand. He started staying in the separate room and recording distorted music sounds. The remaining time, he was gone—digging around the village and the Bowery in lower Manhattan.

Mel and Alan smoked pot as the sun rose and as the sun set.

I think that beginning to get high and beginning to be introspective is that quality that happens when you're a cannabis user . . . like for Alan . . . not trying to escape, but that's always driving inner.†
— Mel

And the occasional LSD trip had an even more spirited effect on his drawings.

During seven consecutive days of LSD, he did something in the order of 120 self-portraits . . . they're extraordinary . . . he's in his hotel room, slashing his wrists and bleeding on the paint on the drawings.‡
— Mel

Self-Portrait, 1970. *Photo by Mel Auston*

Between Alan never being home and his lack of communication with Mariette, their connection, their bond, their relationship—was disintegrating.

* Mariette Bermowitz, *Mindele's Journey: Memoir of a Hidden Child of the Holocaust* (self-pub., CreateSpace, 2012), 212, Kindle.
† Interview with Mel Auston, October 2022.
‡ Ibid.

Alan was into music now and was busy with new projects. When
he was at home, he holed up with a friend in his room, recording
. . . [e]erie, twisted-sounding pieces I found disturbing. . . . I never
complained that it bothered me, nor did he ask what I thought. He was
too absorbed in what he was doing to notice me at all. I understood
only too well what the title of one of his pieces, *Methadone Mary*,
represented, and it added to my feeling of alienation from him.*
—Mariette

***

And Then There was Iggy

It was the third of September 1969. Mel raced to Alan's place and banged on the
front door. Alan opened it.

"What is it?" he asked, moody.

Mel didn't care.

"Come on! We're going to be late!"

Then Alan remembered they were going to see MC5 that evening. Opening for
them were the Stooges, fronted by Iggy Pop. Alan had heard one of their songs
on "The Nightbird," Allison Steel's radio show, and was gripped by its rawness.

He had just had a blowout with Mariette who was sitting on the sofa, in tears.
Alan approached her.

"I'm sorry," he said.

Only tears.

"I'll be back later."

He threw on his jacket and joined Mel outside. They ran down the block to the
E train and took off for the Pavilion in Flatbush.

***

Originally built for the 1964 World's Fair, the New York Pavilion was host to
many rock groups in 1969.

That night, MC5 were hot, having hit big with their album *Kick Out the Jams*
and they were ready to blow the audience away but, in reality—Iggy took over.
He became the headliner—molding and constructing a revolutionary experience
for the audience—redefining rock 'n' roll.

His set was complete mayhem and seriously challenged the audience. Not only
did Iggy curse at them, but he hit himself with the mic, ripped off his clothes and

---

* Mariette Bermowitz, *Mindele's Journey: Memoir of a Hidden Child of the Holocaust* (self-pub., CreateSpace, 2012), Kindle.

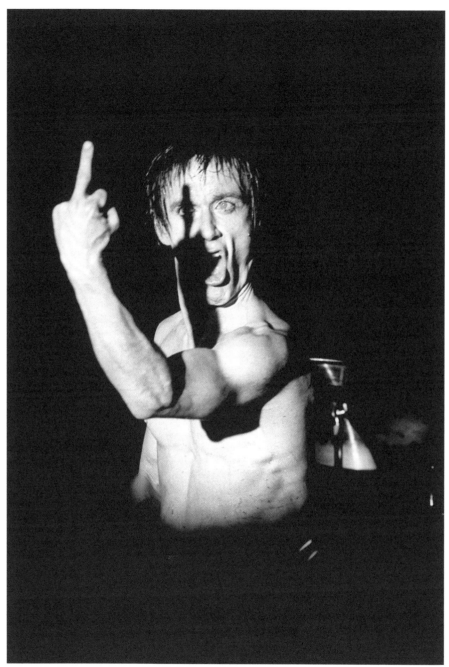

Iggy Pop—Raw Power, 2014. © *Photo - Mats Bäcker*

cut himself. He was bleeding throughout the show. It wasn't anything a rock 'n' roll audience had seen before.

And it deeply divided everyone.

> The music [was] incessant and pounding . . . loud and insane.
> Iggy wriggles . . . about on stage in various sexual posturing. He makes
> use of the microphone stand . . . sits on it, lies on it, caresses it . . .
> no doubt appeal to base, broken tastes . . . the loss of civilization.
> [T]hey launch into, "I Wanna Be Your Dog," or "1969," ya know? "War
> across the USA!" And Iggy's jumping in the audience and cutting
> himself up with a broken guitar! He just got crazier and crazier!*
> —Alan

Even more significant and far-reaching was that after Iggy left the stage, Bach's *Brandenburg Concerto* blasted over the stadium speakers.

Alan's attention was immediately seized. His deep respect and love for classical music was now the coda for what he had just experienced. He took this as a sign that Iggy's music was elevated to the level of the great classics, uniting the past with the future. He knew his path in life was about to be seriously altered.

Alan's epiphany was born out of Iggy's inflammatory, anarchic, and inspirational show.

It gave Alan a new universe.

***

> We saw Iggy Pop and that became . . . the beginning of Alan's kind of
> performing . . . he was a nice Jewish kid from Brooklyn until this rose
> up in him, and as it did, [it] looked like it unleashed all kinds of things
> about not only the work that he was doing, but who he was . . . inside.†
> —Mel

Iggy's performance laid down the fertile soil for the world stage eruption of the Sex Pistols, the Clash, the Ramones, and so many more, but with even greater impact, the astonishing restructuring of—Alan Bermowitz.

> Iggy Pop enthralled him with his confrontational theatrics. Vega had never
> considered going onstage, but he wanted a challenge. "I wanted to evolve
> as an artist, because what I saw Iggy do was so futuristic and so new,"
> [Alan] said. "If I stayed a sculptor, a visual artist, I would have stagnated."‡

---

* Legs McNeil, "Alan Vega, Suicide's Main Man," *Please Kill Me*, May 8, 2017, https://pleasekillme.com/alan-vega-suicides-main-man/.
† Interview with Mel Auston, December 2022.
‡ Kembrew McLeod, *The Downtown Pop Underground* (New York: Abrams Press, 2018), chapter 27.

Mel knew that Alan was not like the Iggy character at that show—or that was his hope.

But something was changing.

Alan hadn't been showing his artwork. His vision, his meaning—what he was trying to get out there, to illuminate people of—couldn't be achieved through the visual medium alone.

> It was when I saw Iggy Pop, that's what did it for me.
> That changed my life.[*]
> —Alan

***

> Rock music is something we align with our personalities . . . Jimi Hendrix because that's sex . . . MC5 are stimulation and electricity . . . Beatles are happy stoned thoughts, fresh breezes too. The Rolling Stones are hard knocks and more sex. The Doors . . . something of each . . . mostly dark poetry of the soul. . . . Whatever your favorite band is, it's kind of a parallel of what you are or want to be.[†]

***

Alan was out with Mel nearly all of the time. Then he was crashing in his art studio, which he had relocated to the Lower East Side.

> Mariette had—I don't know what she had to do with him at all. He never talked about her. . . . Not like she didn't exist. He didn't ever say anything negative about her. He just said, "we're different, you know, just like I'm on a different trajectory," which was pretty obvious.[‡]
> —Mel

Toward the end of 1969, Alan made the fateful decision to leave his home life in Brooklyn and dedicate himself fully to the creative process, in whatever form that was to take. He needed to do this to be fair to Mariette and true to himself as an artist.

---

[*] Tom Taylor, "Six Definitive Songs: The Ultimate Beginner's Guide to Alan Vega," *Far Out*, June 24, 2021, https://faroutmagazine.co.uk/alan-vega-suicide-six-best-songs/.
[†] Chris Hodenfield, "MC5 * STOOGES * DAVID PEEL * MOLLOCK: The PAVILION, Flushing Meadow Park, NY," *GO Magazine*, September 19, 1969. http://makemyday.free.fr/gomag.htm.
[‡] Interview with Mel Auston, October 2022.

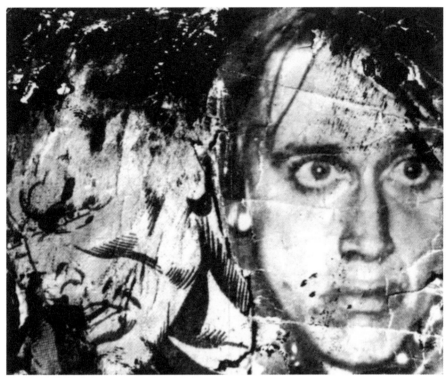

Collage of Iggy Pop by Alan Vega, 1976. *Courtesy Saturn Strip, Ltd.*

Alan came home on New Year's Eve and Mariette figured they would be going to his parents for a midnight New Year's celebration. She went to the bedroom to change her clothes.

***

Yet, that wasn't Alan's plan. He came to the bedroom and pulled out a suitcase and started throwing clothes into it. Mariette looked at him.

"What are you doing?"

"I'm leaving."

"What?"

"I'll call and explain everything," Alan urged. He turned to her and looked at her with deeply felt concern.

"I'm sorry."

He grabbed the suitcase and hurried downstairs.

After a moment, Mariette heard the front door slam shut.

***

> I asked my brother what our mom was worrying about me for.
> He said her worst fear was that I became what I became.*
> —Alan

---

* Luke Turner, "Suicide's Alan Vega in His Own Words," *Dazed*, July 16, 2016, https://www.dazeddigital.com/music/article/25895/1/suicide-s-alan-vega-in-his-own-words.

Courtesy Saturn Strip, Ltd.

6 Reimagined

1970 . . . 1972 . . .

> No man wants to be an artist. He is driven to it.*
>
> —Henry Miller

Alan crashed at a friend's loft on the Lower East Side—now in 1970, a boiling seabed of revolutionary creativity, music, art, and innovation. As a result of his sudden departure, Mariette fell into an extended period of deep depression. She couldn't understand what had happened. Although he appeared aloof and distant, Alan had gone through a profound internal restructuring during the previous two years. He still loved his wife and felt terrible about what he had done, despite the fact that the man who actually had those feelings—didn't exist anymore.

What did exist was a man in search of an entirely new, far-reaching voice. A vital province had been unearthed through his drawings and paintings. And after seeing Iggy and the provocative, sweeping effects he achieved with those watching and listening to him—Alan knew he had to step into another form of expression—of revelation. Visual art had been and would continue to be critical to him, but now—the visual, music, sound, performance began to fuse for Alan, which thoroughly challenged, terrified, and exhilarated him.

> As a kid, I wrote a list of all the things from one to 100 of what I want to be in life. And at the bottom was . . . artist or musician . . . especially [on] stage. . . . I was terrified of getting on stage.†
>
> —Alan

---

* Henry Miller, *Tropic of Cancer* (New York: Grove Press, 1961).
† Paul Tschinkel, Inner-Tube Video LLC.

***

In late '69, Alan became involved with the Art Workers Coalition and partici-
pated in protests against MoMA and other museums in New York about their
treatment of artists and the museums' positions on the Vietnam War.

He then moved into the space run as MUSEUM, The Project of Living Artists
(The Project)—a venture he cofounded and helped obtain funding for from the
New York State Council for the Arts.

Located on West Broadway in SoHo, it was a 5,000-square-foot loft opened
twenty-four hours per day for artists to come create, display, or perform their
work. It was free and open—welcoming anyone seeking to develop their art without any commercial interference.

At one of the meetings of artists belonging to MUSEUM, Alan outlined a set
of demands:

Demands from the Museum Liberation Front

1. MUSEUM should be opened 24 hours a day.
2. All systems of exhibition, including selection groups, be abolished.
3. All exhibits should be changed every day.
4. All exhibits should be opened to anybody wishing to exhibit.
5. All works should be unprotected, uninsured, unsalable, and anonymous.
6. The right be given to any Artworker to have his work on the premise from
   one day to eternity or for as long as he desires.
7. The right be given to any Artworker to remove a work, change a work, or
   destroy a work of any other Artworker who has work on the premise.*

> The outcasts of the art world forming a true community in the blurred
> edges. It [was] the antithesis of the Factory governed by Warhol.†
>
> —Alan

Alan moved in—or squatted—and became the janitor to earn his keep. He
had a room in the basement and was paid a nominal fee per week. He still had to
get his food from the throw-outs dumped in the back of restaurants and super-
markets around the neighborhood.

***

"Bleh! What is this?" Alan throws a dark red sandwich back into the garbage as the
lights in the back of the Italian Bistro go off.

Looking down at it, Mel shakes his head.

---

* Mathieu Copeland, *Alan Suicide Vega, Infinite Mercy* (Museé d'art Contemporain de Lyon, 2009), 58.
† Alexandre Breton, *Alan Vega: Conversation with an Indian* (Le Texte Vivant, 2017), Kindle.

"Looks like a meatball sub," Mel said.

"No—it's something else—it tastes like dirt," Alan shoved aside the paper plates and bags inside the dumpster.

"I don't think you have much choice. I think you need to start getting into dirt. Maybe add some spices." Mel laughed.

"No way!" Alan replied. Then he tossed a half-eaten filet-mignon back into the garbage.

"I'd rather starve!"

***

The general sense of The Project was, despite its aspiring pull for artists, those who lived in the space or crashed there were essentially homeless—a reality with which Alan had become well acquainted.

During his early time there, he started focusing on and fine tuning his light sculptures. Years earlier, he had essentially shifted from painting to sculpture. While working on a painting one day, he found he wasn't getting the shade of purple he wanted so he moved a light bulb across the painting, watching the changing tones of color. Alan eventually stuck the light bulb directly onto the painting, locked in the color and in effect became a sculptor.

> Composed of differently shaped bulbs, neon lights, cables,
> adapters, multicolored light strings, to which were added
> images, TV sets, and all sorts of objects, the works were
> like profane reliquaries, attractive yet disturbing.*

Alan realized how critical light was to the creative process and how visual art was perceived. This understanding energized him.

> I was able to control the color because I was controlling the light. And
> that really, that was it. . . . I began to realize that painting or all art for that
> matter is about light. And depends upon light. If you . . . have no light
> in a room, you can't see a painting right . . . or anything for that matter,
> right? You need a light. So I went to the source, the light and the colors.†
> —Alan

Alan's work started to generate serious interest from the evolving art world elite in SoHo. In the early '70s, Ivan Karp, who had helped run the Leo Castelli Gallery for ten years, had recently opened his own gallery—OK Harris. It was

---

* Alain Berland, *Alan Suicide Vega Holy Shit*, Slash, 2012, https://slash-paris.com/en/evenements/alan-suicide-vega-holy-shit/sous, 2012.
† Paul Tschinkel, Inner-Tube Video LLC.

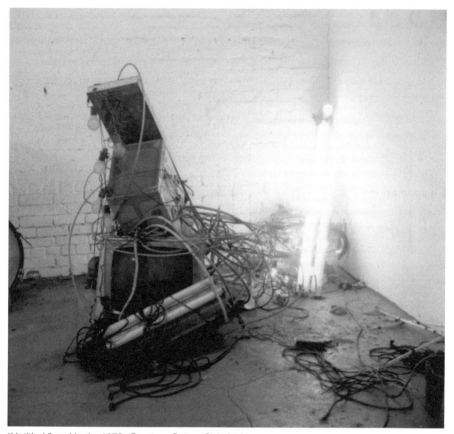

"Untitled," OK Harris, 1972. *Courtesy Saturn Strip Ltd.*

the second gallery to open in the fast-developing SoHo Art District. And one of Karp's first shows was Alan's light sculptures.

Mastermind behind the careers of Andy Warhol, Roy Lichtenstein, and Robert Rauschenberg, Karp found Alan's work highly innovative—as he was turning overlooked objects into art.

He was creating sculptures consisting of complex structures of lights and wires combined with discarded materials he found on the city's curbs next to garbage cans.

Alan's art was something people had never seen before.

It was controlled chaos. From the broken-down, neglected, and destroyed city streets, Alan was bringing in pieces to be embraced, analyzed, and treasured.

> [A]nti-art that recycles all the waste of a consumer society.*
> —Alan

---

* Alexandre Breton, *Alan Vega: Conversation with an Indian* (Le Texte Vivant, 2017), Kindle.

When Karp ventured into The Project and came across Alan working on his floor pieces, he was seriously intrigued and pulled Alan in.

> I love what you're doing and I want to give you a show.[*]
> —Ivan Karp

> My sculpture is an example of Punk visually, a not-give-a-shit attitude about just piling up a load of garbage and proving it could look good too. . . . I found TVs in the street . . . would go into these light stores and shove lights into my pockets . . . occasionally I throw in radios . . . four or five radios playing different stations. . . . People won't get close to the sculpture . . . there are lots of broken wires, smashed bulbs, chains, broken glass, and other kinds of things that just threaten people.[†]
> —Alan (Bermowitz) Suicide

When the shows were finished, Alan threw out the sculptures he had created. He challenged our deeply held beliefs about what art—and music—symbolize.

As Alan's most fervid, committed backer, in 1972, Karp arranged for him to have a solo show at Gallery Marc in Washington, DC. Mel had a station wagon, and he agreed to make the road trip and transport the works while shooting a 16mm film of the entire event.

***

Mel and Alan get on the New Jersey Turnpike and speed forward. Halfway through the trip, they turn off into a Philadelphia rest stop. After downing some cheeseburgers and fueling up, they jump back into Mel's station wagon. Mel takes a few tokes off a joint and Alan drops a hit of LSD.

They arrive in Washington near 2:30 a.m. but before finding a place to crash, they head to the Jefferson Memorial. The place is deathly quiet. Alan is still tripping. They roam outside the memorial and wave to the staunch Jefferson, mounted in the middle of his shrine guarding the American dream. They run up the stairs and jump around the memorial as the late-night stars stream above.

After a few moments, buzzing around the statue, roaring and screaming, security personnel guarding the memorial approaches them and orders them to leave.

"Isn't this place open all the time?" Alan asks. "Isn't it available to all of us—we Americans?" Mel coughs up a howl.

The security guard raises his baton, and ushers Alan and Mel to the steps. They end up parking near the gallery on P street and fall asleep inside the car.

---

[*] DJ Pangburn, "An Art Punk Legend Rises Again with Two Posthumous Shows," *Noisey*, 2017, https://www.vice.com/en/article/padm49/alan-vega-punk-legend-suicide-posthumous-art-shows.
[†] Ibid.

The next day, Alan and Mel help mount the show at Gallery Marc. That evening, when the art connoisseurs arrive, Alan and Mel are like aliens from another planet. The crowds wandering through the gallery include "Jackie-O" styled ladies painted in tailored suits and pillbox hats sipping white wine while their cigar-smoking male companions discuss world affairs.

Meanwhile, Alan, looking deranged, sits in the corner occasionally swigging from a bottle of Jack Daniels and shifting the sculpture pieces around. No one goes anywhere near him.

> [He was] . . . like a painter who painted with his eyes closed.*
> —Marc Hurtado

***

Meanwhile, back at The Project—while Alan's visual art and sound experiments developed alongside the array of other artists, musicians, poets, and radicals expressing their worldviews—bands and performers started playing out their repertoires at The Project, as well.

Alan pulled together people—friends and those who had been wandering through the space—to join in creating the music and sounds. They would hammer on pots and pans while Alan and Mel manipulated a machine creating distorted sounds of static and reverberations. As the beat and the energy ruffled through, Alan screeched out his own sounds and words.

> Six, eight people just banging on pots with Alan shrieking and
> sometimes doing music behind it. That's how the whole thing started.
> I made a light piano right outta the lighting store. It had these little
> keys and you push on it and it lights up whatever circuit it's plugged
> into . . . red and blue lights, and Alan did whatever he was doing with
> making up music at that time . . . it was all with a lot of feedback and
> a lot of craziness and him beating himself with a microphone.†
> —Mel

And then, one fateful evening, Martin Rev joined in.

Taller than Alan with big dark curly hair and ripped, beaten-down clothes, Marty had played at The Project a number of times with his band, Reverend B. Alan actually joined them once with a tambourine.

The Project had always been fascinating and inviting to Marty. He found it a safe and interesting place. The people there—the artists, the musicians—were

---

* Interview with Marc Hurtado, March 2023.
† Interview with Mel Auston, December 2022.

Alan at the opening of the Gallery Marc show, 1972. *Photo by Mel Auston*

focused and energized with what they were creating and there was a lot of discourse on political art, fighting the injustices of Vietnam, the future of performance. People were exploding with emotions and inspiration.

When Marty entered, he saw Alan playing with feedback sounds and reverberations on an amp and his friend, Paul Liebgott, with a guitar making obscure, irregular sounds. Marty grabbed nearby objects and started making the sound of a beat. This evolved into a remarkable meeting of mind and purpose.

> [The Project] was like a refuge—a home away from home—and Alan
> needed the same thing. We'd end up jamming like this, then Paul would
> leave early and we'd meander, walk in the city and leave in [the] early
> hours . . . to a bakery in Little Italy that would open at 5:30 am, we'd
> split a bread and he'd take the subway downtown and I'd go uptown.
> At some point he said to me "let's start a group." Alan and I were finding
> ourselves in the same space almost nightly. That's how it started.*
> —Marty

Alan and Marty became closer and they spent nearly every day together. They talked and dug into each other's histories. As they did, the building blocks of their collaboration came together. Alan had great veneration for Marty's background in jazz, his use of two keyboards and how vital it was to their sound. And Marty was intrigued by Alan's passion and vision.

> I was impressed with Alan's total dedication to his art and to
> developing further. And the first of his works I saw, the pen and ink
> drawings he had already been doing previously, were exceptional.†
> —Marty

Alan's intensity—his demeanor and approach—revealed fireworks exploding inside him, and Marty connected with that energy. They experienced symbiotic moments with each other which defined their lives for decades.

During the early years of their collaboration, they performed a few times at The Project. At first, it was the three of them—Alan, Marty, and Paul. Later, Marty's wife, Mari, joined them on drums. But that setup didn't last long. Mari had children to take care of and Paul couldn't handle the savagery at the gigs.

They then mutated into a configuration of only the two—Marty on a keyboard and Alan in front singing—or not.

> [T]hey shared a mutual desire to create the loudest, most
> confrontational statement they could at a time when
> commercial motives and complacency seemed to be
> replacing the anger, protest and invention of the sixties.‡
> —Kris Needs

---

* Mathieu Copeland, *Alan Suicide Vega, Infinite Mercy* (Museé d'art Contemporain de Lyon, 2009), 35–37.
† Interview with Martin Rev, January 2023.
‡ Kris Needs, *Dream Baby Dream: Suicide: A New York City Story* (Omnibus Press, 2017), 121, Kindle.

Marty and Alan, early '70s. © *GODLIS*

As they built their unknown band, they decided to name themselves "Suicide."

> [It]was inspired by the title of a "Ghost Rider" comic
> book issue that was titled "Satan Suicide"*
> —Alan

The word nailed their perspective on society at the time. Yet, it wasn't that simple. Over the years, Alan would often say what the band and its name was about—and that they probably should've been named, "Life." Suicide was a provocative word—a word eliciting fear, disorientation, and despair.

> We were talking about society's suicide, especially
> American society. New York City was collapsing.
> The Vietnam War was going on.
> The name Suicide said it all to us.†
> —Alan

Alan was calling himself "Alan Suicide" when Ivan Karp originally set him up at his gallery. He later became "Alan Vega" because he found the name "Suicide" was too off-putting.

---

* "Ever Heard of . . . Alan Vega?" *Underground*, January 27, 2022, https://underground-england.com/ever-heard-of-alan-vega/.
† Simon Reynolds, "Infinity Punk: A Career-Spanning Interview with Suicide's Alan Vega," *Pitchfork*, July 19, 2016, https://pitchfork.com/features/interview/9917-infinity-punk-a-career-spanning-interview-with-suicides-alan-vega/.

> A name and a birth with two bases. An artistic birth that replaces
> an original civil status, corrects it and erases it without hesitation.
> . . . "I'm Vega. I did it because I wanted to distance myself from the
> Suicide name. But that's not the only reason. Suicide became an
> obstacle, as it was often censored just because of our name."*
>
> —Alan

He also chose the name "Vega" because one of the brightest stars in the constellation "Lyra"—one of the Sun's closer neighbors—is named "Vega." It tied in with his lifelong love of astronomy and being at one with the universe.

***

Karp ended up bringing Suicide in to perform at OK Harris for their first gig outside of The Project.

Their show was billed as "punk" music—the first time of its use in this context, after Lester Bangs gave birth to it.

> I was showing my art, my sculptures at this pretty big gallery . . .
> [w]e billed it as a "punk music mass." Up until then, that word had never
> been used except in an article in '69 by Lester Bangs. He did a thing in
> *Creem* . . . on Iggy Pop, and the word punk was used for the first time.†
>
> —Alan

They were hated by most of the audiences who saw them. They continued to perform regularly at The Project and receiving not-great responses. It all established for Alan a stronger sense of purpose. Not having been acutely aware of it and coming to terms with his fear of performing onstage—these early gigs fed Alan's inner logic as to why this band, these shows, were important to his vision.

During the next couple of years, Suicide performed at more galleries downtown and was eventually able to perform at the Mercer Arts Center, a preeminent "avant-garde" performance space where Wayne County first performed, The New York Dolls had a once-weekly gig, as well as The Modern Lovers and then—Suicide.

The problem was that initially, the operator of the Mercer Arts Center, Sy Kabak, wasn't too hot on having Suicide perform in-house. So, one day, Alan waited outside Sy's office with Marty to speak with him. They ended up sitting there for days and days until Sy gave his OK.‡

---

* Alexandre Breton, *Alan Vega: Conversation with an Indian* (Le Texte Vivant, 2017), Kindle.
† Aaron Richter, "Read a Rare Alan Vega Interview from 2008," *self-titled*, 2016, https://www.self-titledmag
.com/interview-alan-vega-suicide/.
‡ Interview with Lary Chapman, April 2023.

PUNK MUSIC
by
SUICIDE
Friday, November 20, 1970 8 PM
at
OK HARRIS
465 West Broadway, New York

Invitation to Suicide show at OK Harris, 1970. *Courtesy Saturn Strip, Ltd.*

Tiffany Club designed poster, Edinburgh, 1978. *Author's Collection*

But Suicide still found many people leaving or ignoring them. Yet, that wasn't the point to Alan. He was where he wanted to be—expressing himself in ways which truly reflected him and his ideology.

Look at the world. Open the front page of any newspaper,
and you've got violence all over the place. You
confront it, man. There's nothing you can do.*
—Alan

[H]is sound structures describe the city in which he always lived, New
York. You can almost hear the fire truck sirens, car horns and subway
sounds in his music. They're as violent as the city itself; we find the same
seething madness that emanates from the volcanic energy of New York.
Alan Vega describes not just a city or a society but a space that is created
from all of its sounds and light; he reconstructed the outside on the inside.†
—Alexandre Breton

***

The only truth is music.‡
—Jack Kerouac

---

* Aaron Richter, "Read a Rare Alan Vega Interview from 2008," *self-titled*, 2016, https://www.self-titledmag
.com/interview-alan-vega-suicide/.
† Alexandre Breton, *Alan Vega: Conversation with an Indian* (Le Texte Vivant, 2017), Kindle.
‡ Jack Kerouac, *Desolation Angels* (New York: Penguin), 1965.

7 MIA

1972

We are as forlorn as children lost in the woods. When you
stand in front of me and look at me, what do you know of
the griefs that are in me and what do I know of yours?[*]
—Franz Kafka

It was February 1972 when Alan's mother, Tillie, became ill. She had suffered a heart attack. She was taken to the hospital and died not much later. She was fifty-seven years old. The death sent chilling shocks throughout the family. Adding to the level of distress was the inability to find Alan to let him know. Where was he? Alan's feelings for his mother had always been very warm and caring.

He just loved his mom.[†]
—Mariette

Despite her deep concern for him and the perplexing person she felt Alan had turned into, Tillie loved him unconditionally.

The family was anxious to find Alan. They knew he would be heartbroken to miss her funeral—to miss everything.

At the same time, Alan's brother Robbie had been hospitalized in Maryland, where he lived with his wife, Sue, and their children, Amie and Beth. Robbie's illness was unknown to Alan as well. No one could find him.

He had never informed his family of anything going on in his life—where he lived, what he was doing. There was no known direct phone number.

---

[*] Franz Kafka, "Letter to Oskar Pollak" (1903); cited in *Briefe*, ed. Max Brod (Berlin: Schocken Books, 1958), 27.
[†] Interview with Mariette Berkowitz, September 2021.

Alan, self-portrait. *Photo by Liz Lamere*

Alan had disappeared for painfully experienced reasons. He always felt he was the black sheep. He believed in his heart they didn't want to know him, that they weren't interested in what he was doing. He thought he broke his mother's heart when he didn't become a doctor or physicist and even more so when he left his family life to pursue his art. He felt that after all his mom had sacrificed for her family, he had let her down. The way Alan perceived it, they had disowned him.

Since Robbie was in the hospital and Alan was nowhere to be found, both of Tillie's sons missed her funeral. Although Robbie eventually recovered and returned home, Alan remained missing. It hurt and confused Robbie as to why his brother insisted on keeping an impenetrable distance. They were brothers—their only brothers. They had scrambled and laughed and beaten each other up. They had always been close—or at least Robbie thought they had.

Tillie. *Photo by Alan Vega, Courtesy Saturn Strip, Ltd.*

My biggest problem was the fact that Alan didn't try letting us know where
he was. It hurt Robbie a lot . . . that he didn't know where Alan was.*

—Sue, Robbie's wife

Keeping his distance became a state of existence for Alan. At the time, it defined him. It was all he knew. It was how he survived—not looking back at the past and living entirely, completely, in the present moment. He was a nomad. Whenever he moved somewhere, it was just him and a suitcase.

***

My mother was really beautiful.†

—Alan

---

* Interview with Sue Bermowitz, October 2021.
† Kris Needs, *Dream Baby Dream: Suicide: A New York City Story* (Omnibus Press, 2017), 162, Kindle.

8 Permute
1972 . . . 1974 . . .

Art is not what you see, but what you make others see.
—Edgar Degas

The Project of Living Artists closed and relocated to Greene Street. Alan moved to a basement space there. He didn't have a job and was surviving on minor sales of some of his artwork and a stipend for helping at The Project. Life was not easy. But it was very much where he wanted to be.

Photo by Mel Auston

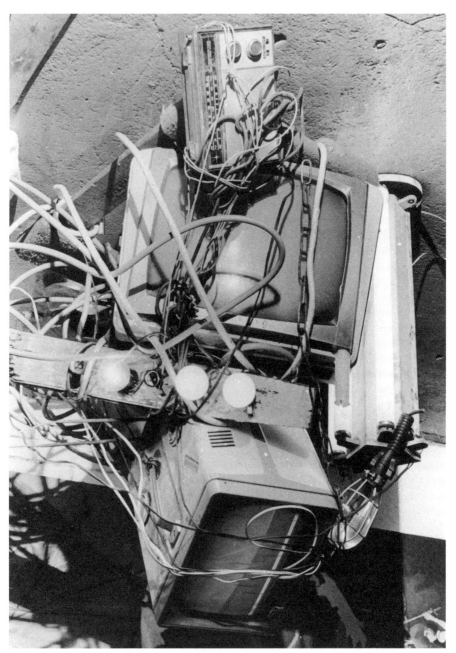

OK Harris, 1973. *Courtesy Saturn Strip, Ltd.*

Alan's focus was turning more to Suicide, but his artwork continued to emerge. In 1975, Jeffrey Deitch saw one of Alan's shows at OK Harris and was blown away. Today, a preeminent art collector and dealer, Deitch had been working for the John Weber Gallery in the 1970s, when he came across this early show of Alan's sculptures.

> Something that I loved about the aesthetic is he would do
> a genius sculpture and then just take it apart, put the parts
> in a box. And then if there was another opportunity to make
> another sculpture, he'd make another sculpture using the
> same parts . . . it's this all-over approach to composition.
> It's this controlled chaos.*
> —Jeffrey Deitch

Deitch took a strong interest in Alan's work and when he grew into a highly regarded curator, he presented a full exhibition of Alan's work at his gallery in SoHo entitled "Collison Drive"—thirty years later.

***

Jeffrey Deitch
Art Dealer, Curator
February 2023
I remember very, very clearly walking into OK Harris and stumbling on an exhibition and something I remember—there was a convention of black vinyl press type he put on the wall with the artist's name and it said, "Alan Suicide." But what he had done is he had scratched it out. So, there were these scratches going through it and it was incredible. It was so much part of the aesthetic. There were a number of these really great innovative light TV pieces, and I just thought they were phenomenal. I loved them. It was the most exciting development that you could connect with—anti-form sculpture.

I was first exposed to Alan as an artist. At the same time, I was going almost every night to CBGBs and sometimes Max's. I was out there all the time. I was having such trouble getting to work at 10:00 a.m. because I was out sometimes till 5:00.

Everyone would stand around on the sidewalk in front of CBGBs and it's not like you had to go to another bar or something. It didn't matter—you just stood around. I was so intrigued by this. For me, the best bands there were just an extension of sculpture.

So, I orchestrated a situation where I would write the gallery newsletter, so I didn't have to come in at 10:00 anymore. It allowed me to stay up all night.

And then another just astonishing thing was when I saw Suicide onstage for the first time.

It was a shock, a level of astonishment equivalent to seeing a sculpture. It made such an impact on me. Wow. Suicide's definitely my favorite of all the bands that emerged during that period.

---
* Interview with Jeffrey Deitch, February 2023.

What the most amazing thing is of course—there was Marty in the back with this kind of visor over his head, and he was not making a gesture—it was so different than any rock band.

One of the things that made the most impact on me is they finished their set and the beat box—whatever Marty had—was still going. And I just thought that was unbelievable, as an aesthetic gesture that here there's the performance and then they leave—and sound still coming out of that box.

I just thought that was really brilliant—made it like a kind of sculptural performance.

And the other thing I just loved about the band is it was so New York—totally New York—this fusion of Doo Wop from the Bronx Street corners. Then the whole heritage of underground music—it's tough, dark—totally New York. And there were audiences that did not feel as good as I did about them but the hostility—that was the whole point.

But I would say that for the most part, the audiences at CBGB were very enthusiastic. Of course, I know about the shows in Europe but they had big followers.

So, one of my goals was to meet Alan. I was spending a lot of time with the photographer, Marcia Resnick. She knew Alan from Brooklyn. And she orchestrated a meeting with Alan and I remember very vividly when I met him. We were talking and he was joined by two fans who came from New Jersey and they were both wearing black T-shirts with white "suicide" lettering that they had made themselves.

I remember our conversation—I asked," So, who's your favorite artist?" And Alan whispered to me—he didn't want anyone else to hear—he whispered: "Jackson Pollack."

He comes right out of Jackson Pollack. He animates Jackson Pollack.

At that point I was twenty-one, twenty-two years old and I expressed my enthusiasm about his work, and that I wished I could do something with him sometime. I attended more of his performances and occasionally crossed paths with him. Then years go by and around 2001, I had heard that Suicide did this revival performance for New Year's Eve someplace downtown, and I was determined to reconnect with Alan and put on an exhibition.

I remember this particular assistant of mine who was also a fan of Suicide and we tried to contact Alan. It wasn't easy but I got in touch with his manager, who was his wife, and we arranged a visit.

I met with Alan and he was the same. And the first sentence out of him was "I've been waiting thirty years for you to come back to me." He remembered me.

So, we created a great exhibition and there were still parts for one of the vintage mid-'70s pieces, which was the centerpiece of our show. And we added some new work, some of the cross pieces—it was a great show, and it was such a sensation with the younger generation.

I wanted to place a vintage '70s floor piece but Alan was never able to find one. It was in his DNA to create something and then throw it out.

It's this controlled chaos—very black and white . . . very American . . . very New York. Abstraction of a stream of violent romance. The American experience. ■

***

During the mid-'70s, Alan became friends with Edit DeAk, an art critic who wrote for *Art in America* and *Art Forum* and worked at the Artists Space gallery. DeAk cofounded the publication *Art-Rite* with William Robinson and Joshua Cohn, which was distributed throughout SoHo and the rest of lower Manhattan. It was a free art magazine whose goal was "coverage of the under covered"*—artists ignored by the establishment—because *Art-Rite* had "a loving relationship with the art world."†

Edit became good friends with Alan when she met him at his OK Harris show. She was completely thrown in awe at his work and steered him to Barbara Gladstone for a show in the early '80s. But even more critical, she invited him to edit Issue #13 of *Art-Rite* magazine.

The issue was:

> harsh and punky . . . mostly a group of found photographs
> invoking speed, violence, and rock 'n' roll.‡

Not much later Edit made a Super-8 Film with William Robinson imparting the epic song, "Frankie Teardrop," which Edit described as a

> homicidal punk epic . . . this is probably the closest
> American Punk has gotten to English Punk.§
> —Edit DeAk

As part of a discussion on the evolving "video art" world in SoHo, the *New York Times* noted Edit's and Robinson's contribution: "a narrative film called 'Frankie Teardrop,' an urban ballad of a mental breakdown."¶

---

* William Grimes, "Edit DeAk, a Champion of Outsider Artists, Dies at 68," *New York Times*, June 22, 2017, https://www.nytimes.com/2017/06/22/arts/edit-deak-dead-downtown-art-critic.html.
† David Frankel, "On *Art-Rite* Magazine," *032c* 9 (Summer 2005), https://web.archive.org/web/20120320033817/http://032c.com/2005/on-art-rite-magazine/.
‡ Ibid.
§ Mathieu Copeland, *Alan Suicide Vega, Infinite Mercy* (Museé d'art Contemporain de Lyon, 2009), 64–67.
¶ John J. O'Connor, "TV: 'SoHo' Programs on Video Art," *New York Times*, June 4, 1979, https://www.nytimes.com/1979/06/04/archives/tv-soho-programs-on-video-art.html.

The film is now part of the permanent collection at MoMA.

> Alan Suicide's talent flourished on his haunting thanatos instinct,
> but the world's sense of itself finally caught up with him. The wild
> spreading lateral crawl of end-of-civilization sensibility ha[d] arrived to
> Alan Suicide on mutual turf: decayed.*
> —Edit Deak

Edit also went to many of Suicide's shows and found a searing tie to Alan's artwork.

> I saw many performances and the reaction after Suicide's
> performances would make you speechless.†
> —Edit Deak

***

In the early '80s, Alan started creating sculptures with a foundation of wood in the shape of a cross. The crucifixes were a new expression for him. He was living in a world of destitution—no money and a meager existence—the very world inhabiting the crucifixes he was creating.

Edit was fascinated by the pieces and set up the meeting with Barbara Gladstone, who was opening her first gallery downtown in the SoHo district. Gladstone became very interested in doing a one-man show of Alan's work.

> I was going from uptown to downtown . . . [a]nd I
> thought he was a perfect way to express that.‡
> —Barbara Gladstone

On the crosses, Alan attached lights, wires, cultural icon images, bloodied boxer's faces ripped from magazines and jumbles of discarded electronic component parts found on the street.

This first one-man show launching the opening of Gladstone's new location in SoHo soon became the hot place to be, and the opening was packed with the glitterati of the art, music, and fashion worlds.

---

* Mathieu Copeland, *Alan Suicide Vega, Infinite Mercy* (Museé d'art Contemporain de Lyon, 2009), 64–67.
† Ibid.
‡ M. H. Miller, "Killing Us Softly: The Art Career of Suicide's Alan Vega," *ARTnews*, July 26, 2016, https://www.artnews.com/art-news/news/killing-us-softly-the-art-career-of-suicides-alan-vega-6722/.

"Marilyn," Gladstone Gallery Exhibition, 1983. *Courtesy Estate of Ric Ocasek*

[He] showed neon crucifix assemblages, made of pieces of found
metal that were kind of put together in a sort of arte povera manner.
. . . The gallery had no overhead lighting, so the only light source for
the exhibition was the sculptures themselves. It was very moody.*
—Barbara Gladstone

* Ibid.

Gladstone told Alan that if they moved the light sculptures, which were usually living on the floor, up onto the wall, she was sure she could sell them—and she did. Julian Schnabel bought one of the biggest pieces, Ric Ocasek bought several, as did an established collector from Washington, DC.

His evolving crosses reflected his longtime conflicted fascination—Jesus and the Catholic structure with its power as one of the most revered and ancient symbols. He was also deeply moved by the structure of the cross—two dissecting lines that would meet in the realm of infinity.

When Alan lived in Brooklyn with Mariette, they traveled to Brussels to visit the convent where the nuns lived who had saved and cared for Mariette.

During this trip, Alan insisted on a committed, fervent journey to the Unterlinden Museum in Colmar, France, to see the work of Matthais Grünewald, a legendary painter from the early Renaissance period. Grünewald's most famous work, which Alan had traveled to specifically study, was "Isenheim Altarpiece." The work includes two enormous wings surrounding the middle panel which depicts the poignant and harrowing crucifixion of Jesus Christ.

> The horribly wounded, etiolated, crucified figure of Christ, dead or close to death, is flanked by the pointing St. John the Baptist, the desperately praying St. Mary Magdalene, and the traumatized Virgin Mary, who is held by St. John the Apostle . . . Grünewald's Christ [is in] a great deal of pain and is covered in sores like a plague victim.*

After seeing this piece, Alan couldn't speak for two days. He was internally reassembled—astonished. This experience would come to affect Alan's artwork in many ways—most poignantly, during the last year of his life when he created his "Spirit Paintings."

> I distrust the name "God" but, yes, I do believe in a higher power, God is in all of us. . . . There is an immense power. There has to be.†
> —Alan

> ***

> I think [Alan is] one of the great artistic innovators of his generation. He's going to end up having much more influence than many artists of his time.‡
> —Jeffrey Deitch

---

* Paul Bonaventura, "Isenheim Altarpiece," *Encyclopedia Britannica*, April 27, 2023, https://www.britannica.com/topic/Isenheim-Altarpiece.
† "Biography of Alan Vega," *Assignment Point*, https://assignmentpoint.com/biography-of-alan-vega/.
‡ Interview with Jeffrey Deitch, February 2023.

9 A Dog with Two Tails

1975 . . . 1976 . . . 1977

> Start with what is right
> Rather than what is acceptable.*
> —Franz Kafka

As the year wrestled forward, Alan and Marty played around a half-dozen shows at various places in the city including The Project. Sadly, The Mercer Arts Center collapsed in 1973 due to faulty construction. The Dolls, the Modern Lovers, and other bands that had been performing there started working the burgeoning nightclub scene—including Suicide.

Although Suicide's first nightclub show was at CBGB—A dark, crowded, wood-stressed venue on the Bowery with a halfway house for homeless men upstairs—Hilly Kristal, the owner, was shaken when he saw their performance. He spoke to them afterward, near tears: "I hope you're not planning for this to be your career."

> [I]t would be another three years before they were
> invited back to play there regularly.†
> —Kris Needs

The following year, they were brought into Max's Kansas City, recently reopened under the aegis of Tommy and Laura Dean. It was located on Park Avenue South across from Union Square. On the second floor was a small club with a bar near the front and a stage in the back, a restaurant on the first floor and a

---

* Franz Kafka, *The Castle and The Trial* (New York: Alfred A. Knopf, 1956).
† Kris Needs, "Suicide: The Terrifying of NYCs Outer Punks," *Louder*, January 16, 2020, https://www.louder sound.com/features/suicide-the-terrifying-world-of-nyc-s-outsider-punks.

Photo by Frédéric Brugnot

third floor where Peter Crowley, the club's new booking manager, administered his magic.

Peter had booked Suicide regularly during the past year at Mother's—a gay club across town. When he started at Max's, he immediately brought them in—and it became home.

> We [were] much more of a Max's band than a
> CBS band. That's how we got started.
> Peter opened up the world.*
> —Alan

Peter also arranged to put the one recording by Suicide—a rare single which included an early version of "Dream Baby Dream" titled "Keep Your Dreams"—on the club's jukebox. Then he put Suicide on the compilation album, *Max's Kansas City 1976*, which included bands that appeared at Max's.

Peter Crowley took Suicide seriously.[†]

***

Peter Crowley
Music Director
Max's Kansas City, 1975–1981
January 2023
What did you think of Alan as the man—given the character of his performances—his fury and energy onstage?

At first, I saw the Iggy influence . . . and the stark contrast between Alan's red hot action and the cool, jazz-like foundation that Marty provided. Later on, I picked up on Alan's (Maoist?) revolutionary mission.

Did you spend much time with him outside of the shows?

Some, but not a lot. We hung out in my office. I'd give him show biz advice and he'd advise me on matters of a personal nature.

What did you see, what did you sense, and perceive was unique and remarkable about Suicide that so many others didn't get?

I've always avoided the "music appreciation" approach to music appreciation. I liked Suicide (in '75) in the same way I liked Bo Diddley (in '55), Little Richard ('57), Hank Ballard ('61), VU ('66), The Stooges ('69), Ramones ('74), etc. Never tried to analyze why. They just knocked me out.

I saw they were getting nowhere as an opening act, so I made them headliners. I also believed they could be recording artists, so I asked them to record for me. (Marty Thau told me he'd always thought of them as only "performance artists" until he heard "Rocket USA" and "Ghost Rider" on Max's jukebox.)

---

* Kris Needs, *Dream Baby Dream: Suicide: A New York City Story* (Omnibus Press, 2017), 202, Kindle.
† Ibid., 195.

Unfortunately, well-meaning rock stars took them on the road as openers . . . perhaps slowing their progress. ■

***

One evening in '76, Michael Alago, former A&R executive with Elektra Records, saw Suicide at Max's and was transfixed. At sixteen years old, he had seen Lou Reed, Todd Rundgren, Alice Cooper, and Bryan Ferry, but when he sat there late that night and watched Marty bang out synthesized distorted sounds and Alan moan, wail, and run into the audience, he was mesmerized.

> I remember getting out of my seat at the table and if you were
> looking at the stage to the right, there were these small steps,
> right at the edge. . . . I ran and I just sat there. I was enthralled.
> I had never heard anything like it in my life.*
> —Michael Alago

Alago was completely transformed by Suicide's music and Alan's performance. He sensed he was seeing something unmatched, without equal.

> All the noise that you heard come out of Marty's keyboards was
> never the same twice. And then Alan hits the stage and he's hootin'
> and hollerin'—it was like the bastard son of Elvis. . . . It got pretty
> insane because Alan was known for hitting himself with the mic,
> and bleeding. . . . [H]e knew how to clear a room really fast.
> I loved every waking moment of it.†
> —Michael Alago

After the set, Alago raced upstairs to the backstage dressing room to tell Alan how incredible he thought Suicide was that night.

> I walked up to Alan and I told him how much I loved the
> music. He looked at me like he couldn't believe that this
> young, sweet kid loved the music of Suicide.‡
> —Michael Alago

That was the beginning of a long, warm friendship lasting until Alan died. And when Michael was hired by Elektra five years later in A&R, he became important for Alan after he was signed to the label.

---

* Interview with Michael Alago, January 2023.
† Ibid.
‡ Ibid.

Alan and Michael, 1976. *Courtesy Michael Alago*

As they played Max's more regularly, Suicide became increasingly popular—in the sense that more people wanted to see what they had heard about this strange, wild, unusual band—curiosity gripped the punk crowd.

> That audience grew fairly slowly, but it doubled every time because people would go and tell their friends, "You have to come and see this band that's different from everybody else." Every show had a few more people than the one before, until they were really, really headliners. There would always be the newcomers who would scream and run out of the club, but there was also a contingent of rock'n'roll royalty that loved 'em. Many people still didn't realize they were watching this futuristic thing that [had] Elvis, the Stooges and doo-wop in it.*
>
> —Peter Crowley

---

* Kris Needs, *Dream Baby Dream: Suicide: A New York City Story* (Omnibus Press, 2017), 201, Kindle.

Suicide at CBGB, 1977. © *Bob Gruen/www.bobgruen.com*

With Debbie Harry and Paul Zone at Max's, 1976. *Photo by Michael Alago*

Then, Suicide began headlining and playing at other nightclubs, as well as CBGBs.

The world of evolving acceptance was a true life-spring for Alan. He had become used to Suicide being misunderstood and disliked by large parts of the audience. It was comforting to his soul to receive support and positive energy from Peter as well as other bands and musicians and the growing public contingent fascinated with his performances.

***

A unique genius.
—Debby Harry

Suicide were regulars at Max's and always supportive to other bands on the scene. After seeing the first Ramones gig, Alan told Joey and Johnny they really had something special and to stick with it.

And when he met a teenaged and angst-driven Lydia Lunch, Alan encouraged her when she channeled her extraordinary energy into a band. He was a firm believer in the power of perseverance and felt a strong sense of community and shared purpose with the other musicians he came in contact with on the scene, such as Debbie Harry, Paul Zone, Mark Mothersbaugh, and many others.

Alan with Gerald Casales and Mark Mothersbaugh of the band Devo, 1979. © *Ebet Roberts*

***

Bob Gruen
Photographer
June 2023

I met Alan at Max's Kansas City when he was playing there with Suicide. They were of course very different than any of the bands who played there. They weren't a band; they were a singer and a guy with multiple electronic keyboards making loud angry sounds. They were a "love 'em or hate 'em group." Some people loved them and most hated them. I remember one night when the N.Y. Dolls played until 3:00 am to a sold-out crowd, but after the show the owner, Tommy Dean, wanted to go home so he put Suicide back onstage and within ten minutes the place was empty.

I became friends with Alan in those years. We drank a lot, smoked strong Lucky Strike cigarettes, and enjoyed a "Rock & Roll" lifestyle of late nights and lots of joking and laughing. Alan had a very cynical sense of humor, which I shared with him, and we used to crack jokes back and forth for hours.

I saw Alan on the road a few times, The Clash was a group that thought Suicide was the cutting edge of the future and I was there when Suicide opened for the Clash on a tour of England. At that time in the mid-'70s the punters there thought it was fun to spit on the punk bands as a way of "being in touch with them." They loved spitting on Suicide and I have a video of them receiving so much spit that it looks like they are playing in the rain; Alan seemed to like the fact that he got the audience to react so much. Each night he would hit himself on his cheek with his microphone and open a cut and bleed down his face. It was the same small cut each night and it made for a very dramatic, frightening scene.

In the late '80s and early '90s I used to hang with Alan on Sunday nights at the Limelight club. Sunday was the night young rock musicians would come and Alan and I would hold court in a lounge in the middle of the club and kind of be the older mentors to the young crowd. We would keep each other laughing all night.

In 1999 I had a photo session with Alan for a French magazine and that's when I met Dante and saw how happy Alan was with his wife Liz Lamere and Dante. It was really good to see Alan having a good time with his art and music finally being accepted worldwide with new shows and articles extolling the virtues and foresightedness of his work. The last time I saw Alan perform was a Suicide reunion at Webster Hall in the spring of 2015. At that show Alan brought Dante onstage to sing with him and it was great to see the love between them. ∎

***

Alan at the Fulton Street loft. *Photo © 1982/2023 Ari Marcopoulos*

Alan eventually moved out of The Project on Greene Street. He headed further downtown to a commercial space in a mercantile building on Fulton Street. The first floor housed a yoga center. Alan affectionately referred to the customers as the dancing "Yogies."

The space was one room with no furniture except a mattress on an empty cement floor. And there were endless cockroaches on the walls, the floor, and under his mattress.

He kept his room lit by red lights because it turned the shit hole into a palace—the red light changed the whole ambiance. It created a more pleasing spiritual presence while disguising the annoying little creatures.

There was no bathroom except a commercial lavatory on Alan's floor. Nor was there a kitchen or food storage space. Alan regularly went to Chinatown to eat and buy cigarettes. He was very much alone in the Fulton Street space but comfortable with it. Being so low on money and resources didn't bother him.

When he went to dinner in Chinatown, he often met with his new girlfriend. She didn't see him much at the Fulton Street space because of the roaches and the chilliness everywhere.

The cold in the building was biting. On the weekends, there was no available electricity and thus, no heat or protection from the bombarding subzero temperatures, and Alan didn't have enough blankets to fight it off.

During the deep winter of '81, Alan developed pneumonia. He struggled in the cold in his room and could barely sleep. Then one night after a bout of severe coughing, he heard him.

***

"What are you doing?"

"What?" asks Alan.

"You're playing my music."

Alan's eyes watered. He looked closer. It was Elvis!

"I love your music, man!" cries Alan.

"You're not done yet," Elvis said.

Alan starts shaking. The cold was hurting him. He feared he was dying.

"What?"

"You can't go. You're not finished."

Just then, Alan fell out and when he awoke the next morning, he felt better—through his coughing and trembling, he felt better. Then he remembered Elvis. "What? . . . Oh my god," he thought to himself. And a deep smile crossed his face.

***

As Suicide performed more, Alan noticed there was interest weaving around other bands to get them recording contracts. He and Marty understood the far-reaching impact recording Suicide's music could have—and they wanted in.

Marty Thau, manager of The New York Dolls and previous head of A&R for Paramount Records, found Suicide fascinating. Thau was captivated when he heard their tracks on the Max's jukebox. He was unsure at first, but when he heard the recording of "Ghost Rider" he believed their music would do well on record.

He signed them to a contract on Red Star Records. With Roy Trakin, minister of information at Red Star, and producer Craig Leon, Suicide set out to create their first album.

> Confronting an audience with songs full of lurid, murderous imagery
> and distressing urban angst, combined with a deafening and immensely
> physical mixture of droning, rhythmic, electronic grinding repetition,
> was just part of a show that some bewildered critics didn't understand,
> and viewed with sneering disbelief and suspicion. But, as masters of
> their domain, Vega and Rev knew exactly what they were doing.*
> —Marty Thau

***

* Kris Needs, *Dream Baby Dream: Suicide: A New York City Story* (Omnibus Press, 2017), 153, Kindle.

Suicide's first album. *Courtesy Saturn Strip, Ltd.*

They recorded in a studio in northern New York called Ultima Studios. The building was shabby and run-down, and in early 1977, the studio was sparse and basic.

> It was totally analog of course, with a couple of delays. The console was
> extremely microphonic; the equalization was tuned in octaves of A and
> you could really overdrive sends if you wanted and this actually helped
> [Suicide's] sound. It didn't have much separation but there was "a booth."*
> —Craig Leon ,

Alan and Rev recorded the entire album while performing live—in about a
half-hour—with the exception of "Frankie Teardrop."

---

* John Doran, "Blown Out '77: In the Studio with Suicide," *The Quietus,* July 15, 2019, https://thequietus
.com/articles/26801.

Suicide performing with Ric Ocasek, 1989. © *Ebet Roberts*

After leaving the studio that first day, Alan read a newspaper article about a factory worker who had lost his job, killed his wife and baby, and then himself. He knew this was the story the song needed to tell and the next day he rerecorded his vocal for the song "making it arguably the most harrowing and intense ten and a half minutes of audio ever committed to tape."*

Yet, during the final mixing, Craig Leon had to go to LA for a previous production job. Everyone was thrown and weren't sure what to do. Thau decided to take over despite not having any experience in production work. He ended up "[g]etting inspiration from a huge bag of grass."†

After a couple of weeks, Craig returned, and he and Thau completed the final mixing of Suicide's first album.

***

Although initially giving the album a dismissive review, *Rolling Stone* placed it on its list of 500 greatest albums of all time in 2012 and 2020.‡

Liz: When Alan learned of the Rolling Stone listing he said, "This is the slowest Suicide in the history of mankind. I guess we really were ahead of our time."

***

---

* Ibid.
† Ibid.
‡ See https://www.rollingstone.com/music/music-lists/best-albums-of-all-time-1062063/suicide-suicide-2
-1062735/.

Roy Trakin
Journalist
Minister of Information, Red Star Records, 1977–1978
December 2022

The relationship between Alan and the audience was always so interesting. He would toy with them. I know he was a professional wrestling fan too. And he really enjoyed being the bad guy, which was so absolutely 180 degrees from what he was off the stage, where he was a pussycat, a sweet, sweet man who had a heart so large.

I think he was a bit of a sadomasochist. I remember him slapping his face really hard. I think there was a bit of self-loathing to what he was doing. But there was this sense we're all in this together. You know, we're all Frankies—we are all Frankie Teardrop. We all have these emotions and feelings of loathing, and we all want to just connect. And Alan's connection took such an aggressive form, but ultimately, he just wanted to bring you into his circle. It was remarkable. And he'd be the first to admit he could clear out a room faster than almost anybody ever could.

But once he cleared out that room, the ones who remained were totally there. And whoever it was, I mean, it could be two, it could be three, it could be a half dozen, but they were mesmerized.

Marty Thau—he was a true believer. He had faith in this and Thau was someone who saw the artistry. Being the manager of the New York Dolls at the time—of course, the primary example of a band you either loved or hated with no in-between—it was the same deal with Suicide. I mean—coming out with that name. It was an "in your face" kind of name.

But as is often written about them, it wasn't about death—Suicide—it was about life—it was about rebirth. And that Elvis Costello gig was amazing. Alan worked the crowd up to a fevered pitch. And then Elvis, who was a friend and admirer of them, played a very short, angry set. Then he went off and wouldn't come out for an encore. The fans went absolutely out of their minds. They started pulling tiles off the ceiling. They started throwing chairs. And I remember Alan and Marty and I had to run out the back door. We literally had to escape on those cobblestone streets in a car. Oh my God—we were literally being chased with pitchforks and torches. It was like Frankenstein.

You looked at Alan and you realized he was the sum of various influences. He admitted to Iggy and Elvis Presley. And I know he was a fan of Sinatra and that crowd. He'd always have a cigarette and sometimes he popped the cigarette into the audience and there was something really funny about it. I mean, there was a sense of humor there. People thought they were so foreboding with Rev back there in his black goggles.

But to me they were like Vladimir and Estragon from *Waiting for Godot*. They were Abbott and Costello, they were Laurel and Hardy, you know, they were a classic comedy. But also, my critical philosophy has always been finding the common thread in seemingly disparate elements kind of like a Hegelian thesis, antithesis and that was what attracted me to them.

When Marty Thau signed them to Red Star, they were reviled on the local scene. I mean, you know, Christgau—the renowned music critic—hated them. All the people who mattered hated them. They were pariahs on the local scene.

They weren't a rock and roll band. Martin Rev is one of the most brilliant musicians—the Mozart of the time. People will be remembering these guys and going back and rediscovering them. They were fifty years ahead of themselves in 1974 and by the time they ended, they were still twenty years ahead.

And Alan's art—he was truly the ultimate punk artist in that he recycled—he took things other people considered garbage and had thrown out on the streets and made sculptures. Alan wasn't just a singer in a band. He was an artist. His life was a work of art.

There's a certain point at which noise becomes music and causes you to completely change your mind about what music could be or what sound is.

There was such a conceptual aspect to what Suicide were doing. I spent a lot of time with Marty Thau in the studio, and I remember remixing—I think it was "Dream Baby Dream" with Rev—and remixing and remixing that song and Thau would get upset about the obsessiveness of the work.

In the post-production, you hear the echoes and the overlapping and the way noise becomes music—you hear the harmonics in it. This was twenty-first-century dance music. It's got a beat. And you can dance to it. I saw amazing performances by Suicide. It was truly a privilege to watch them. ∎

***

A key song for Alan—"Frankie Teardrop."

> Then you hear "Frankie Teardrop" for the first time
> and nothing in your record collection or your life—
> outside of war—prepares you for the storyline.*
> —Henry Rollins

---

* Ron Hart, "Henry Rollins on How Suicide's Alan Vega Changed His Life," *Pitchfork*, July 20, 2016, https://pitchfork.com/thepitch/1235-henry-rollins-on-alan-vega/.

"Frankie Teardrop" live, Eric's Liverpool, 1977. *Author's collection*

. . . one of the most amazing songs I ever heard. *
—Bruce Springsteen

* Frank Rose, "Alan Vega Ignored the Art World. It Won't Return the Favor," *New York Times*, June 23, 2017, https://www.nytimes.com/2017/06/23/arts/design/alan-vega-ignored-the-art-world-it-wont-return-the-favor .html.

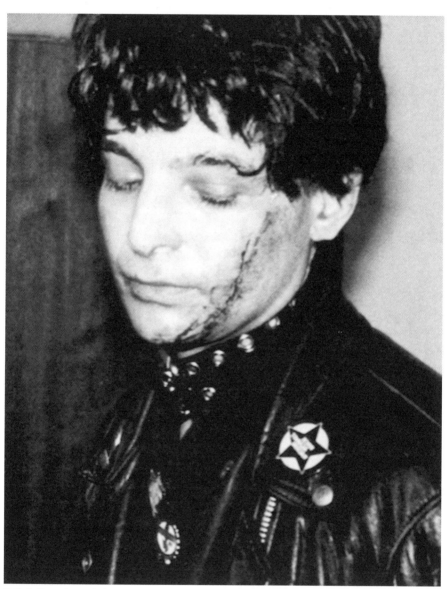

10 Bestial

1977 . . . 1979 . . . 1983 . . .

The sound of blood is the blood of sound.*

"Frankie Teardrop"

Twenty year old Frankie
He's married he's got a kid
And he's working in a factory
    He's working from seven to five
He's just trying to survive
Well let's hear it for Frankie
Frankie Frankie
    Well Frankie can't make it
'Cause things are just too hard
Frankie can't make enough money
Frankie can't buy enough food
    And Frankie's getting evicted
Oh let's hear it for Frankie
Oh Frankie Frankie
Oh Frankie Frankie
    Frankie is so desperate
He's gonna kill his wife and kid
Frankie's gonna kill his kid
Frankie picked up a gun

---

* Alexandre Breton, *Alan Vega: Conversation with an Indian* (Le Texte Vivant, 2017), Kindle.

Pointed at the six month old in the crib
Oh Frankie
Frankie looked at his wife
Shot her
"Oh what have I done?"
Let's hear it for Frankie
Frankie teardrop
Frankie put the gun to his head
Frankie's dead
Frankie's lying in hell
We're all Frankies
We're all lying in hell*

Many audiences continued to dislike them.

Suicide's innovative sound and live performance—so punk even the punks hated them—was met with increasing hostility. Alan and Marty were driven to break new ground in the world of rock 'n' roll historically inhabited by guitar-driven music—with non-rock 'n' roll.

When Peter Crowley set them up as regulars at Max's, Alan found himself continually redefining his performance—never performing the songs the same way twice.

Alan was going into the audience before we even had tables.†
—Peter Crowley

He wedged himself into the audience, breaking down the barrier between them. And it wasn't long before the provocation became a regular, known, expected part of Alan's shows. Not only was he busting down the wall; he was employing a strategy of shock and awe to clarify: "this is not for fun, people."

Alan . . . used to wear knives and punch his own face.
He'd also whip the stage with a motorcycle chain.‡
—Arthur "Killer" Kane
New York Dolls' bassist

It was seen by many in the audience as intimidating and then frightening. Many wondered if he would be inflicting harm on them.

---

* "Frankie Teardrop" by Alan Vega and Martin Rev.
† Kris Needs, *Dream Baby Dream: Suicide: A New York City Story* (Omnibus Press, 2017), 203, Kindle.
‡ Henry Irvine-Scott, "Suicide Is Fearless," *Record Collector*, January 21, 2014, https://recordcollectormag
.com/articles/suicide-is-fearless.

But that's not what happened—ever. Violence as a consequence was not his end goal.

> He's working from seven to five
> He's just trying to survive
> Well let's hear it for Frankie*

As the band secured their place in the evolving avant-garde landscape, and the reconstruction of rock 'n' roll within the downtown rock clubs, Alan continued redefining his art.

The visual and the performing were integrating.

The powerful imagery depicted in his artwork—and the fevered drive trying to wake up the world—bled into his onstage stance. It was intended outrage and passion built into his performances. He had an objective.

> They gained a particular reputation in the scene, because their first shows were very confrontational, instigating violence. In some shows, Martin and Alan dressed up as artsy street thugs, and Vega became infamous for brandishing [the] length of motorcycle drive chain onstage. Their look and their performance altogether were not well-received by the audience, who often booed them from the get-go. Martin Rev compared the feeling of stepping onto the stage to war, as if they were going into the trenches.[†]

The intensity at the heart of his onstage world was not caused by a dislike or hatred of the audience or any person in particular. The fury was a burning seed crawling out of the soil of society—the wars this country were perpetrating, the continuing oppression of the poor and disenfranchised, the endless lies the government stood by, and the state of disgust and disease of New York City—everywhere.

> In private he is the most courteous and affable man in the world, but at the same time the anger in him is not in any way faked. . . . This double tension has been visible in Vega's work since his apprenticeship years with Ad Reinhardt.[‡]
> —Alexandre Breton

---

* "Frankie Teardrop" by Alan Vega and Martin Rev.
† "Milestones in Music History #3: Suicide, and How Bravery Paid Off," *Insounder*, December 7, 2021, https://insounder.org/milestones-music-history-3-suicide-and-how-bravery-paid.
‡ Alexandre Breton, *Alan Vega: Conversation with an Indian* (Le Texte Vivant, 2017), Kindle.

As Antonin Artaud, the preeminent creator of *The Theatre of Cruelty* in the early twentieth century, delineated:

> [C]ivilization had turned humans into sick and repressed creatures
> and . . . the true function of the theatre was to rid humankind of
> these repressions and liberate each individual's instinctual energy.
> [Artaud] proposed removing the barrier of the stage between
> performers and audience and producing mythic spectacles that
> would include verbal incantations, groans and screams.*

His fury at the complacency of society and government was merely the first ingredient Alan poured into his performances. Growing out of his outrage was his desire to illuminate—that he, Marty, Suicide—were not there to entertain. Alan was deeply committed to showing that despite the audience's expectation after paying the entrance fee and sitting down with a drink, to be amused, distracted—that was not on the agenda.

Like Artaud's perspective, the key was to bring art and performance to the audience with an undeniable truth which isn't cloaked in the pretenses of entertainment.

> Artaud sought to remove aesthetic distance, bringing the audience
> into direct contact with the dangers of life. By turning theatre into
> a place where the spectator is exposed rather than protected,
> Artaud was committing an act of cruelty upon them.†

That was Alan's passion—his commitment to not entertain, to not let the audience off easy.

> I hated the idea of going to a concert in search of fun. Our attitude was,
> "Fuck you buddy, you're getting the street right back in your face."‡
> —Alan

When he threw the street at them, audiences expressed their intense discomfort with screams of: "Go home!" "You suck!" "Fuck you!"

---

* Editors of *Encyclopaedia Britannica*, "Theatre of Cruelty," *Encyclopedia Britannica*, March 6, 2016, https://www.britannica.com/topic/Theatre-of-Cruelty.
† Natasha Tripney, "Antonin Artaud and the Theatre of Cruelty," *British Library*, September 7, 2017, https://www.bl.uk/20th-century-literature/articles/antonin-artaud-and-the-theatre-of-cruelty.
‡ John Wilde, "Every night I Thought I'd Be Killed," *Guardian*, July 31, 2008, https://www.theguardian.com/music/2008/aug/01/popandrock.suicide.

Some nights . . . we'd barricade the doors, so nobody had any choice
but to stay and listen. Every night it was like a fucking revolution.*
—Alan

***

By stripping away convention, Suicide confronted listeners with
what they feared most; namely, themselves. When people went
to Vega and Rev for more standard or predictable versions of
entertainment, they were forced to marinate in the very states of
being that they most feared—emptiness, loneliness, confusion. By
not providing the conventions on which their audience so desperately
depended, Suicide caused anger, panic and revulsion.†
—Michael Friedman, *Psychology Today*

***

In the fall of 1978, a college DJ in Albany, New York—Kevin Patrick—got
hold of the first Suicide album and found it so fascinating, he sent it to Howard
Thompson—then at Bronze Records in London. Howard was equally captivated
and signed Suicide to Bronze records. He then set up shows to have Suicide open
for Elvis Costello and the Clash on their European tours.

A few years later, Howard moved to New York City and became head of A&R
at Elektra Records—with whom Alan was eventually signed as a solo artist—and
Thompson brought Kevin with him on his A&R team.

***

Kevin Patrick
Record Company Executive
A&R Elektra Records 1984–1988
April 2023
Well, Howard Thompson and I originally met when he was a junior A&R guy
at Island Records, and I was the program director of a pretty prominent college
radio station that had a big reach in the upstate New York and Toronto area. I
always loved British music from day one. And I wrote a letter to Howard Thompson about a punk band he represented who I played a lot on the radio station.

By 1978, Howard had moved to Bronze Records and I sent him the first Suicide album. And he was playing it constantly in the office. He talks about how
stunned he was at its power.

---

* Ibid.
† Michael Friedman, "The Beautiful Randomness of the Band Suicide," July 18, 2016, https://www.psychology
today.com/us/blog/brick-brick/201607/the-beautiful-randomness-the-band-suicide.

Howard would visit New York often and during one of his early visits, we went to visit Alan on Fulton Street.

It was a shell of a loft. Maybe there was a mattress on the floor and some big cardboard box that doubled as a coffee table, a dilapidated TV set with a couple of coat hangers for antennas. And I remember in the fridge there was nothing but a six-pack of beer. In the back corner of the place was this heap of stuff, clothes and whatnot—that was basically Johnny Thunders stuff piled up there and Thunders was passed out in the middle of it.

Howard eventually moved up in the ranks and went pretty quickly to Columbia records in New York. He was there for a year or two, and Bob Krasnow at Elektra offered him the opportunity to run the brand-new Elektra A&R department.

So, Howard called me: "Listen, I can hire an A&R staff." So, I joined him.

As soon as I got to Elektra—they were starting on Alan's second album, *Just a Million Dreams*, and Howard was putting it all together. All those conversations in planning it happened down at the Gramercy where Alan was living. The pattern was—we would start in the bar, and maybe we'd go up to Alan's room for a bit, and then we would go to Danceteria until 4:00, 5:00 in the morning, and then back to Alan's. This became the daily routine. And Alan and I, we just kind of hit it off.

I think we had a commonality in that when we were in the thick of stuff, we could zone out whatever we weren't interested in. And we seemed to have zero interest in similar things.

He was happy with his relationship with Chris Lord-Alge. He was happy with Elektra because he was happy with Howard. And that's really all that needed to happen.

We were all super excited and it felt like it was going to be a competitive album at the time. It was going to be very Alan, but it was also going to be able to stand successfully in the programming world alongside bands like the Cars, which were kind of electro-rock, cutting edge. Believe it or not at the time, it looked like Alan was going to get in the fast lane because of this record, the same lane that Television or the Ramones and people like that, couldn't seem to get into. And I think there was some great confidence in it. He was a very up person at that time. And he had that whole regalia on with . . . the red and black, fringe jacket and his cool shoes.

One time, there was a blizzard and we were uptown near the Beacon in this little skivvy sort of bar. And we went in—where one of us knew somebody that was selling some drugs. And we get some coke. And the thing was—cabs were in low supply because of the weather, and the two or three that slowed down to pick us up—as soon as they saw Alan, they just stepped on it. So . . . I had Alan hide in the doorway and I got the cab.

Alan, Kevin Patrick, and Andrew Eldritch, 1985. *Photo by Howard Thompson*

We were always together at night going to Danceteria. It was our thing. We talked about everything. But it would never hold his attention to go back and talk about old recordings that he had released.

Alan and I would hang out with Joey Ramone a lot, too. They had a really solid friendship for a long time. Of course, now that Joey has passed away, we can't get any further information about their friendship, but they would have long conversations.

At the Artists Space dinner . . . Kim Gordon was speaking at this event where Alan was being honored as a visual artist, and she was elaborating on the influence that Suicide had been to Sonic Youth . . . she was talking about this whole experience and the uplifting artistic result of it for her—and Alan turns to me and says, "Who is this chick?"

To me, Alan was just a really kind, generous, and gentle person. When the lights came down and Alan would be onstage—he was showing the audience what the world really looked like.

I feel very lucky because I was on the gentle side of him. And there was never anything aggressive or harsh or mean or humiliating that Alan did or said to me or any of his friends. ■

***

In 1978, Suicide opened for Elvis Costello on his premier European tour. Their first stop was Brussels.

It is renowned because Elvis was riding an exploding star in rock 'n' roll. But rather than follow the release of his second album—*This Year's Model*—with a tour of easy pop concerts promoting his rise, the shows turned into police riots.

As the audience became more hostile and booed and screamed at Suicide that they should go home, Alan tried to finish singing but the crowd became raving mad and raised their fists to get Suicide to go. They wanted "Elvis! Elvis! Elvis!"

> [Suicide] were like a hand grenade at a sweet 16 party.*
> —Miriam Linna

Then, an audience member jumped onstage and ripped the microphone out of Alan's hands. The crowd went wild, applauding and screaming their support. However, Alan was able to get a new mic and started singing "Frankie Teardrop" acapella, but the crowd kept violently harassing him and Marty, demanding they get offstage. Alan screamed:

> Shut the fuck up, this is about Frankie!†

It was savage.

Finally, Suicide left the stage and Elvis came on. The crowd, having been sent into a violent frenzy during the last twenty minutes, was thrilled to see Elvis finally appear.

But Elvis didn't feel the same way. He was furious with the way the audience had treated Suicide and "he made no secret of his outrage."‡ After a short set, Elvis went off the stage and refused to play an encore. A full-on riot ensued.

---

* Miriam Linna quoted in Kris Needs, *Dream Baby Dream: Suicide: A New York City Story* (Omnibus Press, 2017), 250, Kindle.
† Daniel Dylan Wray, "'It Was Like Going into the Trenches': How Suicide Rioted against Plastic Punk," *Guardian*, July 18, 2017, https://www.theguardian.com/music/2017/jul/18/suicide-23-minutes-over-brussels-alan-vega-martin-rev-punk-riot-1978.
‡ "42 Years Ago Suicide Performed Their Legendary '23 Minutes Over Brussels'!" *Peek-a-Boo*, July 16, 2020, http://www.peek-a-boo-magazine.be/en/news/2020/42-years-ago-suicide-performed-their-legendary-23-minutes-over-brussels/.

> [W]hen Elvis Costello didn't perform an encore, the crowd's anger
> erupted. . . . "The audience were tearing the tiles from the walls," Rev
> remembers. "Bouncers had kids in full nelson headlocks as we were
> rushed out . . . [W]e were told it was too dangerous . . . it was a total
> riot." Soon the police stormed the room and discharged tear gas.
> [Howard] Thompson recalls . . . "Fans were tearing the place apart."*

The mayhem was captured in the now infamous recording, "23 Minutes Over Brussels."

They continued opening for Elvis throughout Europe and the shows didn't get much better. But Elvis wasn't worried or concerned. He thought Suicide were revolutionary and he was keeping them on the tour.

In fact, Alan ran into Elvis in London while running an errand and Elvis said, "Do you think you can start another riot tonight? I'm kinda tired and wouldn't mind cutting our set short again."

***

Elvis Costello
Interview May 2023

What did you know about Suicide before they opened for you?

Oh, yes. I still have my copy of that first wonderful record.

What was your reaction after Suicide were booed and forced off the stage by the audience? How did you feel about it?

The riot in Brussels has gone into legend, although even at our last meeting, when Alan visited the set of the *Spectacle* television show on which I was interviewing Lou Reed, we disagreed on the details of the evening. A bootleg has long been in circulation immortalizing the dissolution of Suicide's set with Alan refusing to back down in face of an incredibly hostile Belgian audience. I was backstage, mortified to hear the crowd chanting my name (or at least, "Elvis") in an attempt to chase Suicide off the stage.

I remember Alan offered the mic to someone in the front row, who promptly unplugged it and made off into the night pursued by my rather leery soundman, "Murph" and fisticuffs ensued.

Alan's account was that the evening then proceeded directly into the riot, but that is only partially accurate. I'd been surprised and disappointed by the reaction of the Brussels crowd and being fairly drunk and whatever, got myself pretty indignant. Far from the evening ending with the Suicide performance, there are a number of pictures of me onstage that night, some of me clearly baiting

---

* Daniel Dylan Wray, "'It Was Like Going into the Trenches': How Suicide Rioted against Plastic Punk," *Guardian*, July 18, 2017, https://www.theguardian.com/music/2017/jul/18/suicide-23-minutes-over-brussels -alan-vega-martin-rev-punk-riot-1978.

the crowd. The Attractions and I played a short, if not entirely incoherent set designed to further enrage the audience when they didn't exactly get the pleasant "New Wave" band they apparently had been expecting.

We came off and nobody really called for an encore but started smashing things and then we heard the sound of horse's hooves outside.

Did you speak with Alan and Marty after the riots started?

I don't recall us discussing anything after the riot broke out, but we all had to wait until the crowd and police had dispersed. I don't think any of us expected the evening to end with a cavalry charge.

What were your feelings about them as a band?

Those years were about jolting rock music coming out of a tedious orthodoxy to which it is soon sadly returned. Alan and Marty were experts in "jolting," and I continue to find inspirations from Marty's distorted drums machine and you can take many of Alan's songs and revisit them the way Bruce Springsteen did. They would hold up the way any great rock 'n' roll song might, so long as you don't clutter them up with too many instruments. ∎

***

Things became exponentially worse when Suicide opened for the Clash on their UK tour later in the year. They were too punk for the punkers coming to see the crème de la crème of punk.

> Every Suicide show felt like World War Three in those days.*
> —Alan

At Glasgow, the crowd was going crazy, demanding Suicide get off the stage when Alan screamed at them, "You fuckers have to live through us to get to the main band!"† at which point, someone threw an axe at Alan's head.

It missed him.

By a hair.

> Every night I thought I was going to get killed. The
> longer it went on, the more I'd be thinking,
> "Odds are it's going to be tonight."‡
> —Alan

Not everyone was predisposed to hate Suicide. One night in Germany, the full lineup of Kraftwerk stood front and center up by the stage in their typical outfits

---

* John Wilde, "Every night I thought I'd be killed," *Guardian*, July 31, 2008, https://www.theguardian.com/music/2008/aug/01/popandrock.suicide.
† Ibid.
‡ Ibid.

Photo by Catherine Ceresole

of formal suits. Alan didn't know who they were or what to make of this enigmatic crew and proceeded to taunt them. But after the show was over, they came back-stage to introduce themselves. Alan was very surprised.

***

For Alan—the violence and the riots, the police, the tear gas, the anger and near-death moments—it all made sense. He would be found watching in amazement as he saw the police racing in and rounding up audience members. It was all part of the truth, his existential authenticity.

> Art is played out between two poles: the celebration of life and the celebration of death. Creation and destruction in the same gesture. It was the street being played out on the stage, with all its blank violence and distress. No Future was the slogan for the punk generation of 1977.*
> —Alexandre Breton

***

> [H]e was a true and uncompromising artist who cannot be defined by one record or one crazy night in 1978.†
> —Elvis Costello

---

* Alexandre Breton, *Alan Vega: Conversation with an Indian* (Le Texte Vivant, 2017), Kindle.
† Interview with Elvis Costello, May 2023.

11 Gloria

1977 . . . 1980 . . . 1983 . . .

> I do not believe in God and I am not an atheist.*
> —Albert Camus

And then there was Ocasek.

> When I work with him, I know I'm in God's hands.†
> —Alan

Life had become a bit crazed and breathless. Elvis Costello and the Clash were only the beginning. Suicide had started to get even more interest from others well positioned in the industry.

Alan had some money left over from the Red Star Record advance and he was earning a little more from Suicide's gigs. The quality of life had improved. Alan's girlfriend, herself an artist, was not making much money, so Alan supported them both.

Fate often brings surprising turns, and it did for Alan and Suicide when Ric Ocasek, who had recently started his band the Cars, went to see Suicide perform at the Rat Club in Kenmore Square in Boston.

It was early 1978. Ocasek had heard Suicide's first album and had become a devout fan. When he saw them perform, he immediately headed backstage after the gig ended—to express his admiration.

This night was before the release of the Cars' first album.

---

* Albert Camus, *The Notebooks 1951–1959* (New York: Alfred A. Knopf, 1965).
† Elisabeth Vincentelli, "Just What They Needed," *New York Times*, October 17, 2004, https://www.nytimes.com/2004/10/17/arts/music/just-what-they-needed.html.

UNIVERSAL AMPHITHEATRE 1979
THE
CARS
ON THE ROAD 1979

WITH SPECIAL GUESTS **SUICIDE**

TUESDAY, WEDNESDAY & THURSDAY
SEPTEMBER 4, 5 & 6

TICKETS AVAILABLE AT UNIVERSAL AMPHITHEATRE BOX OFFICE, TICKETRON, TELETRON,
CHARGELINE AND MUTUAL OUTLETS
100 UNIVERSAL CITY PLAZA   LOS ANGELES, CA. 91608

Author's Collection

When their album, *The Cars*, was finally launched in 1978, it had a massive effect. The band became enormous. Then when their second album, *Candy-O*, came out the following year to even greater audience praise, Ocasek wanted nothing more than for Suicide to open for them on the Candy-O tour.

Ocasek had taken a fierce, enduring interest in Suicide and when he and Alan met, it became a friendship for life.

> I was freaked out by him. I was scared to go up to Alan—he was pretty aggressive then, pulling people up on stage and confronting them. But he had the anti-show. They would do everything they could to have people throw them off the stage, even when they played in Los Angeles, at Hollywood Bowl. We had them open for us on a tour and we played in arenas, and before they got to their second song, they got booed. . . . All the critics loved them. But the people didn't get them. They were the real deal. . . . Those guys were artists.*
> —Ric

Ocasek was struck by the intense energy of the music and Alan's performances.

> One of the many things we loved about Suicide was they were the only band that was actually louder between songs than when they were playing. It seemed like there was all this primal noise that existed somewhere, maybe in space, or the Earth's core, that they would somehow harness and channel into their songs. Of course, they drove everybody out of the club except a few hardened devotees, so Alan had lots of room to walk out across the tables.†
> —Ric

When Suicide arrived at the Amphitheater in LA to open for the Cars, the promoters presented a list of things that would be inappropriate for Alan to do:

Swearing
Breaking bottles
Cutting himself
Inciting mayhem

---

* Roger Catlin, "Ric Ocasek, The TVD Interview," *Vinyl District*, February 15, 2019, https://www.thevinyl district.com/storefront/2019/02/ric-ocasek-the-tvd-interview/.
† Kris Needs, *Dream Baby Dream: Suicide: A New York City Story* (Omnibus Press, 2017), 213, Kindle.

When they informed him of the rules, Alan looked at them. Then his eyes spanned across the hills behind the Amphitheater.

"Bob Hope's mansion is right up there. God forbid we disturb the peaceful enjoyment of his home," he said.

Ocasek stepped in and instructed Alan to let the fuck-bombs fly.

> Vega and Rev court the anger and outrage. In the much explored world of rock, they apparently feel there must be room for a group that everyone can hate. To draw the audience hostility, the pair smothers itself in snobbish art-rock trappings. Vega struts around the stage turning up his shirt collar in mock conceit and sings with the super-confidence of a rock messiah.*

The audience was far from impressed. Alan fired wild vulgarity, escalating the situation. People threw garbage, shoes, cups of beer, coins—anything they could find—at him. Alan screamed every possible obscenity right back. And because he had been devastated by the Dodgers move to LA in 1958, he screeched:

"You suck just like your Dodgers!"†

Although the promoters had wanted to get Alan off the stage immediately, Ocasek informed them the Cars wouldn't perform if that happened.

The rest of the band agreed.

When Suicide's set ended, the Cars came onstage and Ric flew open with, "How are you motherfuckers doing tonight?!"

> The irony was that the Cars could be so conservative on stage and yet select an opening act as adventurous as Suicide. . . . By the end of [their] second number almost everyone in the 5200-seat Amphitheater was booing, shouting insults, or heckling Suicide. It's easy to see why the joke in New York . . . is that audiences wish the duo would live up to its name.‡

After the show, Alan went to get something to eat. As always in New York—he was dressed entirely in black leather—and his jacket emblazoned with "Suicide" on the back.

He was directed to a McDonald's located down Kirk Douglas Drive. There were no people on the sidewalk. It didn't register easily with Alan that LA was a car culture and people drove—they didn't walk—like in New York. After a few

---

* Robert Hilburn, "The Cars: Sluggish Road Performance," *Los Angeles Times*, September 6, 1979, https://www.fromthearchives.com/av_mr/VR04_Sep_79c.jpg.
† Kris Needs, *Dream Baby Dream: Suicide: A New York City Story* (Omnibus Press, 2017), 238, Kindle.
‡ Robert Hilburn, "The Cars: Sluggish Road Performance," *Los Angeles Times*, September 6, 1979, https://www.fromthearchives.com/av_mr/VR04_Sep_79c.jpg.

blocks, a police helicopter suddenly appeared flying above him and shined a beam of light on him.

"Get off the street ya vagabond! Move it!"

Alan quickly looked up and felt fear pulsing through him. With what he had heard about the LA police, he made a fast run for it.

***

Soon thereafter was Alan's "Presley period"*—getting a taste of Ric's lifestyle and the bubble of rock stardom:

> [H]e shows off his wonderful treasures and gets ferried
> around by the King's own limousine driver!†
> —Alexandre Breton

The Cars went on to cover Suicide's song, "Rocket USA" and Suicide supported them on the Midnight Special—a popular late-night variety TV program showcasing music and comedians—in late September 1979.

Wolfman Jack—a well-known DJ and performer—was the host. At the rehearsal for the show, though, Wolfman was freaked out by Suicide—their name and their performance—and he demanded Suicide not be allowed to appear.

That's when Ocasek told Wolfman straight and with impact:

"No Suicide. No Cars."

So, the show went on. But Wolfman refused to introduce Suicide when they were set to go onstage. Someone else stepped in to cover for him.

Suicide performed their now-famous song "Dream Baby Dream" followed by "Ghost Rider." Ocasek was thrilled with the ghostly, sublime performance.

***

Ocasek ended up producing their second album, *Suicide: Alan Vega and Martin Rev* in 1980.

The album got very good reviews. It was named one of the best albums of 1980 by *NME*.‡

> Perhaps it's not as renegade as *Suicide*, but it's an arguably
> better, more realized work, and just as essential.§

---

* Alexandre Breton, *Alan Vega: Conversation with an Indian* (Le Texte Vivant, 2017), Kindle.
† Ibid.
‡ *NME*, "*NME*'s Best Albums and Tracks of 1980," October 10, 2016, https://www.nme.com/features/1980-2-1045402.
§ Andy Kellman, "Suicide: Alan Vega/Martin Rev," *Allmusic*, https://www.allmusic.com/album/suicide-alan-vega-martin-rev-mw0000603758.

"Midnight Special," 1979. *Author's Collection*

Marty, Alan, and Ric at the Power Station, 1980. © *Ebet Roberts*

The album was released on ZE Records. Michael Zilkha, co-owner of ZE, was a huge fan of Suicide. He had first learned about Suicide from Howard Thompson and was instrumental in many things happening for the band. He also helped get Vega signed to Elektra Records for his solo work.

***

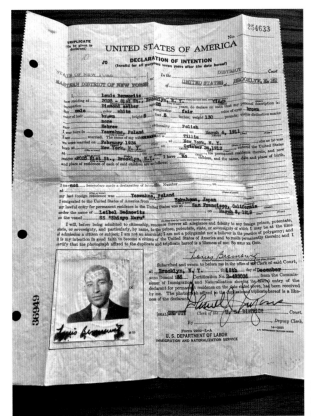

Louis Bermowitz Citizenship Application, 1936. *Photo by Amie Bermowitz*

Baseball team in the Poconos—Alan far left, cousin Marty third from left, 1949. *Courtesy Jack and Riva Levitt Estate*

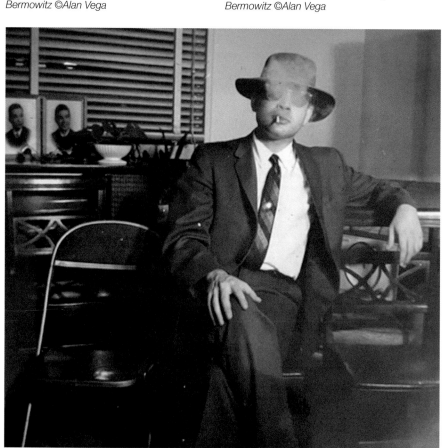

Self-Portrait, 1970. *Photo by Mel Auston*

"I made it past suicide again," early 1970. *Photo by Mel Auston*

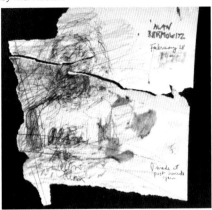

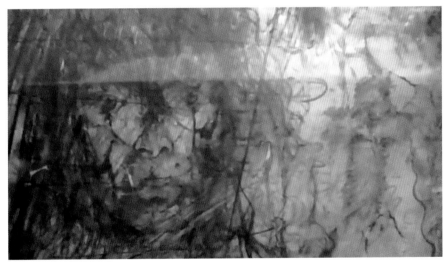

"Untitled," early 1970. *Photo by Mel Auston*

Art-Rite, Special #13 by Alan Suicide, 1977. *Author's collection*

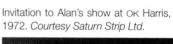
Invitation to Alan's show at OK Harris, 1972. *Courtesy Saturn Strip Ltd.*

"Untitled," Alan Vega, OK Harris, 1978. *Courtesy Saturn Strip Ltd.*

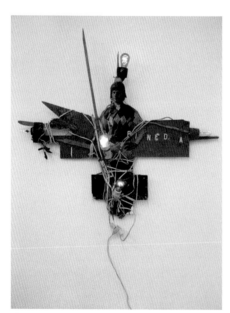

"Pineda," Alan Vega, 1983. *Courtesy Galerie Laurent Godin*

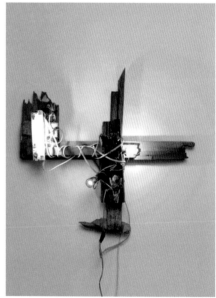

"Dachau," Alan Vega, 1983. *Courtesy Galerie Laurent Godin*

Isenheim Altarpiece (1515). *By Matthias Grünewald—Own work, Pd/Wikimedia Commons*

Max's Kansas City, September 1976. © *Bob Gruen/www.bobgruen.com*

Alan and Marty, Ghost Rider, Copenhagen.
Photo by Liz Lamere

Brussels, 1978. *Author's collection*

Performing at the Brussels concert, June 1978. *Photo by Gie Knaeps*

Dunfermline, Kinema Ballroom, UK, 1978.
Author's collection

*Suicide: Alan Vega and Martin Rev,
1980. Courtesy Saturn Strip, Ltd.*

Kuch, Alan, and Richard Fantina performing, 1980. *Photo by Dori Kuchinsky and Peter Wantula*

Collision Drive, 1981. *Courtesy Saturn Strip, Ltd.*

Play Loud! Production Release, 2023. *Courtesy Saturn Strip, Ltd.*

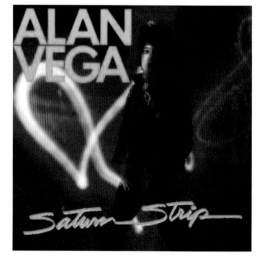

Saturn Strip, 1983. *Courtesy Saturn Strip, Ltd.*

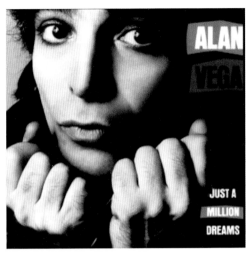

Alan and Liz at the "Be Well, Ramone's
Beat on Cancer," benefit concert, 2004.
© Bob Gruen/www.bobgruen.com

Just a Million Dreams, 1985. *Courtesy Saturn Strip,
Ltd.*

Alan and Toots, Paris, 2004. *Photo by Liz Lamere*

Deuce Avenue, 1990. Courtesy Saturn Strip, Ltd.

Alan and Liz on tour, 1990. *Photo by Catherine Ceresole*

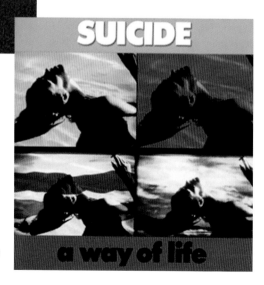

A Way of Life, 1988. Courtesy Saturn Strip, Ltd.

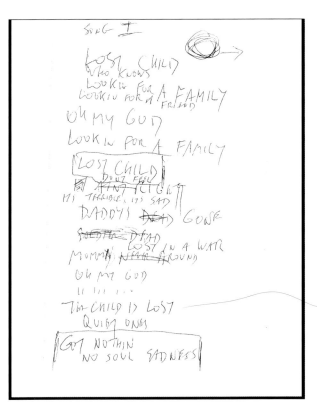

Alan Vega Notebooks. *Courtesy Saturn Strip, Ltd.*

Alan Vega Notebooks. *Courtesy Saturn Strip, Ltd.*

Alan Vega: Deuce Avenue War: The Warriors V3 97, 1991. Courtesy Saturn Strip, Ltd.

Power on to Zero Hour, 1991. Courtesy Saturn Strip, Ltd.

Why Be Blue, 1992. Courtesy Saturn Strip, Ltd.

Momilou's Jesus statue at Hanover Square with *Vega's Marilyn II* Sculpture. *Photo by Liz Lamere*

Alan and Liz wedding reception, 1992. *Photo by Peggy Melgard*

New Raceion, 1993. *Courtesy Saturn Strip, Ltd.*

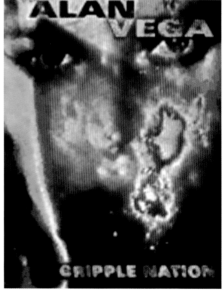

Alan Vega, *Cripple Nation*, 1994. *Courtesy Saturn Strip, Ltd.*

Suicide/Alan Vega Anthology, 1994. Courtesy Saturn Strip, Ltd.

Dujang Prang, 1995. Courtesy Saturn Strip, Ltd.

Extrait du film *"Autour de Vega,"* 1995. *Author's Collection*

Alan and Christophe, 2004. ©
Joseph Caprio

Cubist Blues, 1996. Courtesy Saturn
Strip, Ltd.

Getchertiktz, 1996. Courtesy
Saturn Strip, Ltd.

Michael Zilkha
Publisher
Former ZE Records Co-Owner
February 2023

The first time I saw Suicide was at CBGB's and it was pretty empty. I don't know what night it was—it might have been a Sunday night. And they were being heckled and booed and I hadn't seen anything like it ever and was sort of fascinated by the music. And then I bought their first record as soon as it came out. I had started ZE Records and I just assumed that Suicide was signed because they'd put out a record.

So, I dropped a series of cassettes with the receptionist at CBS in London. About two months later, I got a call from Howard Thompson at CBS. And that was the first time anyone from a major record company had called me. And he said, "Do you like Suicide?" And I said, "I absolutely love Suicide," and he said, "Well, they're unsigned," which I couldn't believe. I mean, it seemed incredible. I was not aggressive in seeking out bands. It isn't like I was going to clubs and looking for bands. It was really who walked in the door and Alan would not have walked in the door. So, Howard gave me Alan's number and I phoned him, and went downtown to Alan's loft, and met with him. He was just absolutely lovely. Not that different from the persona I'd seen onstage in that the persona onstage wasn't frightening—it was committed. I thought he was so sweet. He was an angel.

And then it turned out that "Dream Baby Dream" was just sitting in a studio waiting for someone to pay $4,000 for the studio time. So, I paid the $4,000 and then we put it out as a single and followed that up with the second Suicide album.

But the recording experience was not an entirely happy one because Ric Ocasek was doing us this huge favor, right? We were recording at the Power Station, which costs an absolute fortune, and he was being put up at the Plaza and doing the record for free.

But it wasn't the record I wanted. I had given Ric a copy of "I Feel Love" by Donna Summer, and I had told him that that was what I wanted. Instead, it was more of an art record, and he said, "Well, I've sold seven million copies of an album before this, so who are you to tell me what you want?"

At exactly the same time, Alan was making his first solo record. He would come to my offices on his way to the Power Station and play tracks for me that he'd done at home on a four-track or eight-track or whatever and that was the stuff that I was responding to much more.

There's a lot of the second Suicide album that I do love.

But it wasn't Alan. I feel like maybe the second Suicide album was more Marty's album. I mean, it's got a lot of music in it. Whereas Alan's solo album is basically like a sort of rockabilly record with drum machines and it's superb. So,

I could feel that Alan was conflicted at the time. And even if I think about that Suicide record, even the cover is so fucking elegant with that sink.

But it's not really Alan at all. It's very, very sophisticated. Not that Alan wasn't sophisticated, but he was earthy, he was intuitive, he loved life. He was messy but not shambolic. And that cover and that album wasn't the Suicide that I loved. Maybe it's the next logical extension after "Dream Baby Dream." Because "Dream Baby Dream" is quite different in sound from the first album. So, it started with Ric Ocasek but it's as if Ric really took over.

My beef with the second Suicide record is that it wasn't a dance record, it didn't have the dance hit that I had asked for. I mean, "Shadazz" gets close, but it isn't.

So, Tony Wright had seen Suicide when he made the cover for the second album, and it is fabulous. And you've got the word Suicide and Martin Rev, Alan Vega. And it's got that drain on it, that sink, that very, very plush sink. And then isn't there a little blood? It's totally subversive. And it could equate to Suicide.

Ric was totally committed to the band, and I don't mean to cast aspersions on him. What I'm really trying to talk about was how Alan was making his first solo record at exactly the same time as that Suicide album—and how different they were.

So, Alan started making a new solo record with Ric and he brought it to me. I said, "I'd love to put it out." By then, I had some leverage because of Kid Creole so I went to Bob Krasnow at Elektra and he signed Alan.

Saturn Strip didn't sell like they wanted so Elektra took over. Alan's analysis is correct about what happened with Elektra. They didn't know what they had with Alan.

So, there was a disconnect. And by then I was out of the record business. I stayed friendly with Alan. I loved Alan. And I would go see Suicide play at the Kitchen—I just loved that band.

By the time the second album came out, Suicide were not that scary. They weren't nearly as confrontational onstage.

Alan was just a lovely, lovely artist who was very committed to his life's work, and he wasn't careerist in any way. ∎

Kate Hyman
A&R
Music Consultant
July 2023
My first impression of Alan was that he was a free spirit doing music that was visceral and from the heart.

He *had* to create. I had never heard anything so raw and real. It affected me emotionally and physically. I was lucky to be working at ZE where all five of us felt as strongly. The sounds of Rev and the talk/rhythm of Alan was tribal.

Alan's influence had a huge effect on the way I went forward in my career. He set a bar when it came to originality and gut feelings. I became fearless in looking for artists who were ahead of their time and not playing it safe. "Cheree" and "Ghost Rider" struck me immediately. Like a crooner from the '50s transported into the modern world. I would call the way he wrote—poetry. Also stream of consciousness. The production was sparse and electronic. New sounds, I didn't like electronic sounds but he changed my mind. He would put you in a trance.

The performances were rock, punk, spoken word, and performance art seamlessly rolled into one.

I adored the album cover of the lemmings jumping off a cliff. Not sure who came up with it. . . .

Alan was kind and caring first and foremost. He always asked how my life was before anything else. Not your typical artist. He really was interested and wanted to know. A gentle soul and zero ego. He was fun too. There was one occasion when he had not received his check from Island Records, who distributed ZE Records. I told him to shout in the background while I had Chris Blackwell on the phone that he was going to jump out of my window onto Fifty-Seventh Street. It was hard because we were both giggling but the check got messengered over. We spent ages at CBGB's chatting about everything. He was so relaxed and warm.

His music needed no input. It was his.

As a visual artist he was also ahead of his time. Record companies were always telling musicians to stick to one thing. Now they write books, paint, do Broadway, etc., etc.

I always thought he would be a bit scary. So yes. He was intense and focused but always a gentleman. ◼

***

Suicide went on to do some shows opening for the Cars on their Panorama Tour, but there was a general feeling that the momentum the band had between 1977 and 1979 was now fading.

Neither Alan nor Marty believed that was the case. However, they both sensed they needed to pursue their own musical callings.

While Suicide were recording their second album, Alan was recording his first solo album, *Alan Vega*—and it was vastly different. It was "minimal rockabilly"—a vision he could pursue because it was so different from Suicide. In a similar vein, Marty was recording his first solo album, *Martin Rev*. On the opposite side—Suicide's sound was not affected—it maintained its own power without even a flesh wound.

The duo never split up but went on to record solo albums.*

Alan grew up listening to Elvis, Gene Vincent, and Roy Orbison, as well as a lot of jazz—Eric Dolphy, Miles Davis, Pharoah Sanders. But Elvis and rhythm and blues were near and dear to him. He felt compelled to explore a minimal rockabilly style to which he could sing the blues.

He began working with Phil Hawk, a guitar player from Texas whom he first met at the Drawing Center in SoHo and who had become an undying fan of Suicide.

Having grown up in Texas, Phil had a healthy southern accent. He also had a distinctive twang to his guitar playing. The initial song they recorded, which would be included on Alan's first solo album, was "Jukebox Babe." They jammed together in the studio where Alan guided Phil to play the riff he was hearing in his head while Alan set the rhythm with a drum machine. Together they layered in additional sparse elements. When the album was released, "Jukebox Babe" became a top hit in France and is considered a classic today.

***

Philip Bacon aka Phil Hawk
Musician
April 2023

I met Alan at the Drawing Center in SoHo. I'd just moved to New York from Texas after graduating from art school. By then, I was more interested in playing music than making sculpture. This was late '70s. I was twenty-two or twenty-three.

I had gone to Max's one night and saw Alan play a set with a boom box and Anne on sax. I was blown away by the intensity and focus of Alan's presence onstage. I knew I wanted to work with him. I mentioned the show to a friend, and he knew Alan from the Drawing Center and said they were having a party there in a few days and Alan would probably be there. So, I went. Alan was sitting alone at a piano playing chords. I went over and introduced myself and told him I wanted to work with him. We talked for a while, and he gave me his number and said I should call him.

He said he had a complete picture in his mind of what he wanted. And it was just fortunate that I hadn't been seriously playing guitar for a while, so I didn't have a lot of chops. I had a sound, but I didn't have a lot of technical chops as far as reading music or all that, so it was much more about what it sounded like instead of what the notes were. It was easy for him to work with me because I didn't come in with a lot of baggage.

---

* Alexis Petridis, "Suicide's Alan Vega: A Punk Pioneer Who Shoved the Streets Back in People's Faces," *Guardian*, July 18, 2016, www.theguardian.com/music/2016/jul/18/suicide-alan-vega-punk-pioneer.

We spent many a night into early morning talking art, music, politics, while drinking black coffee, sipping cognac, and smoking cigarettes.

Eventually, we got around to working on music. Alan had a rhythm machine and some effects so he would come up with a track and then work on some vocals and tell me what kind of guitar he wanted to hear. We worked many nights every week for long hours and quickly came up with six or seven songs. Alan got us some gigs around town. Then we went to Boston and played and wound up at Ric Ocasek's house.

He had that big house in Brookline when he was married to Suzanne—he had a studio there so we went in the studio, and we used one of his rhythm machines and put down the rhythm track. And then I think we ran a cord out into the garage for me to play guitar because he didn't want the sound in the same room. Then we got the most sensitive microphone they had in the studio, and Alan and I stood next to each other snapping our fingers next to this microphone in perfect timing with each other. Then Alan put a vocal on it and Ric mixed it down and gave us a reel to reel. So, that was the first version of "Jukebox Babe."

Ric had encouraged Alan to make a solo album and he wanted to produce it, but Alan was set on producing it himself. Alan got a deal with ZE Records.

Our recording studio hours were from midnight till 8:00 in the morning—just Alan, me, and the engineer, Dave. It took us a while to get going. We put down a rhythm machine track then a guitar track, bass track, scratch vocal track, and then we'd go back and replace the rhythm machine track with drums. We kept working it till we got what Alan was looking for. I'd never played bass or drums before, so it was a challenge. We took the drum kit apart and the bass drum, snare, tom-tom, and cymbals were all recorded separately on different tracks along with hand claps and finger snaps.

Thinking about that time, Ric really wanted to produce the record. Marty Thau really wanted to be involved with Alan's solo work too. There were musicians from the scene who really wanted to come to the studio and be part of the record, but Alan had a very clear idea of the sound he was going for and didn't want to be distracted by other people's input. I was lucky that Alan liked my sound, and he knew that I was there to help him get what he was after and would work until we got it.

Soon after the album came out, Billy Idol moved to New York. Gen X had disbanded. Billy was a huge Suicide fan, and he loved the "Jukebox Babe" album. He called me up to see if I would be interested in working on some material with him. This was before he signed with Kiss's manager, Bill Aucoin. Alan and I had a lot of gigs around that time, so I brought Billy to one and the two of them hit it off right away. Alan would have Billy hop onstage and do a number with us at every gig.

Phil Hawk. *Photo by Patricia Nolan*

Remember the infamous PIL show at the Ritz in 1981? A few days before the show they called Alan and asked if we wanted to be the opener—for $150. Alan politely told them they could go fuck themselves.

We opened for Sam and Dave once. But Sam and Dave weren't on speaking terms at the time, so they had separate dressing rooms and we were stuck in the hall. They would enter the stage from opposite sides, do the show, leave and never say a word to each other.

When we started recording, we weren't getting the sound Alan wanted with the guitars I had so I went out and bought a brand-new Fender Tele. That was it—clean as a whistle.

At the time Alan was living on Fulton Street in a loft in a commercial building. He didn't have an account with Con Ed, so all his power came from an extension cord plugged into an outlet in the hall. On the weekends the building would turn off the heat. It was freezing in the winter.

I'm sure I am biased, but the first Suicide album and Alan's first solo album are just special. I think a lot of it has to do with having the bare minimum of equipment and tech. You can hear it, you can feel it—when people have to physically push themselves and their equipment to get what they're after. At Skyline studio and many recording studios at the time, light bulbs served as circuit breakers if the track was too hot. We broke a lot of light bulbs.

Alan's favorite TV show was Kojak. If we were working and a replay of Kojak was on, we had to stop and watch it. "Who loves you baby"?

Alan was always honest in everything he did creatively. I think he made himself more vulnerable on the album we did than he ever did. I'm touched to have been a part of it. ■

***

Alan's first solo album, *Alan Vega*, was released that November, colored by his love of rhythm and blues. He wanted to infuse his music with the sensations he picked up listening to that sound.

> As Suicide's vocal half, Vega was an infuriating electronic shaman. On his own, he creates seductive, '50s-inspired music that succeeds with or without rockabilly revivals. Alan Vega's impact is the result of its spare instrumentation . . . and deceptively simple songs. "Jukebox Babe" transcends a stuttering lyric and solitary riff to engulf its idiom and then the universe. "Lonely" should be the last word (or moan) on that subject. The rest of the album is similarly Zen-like, and no less enjoyable for it.*

---

* Steven Grant and Ira Robbins, "Suicide," *Trousers Press*, https://trouserpress.com/reviews/suicide/.

Alan Vega, 1980. *Courtesy Saturn Strip Ltd.*

Suicide continued to do some shows throughout the year, including supporting the Cars at a couple of gigs in Connecticut—but their energies were dividing.

***

As 1980 eased into 1981, Alan pulled a band together with Mark Kuch on guitar,
Lary Chapman on bass, and Sesu F. W. Coleman on drums. After working with
them on a few gigs, Alan and the band went into the studio to record his second
solo album, *Collision Drive*, on ZE records.

> *Collision Drive* continues the trend started on the first Alan Vega
> album of incorporating Vega's love of '50s rock and R&B. "Ghost
> Rider," which sounded cold, sleek, and mechanical on Suicide's
> first album, now becomes an upbeat rockabilly rave-up.*

---

* Victor W. Valdivia, "*Collision Drive* Review," *Allmusic*, https://www.allmusic.com/album/mw0000841234
?1676295850834.

***

Lary Chapman
Violinist
Bass Player
April 2023

I was in a rock band in Los Angeles back in the late '60s, early '70s. We were called the Magic Tramps and Warhol superstar, Eric Emerson, was our singer. Eric said he could get us a job at Max's Kansas City. So, we drove across country. Max's was really just starting around that time. We did an audition for Mickey Ruskin. Eric Emerson sang. And there was no bass player. It was just our sound that we had developed for many years. And the interesting thing is that Alan was there, and he appreciated us trying to do a new thing, trying to do our own thing. He approached us and introduced himself. And I gotta say, he was one of the nicest people I ever met.

Some time later, I was working at the Mercer Arts Center. I was handling the bookings for rock bands. I had already seen Alan somewhere. I'd seen him a couple of times perform. I was aware of his music, and I was really impressed because here was a guy doing his own thing. And Marty's got this, this little thing you buy for $2.50—a drum machine—the size of a shoebox.

And they had this intensity with this small little sound. I was so impressed. And Alan took on a whole other role as a musician, because as a person, he was just a really nice guy who cared about art and cared about people. I mean, if you were hanging out with him and you fell and tripped, he'd be all over you, taking care of you. He was such a caring person.

Then, when he got onstage and did his thing and became Suicide—it was just this completely other direction that was so intense. I loved it. I really enjoyed it.

Everybody at the Mercer Arts Center had a different room—my band had a room, the Dolls, Wayne County. And I wanted Suicide to play there—and eventually they got a room. People would go to see them out of curiosity because nobody had ever heard of them.

Then, Alan asked Sesu, the drummer in our band, and me to play with him. I know he was playing with Phil Hawk, 'cause I followed him. I went to his gigs and stuff. He was still doing some stuff with Marty, occasionally, sporadically when he was working with Phil. And Phil was a really nice guy.

I remember going over to his loft on Greene Street. I brought my violin and we were talking and hanging out and Alan says, "Why don't you play some violin?" He had an amp. So, I took the violin and started playing. And because of Alan's presence, I took it to the highest level that I could. I played at full volume—high-level intensity—more than I'd ever done. Alan happened to have a trumpet, and he started playing along with me on the trumpet. What an experience that was.

So, we did some gigs with Alan—me, Sesu, Alan, and Mark Kuch, and then we went on to record *Collision Drive*.

After its release, we went on tour. We opened for the Pretenders at the Tower Theatre in Pennsylvania. It was our third gig on tour with the Pretenders.

We were friends with everybody. So, we're playing and we're getting a bad response from the crowd. We're kind of used to that—people are there to hear the Pretenders.

They're starting to yell at us—really nasty. Twenty-five thousand people. They're throwing really big things at the stage and yelling at Alan. It was becoming a little uncomfortable.

And so that night, Mark and I get together with the sound people and we get them drunk. One thing we had the ability to do was out-drink anybody! So, they're drinking and kind of falling on their faces. Then one of the guys says, you know, they're paying us to make you sound bad.

Apparently, it was on instruction from the Pretenders: "Make sure the opening band doesn't sound good."

But it turned out, it wasn't from the band, it was from their management.

I told Alan and he flipped out. He went to Chrissy and she flips out. She starts yelling at her management and threatened to fire them. It got really heavy after that.

So, then we did one of our first gigs on the European tour in Germany. And at the end of the gig, they wanted an encore. Alan was upstairs in his dressing room. The audience wants more and they're banging on the stage. They want an encore. I was giddy because it was so exciting.

But Alan said, "I ain't doing no encore." He was really mad. He was just trying to be by himself. The audience wouldn't take no for an answer. So, they stormed the stage.

Alan ran down the stairs to see what was happening. And they're chasing us through the parking lot. We run into a trailer and close the door and they start pushing the trailer, trying to overturn the trailer. It literally was a riot.

And then we were banned from playing the next three gigs. They said they were scared of us playing again. We were supposed to go to Munich. We were supposed to go to Berlin.

Then Alan says they want us to do a TV show. So that's when we did the Rockpalast show in Cologne.

Alan was such a creative force. I loved that experience with Alan so much. I mean, I've played violin my whole life and I've done some fantastic things in symphonies and rock and roll, but playing bass with Alan was a highlight. Wonderful. ∎

***

Sesu F. W. Coleman
Drummer
April 2023

We met Alan when he came to our Max's show. We kind of connected and stayed in touch. And we went to see an installation of his work at the OK Harris gallery. And there was some kind of connection with Alan, artistically, because our thing was, music was one part of it—we and Alan—wanted to be around people who wanted to bring music and art together.

Things sort of evolved from there. We stayed kind of connected—see each other out and about.

We were kind of doing the glam scene—our band, the Magic Tramps.

It was kind of theatrical and that probably caught Alan's attention.

So, when *Collision Drive* was recorded—it was really hot. I remember that.

He came up to us and said, "I'm gonna be recording a new album. It's gonna be an important album because it's a follow-up to 'Jukebox Babe.' And we're gonna do a tour." He said to me, "I want you to be my drummer—my first drummer."

And I thought, Wow! What an honor! What a thrill! He said, "I want minimal." So, I got the feeling from him like you're going out in the woods, the organic, and you're hitting a tree. That sound, the big hit on a tree in the forest sound. "I want it to be minimal," he said. "Not a lot of cymbals. I don't want any cymbals."

So, we got together and did some rehearsing in the studio, and it was quite easy to pare down to just basic, like a heartbeat. I used my toms a lot. My toms were my ride, my two decks.

It made total sense to me in my relationship with Alan, through the art medium. It was putting music on canvas. It was wonderful.

We were setting the stage for Alan to paint on. That was our role. Lary and I were setting that foundation. It was magical.

When Alan put the guitar on, he became like a shaman.

He was a magical shaman. He was very, very special. Working with Alan brought something out where you had to be in his wavelength to be able to work with him. That's why *Collision Drive* to me was probably the most special thing I've ever done musically.

I stayed with Alan at his place when we were recording. We'd stay up all night to four o'clock in the morning. There was a little black-and-white TV, and it was always on snow. I loved it.

He gave "static" a purpose.

That was a cool thing with Alan. If he did something really abstract and off, he'd say, OK—and he just went with it. He gave sound something ecstatic. In a harmonica solo for instance, there was a point where you couldn't tell where he was hitting a high note or if the mic was just screeching. It all became his solo.

Sesu, Kuch, Alan, Lary, Collision Drive tour, 1982. *Photo by Dori Kuchinsky and Peter Wantula*

I realized that everything Alan said in his work, had some kind of personal place that it came from—for humanity. It wasn't just stardom and all that. It was more the street, the people, you know—life. I always respected that a lot.

One of the most evolutionary things that that I got out of working with Alan—when he showed up, people noticed, but he didn't go out of his way to be a showoff. And I don't know if anyone ever really got him. I mean, in the beginning, people were kind of a little like, Whoa, what's this?

He freaked a lot of people out.

One time, when he started to swing the chain around there was an electric light cord with a yellow light bulb in it. He would come out and hold it and hold it up and stare out at the people, just stare and say: "I'm looking at you!"

People left fast. They couldn't find the exit fast enough.

There was this time, he took this light bulb and he just smashed it and pulled it across his arm and his arm's bleeding. You're watching it and you're just going with it—not even trying to put it in a category. Then he took a bottle of vodka and poured it on his arm.

And there was this time when we were on tour in Paris and we had a day off in between shows and we found this gym. And I love saunas personally. I went to the sauna and went in and shut the door. And I'm just there thinking, "Oh God, this is amazing." Then it's time to cool off. So, I go to the door and I can't open it. It's stuck. I keep trying to open it. Then I look out the little window and there's Alan and Mark looking at me and cracking up. And it's hot!

I just want to say this one thing—Alan was special. He was special at what he was doing, not a lot of people got it. But Alan really offered something out there to the industry, to art and to music. It was always my pleasure and honor to have had the opportunity to know and work with him. I really loved Alan. ∎

***

In 1980, after his band, Generation-X, disbanded, Billy Idol moved to New York. He was impelled to make the move because all the musicians he admired worked and lived there—the Ramones, the Talking Heads, Patti Smith, the Cramps, and Suicide.

> Alan Vega was leading the way to the future. His band was playing this tight groove, machine-rock blues that was old and new at the same time; he had a million influences . . . [o]ne minute he'd be a raging Otis Redding, and the next, a lizard-like Lounge lizard.*
> —Billy Idol

Photo by Gail Higgins

---

* Billy Idol, *Dancing with Myself* (New York: Simon & Schuster, 2014), 158.

Billy had been at the Birmingham gig when Suicide opened for the Clash in '78 and had listened to their first album over and over and over. He was captivated.

> [Alan] would stare straight at Perri and me while he sang the
> ballad "Je t'adore." . . . It was really romantic. "Je t'adore, Perri.
> I love you, I love you, baby." I liked that Alan had a rep for both
> the performance side of his art and also the soft "I love you"
> romantic side, like Suicide's "Cheree," or my favorite,
> "Dream Baby Dream" . . .
> A punk with a heart? What's wrong with that?*
> —Billy Idol

Billy Idol
Singer/Songwriter
March 2023

The first time I saw Suicide they were supporting The Clash in Birmingham—must have been the "Give 'Em Enough Rope" tour or something like that. Of course, I knew about Suicide but the idea you could see them was incredible. The Clash audience just couldn't stand them. That was the thing I watched really. You saw Alan putting up with this audience that was hating what they were doing and just kind of sucking it up in a fantastic way. He would just luxuriate as they were throwing everything at them. I mean, they wanted them to get off the stage.

It's pretty wild of The Clash to put Suicide on before them, the crowd just didn't want to know—they were waiting for The Clash. And that showed you some of the open-mindedness of '75, '76. It was already closing down by late '77, '78—if it wasn't exactly what they thought punk was, they couldn't take it. Whereas for us, Suicide was beyond punk, they were the future, this was the future of music. And look what happened. Even today, we're back with EDM ruling everything and in a way, Suicide were way ahead of everybody.

That's one of the things about Suicide I loved—that a lot of people just didn't understand it—and you could tell. That music today is still futuristic. Jim Morrison in '69, '70, he was on a PBS show, and he was talking about the future of music, and he was saying, "In the future, it's probably going to be just two guys. One guy on a kind of keyboard, some sort of—" he didn't even say synthesizer because they probably were only just being invented then. But yeah, just had a keyboard and a singer. And of course, next minute, that's what Suicide were doing.

And then they were doing this music that actually—a lot of it is really super-romantic. I mean, "Cheree" and even "Dream Baby Dream." It's very romantic in a way, very positive. And yet a lot of people when they heard Suicide, they heard

---

* Ibid., 109.

Billy singing and Alan on guitar. *Photo by Catherine Ceresole*

the exact opposite. They just couldn't stand the rhythms. I don't think they got it. Maybe where we were growing up from—we'd kind of grown up with those organ sounds and those drum sounds.

We'd kind of grown up with all those tangos and cha-cha-chas and all these rumba beats our parents were into—so it was kind of brilliant, that Suicide then took all that and sort of made this crazy, avant-garde music that most people couldn't handle. I mean, if I wanted to end a party—I could drive people out of the room by putting Suicide on. If you got "Frankie Teardrop" on, you drove them right out . . . even "Rocket USA" and "Ghost Rider." Just putting those on—people would leave . . . and especially girls couldn't stand it. It's weird because, to me, a lot of it was super-romantic.

Then when I did get to meet Alan and everything—Alan would sing "Je t'adore" to me and my girlfriend, Perri Lister. He dedicated it to us . . . super-romantic. There's a whole side to Alan that I think people didn't quite understand because of Suicide having the "Frankie Teardrop" side to them. They didn't quite get to the "Cheree" or the "Dream Baby Dream" side.

I can't quite exactly remember when I first met Alan. . . . I saw a gig at the Peppermint Lounge. And then I went to the Rat Club in Boston and that was the first time I'd really hung out with them and got to know Alan.

Only when I got to America did I start to realize, "Oh, he's starting his solo career but he's got Suicide as well." I would go see Suicide with Phil Hawk. We would be standing—me, Phil Hawk, and his girlfriend—in the downstairs of the Peppermint Lounge watching Suicide. And we were the only people in the room smiling. There were only a few other people, most other people just couldn't stand it.

And then Alan pretending to be Otis Redding at times, just being all his heroes—he was fantastic. And then punching himself. That's what he was doing in Birmingham with The Clash, he was hitting himself in the head and bleeding and stuff and falling to the ground and everything. It was fantastic. It was a great performance in Birmingham, and it was great watching him in New York.

That's what I got from most people in punk rock who were really great. Joe Strummer was being Joe Strummer, Johnny Rotten was being Johnny Rotten, Johnny Thunders being Johnny Thunders and there's Alan Vega being Alan Vega. Johnny Rotten wasn't the same as Joe Strummer, Joe Strummer wasn't the same as me. We weren't just trying to be carbon copies of people. That's what I thought when I saw the Sex Pistols. You saw them and you realized, "Man, you can do it." Iggy was like that too—"Wow. You can do it." You don't have to be the greatest musician. It's more about believing in yourself and being committed to it and sticking to it.

There was something sort of liberating about Alan's performance because he gave everything, that's the feeling you got. And I believed in that too. I believe when you perform, you give everything. If you are going to go onstage, there's a level of commitment to your performance, whatever it is. You don't hold anything back. It was very much what Iggy was. It was kind of challenging . . . and Johnny Rotten was like that—challenging the audience. Not entertaining them but challenging them. No saving it for the next night. You're not going through the motions either. There was none of that.

And that's what Alan was like. Alan was his own person. He had his own way of doing things that he stuck to, and you could see that. And he stuck to it through thick and thin. The commitment to performance—not to shrink away or look for an easy way out. No. In fact, he was challenging the audience. He was "If you're going to throw things at me, I can do things to myself that you could never do."

On a personal level, he was very warm. He was lovely to be with. It was great hanging with him. I was starting my solo career in America, so I suppose I was really looking for other people who were doing that and also looking for like-minded people. I worked with Phil Hawk on a song called "It's So Cruel" on my first solo album. So, in some ways, yeah, I was just trying to find out about New York and the people that were there and the other musicians. And that's what we couldn't see in England. We could only dream about seeing Suicide and Alan's solo career but here I was in America, I could drink it in, if you know what I mean. And I could use it in some way to fuel my own career because there was an energy and a commitment that I was looking for—it's right what we're doing, we're right to stick to our guns, we're right to stay true to what we believe in. And well, I had to be Billy Idol, really, that was it, I had to. And I was watching Alan be Alan.

I was vibe-ing off what he was doing. He wasn't thinking about having hit singles or not having hit singles. It was all about being Alan Vega to the tee, to the highest degree. And that's what I was being, Billy Idol to the highest degree. And sort of finding out what that was and mining that seam. I could see Alan doing the same thing. And it wasn't like there was loads of other people that I really admired. It was really incredible.

Alan Vega's solo stuff wasn't just about the music. It was performance art, really. Malcolm McLaren said a really great thing about punk, "If this was about the music, it would have been dead a long time ago." And I think that Alan was a part of that. He was using music to do it as well, to expand his art. It wasn't just something on a wall. His music and his stage performance were a huge part of that.

Then with *Collision Drive*, Alan had that band who wore flares and stuff. I don't know where he got them from, but it was fantastic. They all looked like they just came out of a Holiday Inn or something. They were great, and I love rockabilly, I loved that Alan was sort of going from Suicide then doing sort of rockabilly-based music or very early rock and roll music.

When I was growing up, six years old or so, I was into the sort of pop music of the time in England and you could only go back to the '50s, really. You could only look back to the '50s when you're in 1963 and think about Roy Orbison or Elvis or Buddy Holly or whoever it was, Gene Vincent, Eddie Cochran, Little Richard, Chuck Berry—all of those people, that's all you could go back to. And here was Alan kind of almost doing a similar thing. He was looking back to reinvent his solo career. There was an element of blues behind it.

Alan really did stand by me and was a mentor as well. He was someone I could rely on as a friend. I loved all of it. ∎

***

In 1982, not long after the release of *Collision Drive*, Ocasek and Michael Zilkha approached Bob Krasnow about signing Alan to a recording contract. Although it was highly unlikely a major record label would go through with signing a singer and performer like Alan, he had some serious weight in his corner—and he was brought onto Elektra.

With the advance Alan received from the company, he secured a lease on a loft in the Music Building—a new space with rooms and lofts where musicians could live and rehearse. It was near Times Square and he moved in with his girlfriend.

Michael Alago—who was still Alan's friend since their first meeting in 1976—was initially assigned as Alan's A&R rep at Elektra, but when Howard Thompson joined the company, he took over management of Alan.

Alan went into the studio with Ocasek and Zilkha to record his first solo album for Elektra—*Saturn Strip*.

Ocasek brought in Al Jourgensen from the band Ministry, and they cowrote the title song, "Saturn Drive," as well as the song "Kid Congo," a tribute to the performer.

***

Kid Congo Powers
Musician, Singer
Actor
May 2023
Wow. Alan Vega. "Wow" was the first impression I had as an eighteen-year-old hearing the first Suicide album. I carry that awe to this day.

I never really knew Alan as a friend. I stood fast in my place as a fan. I would meet him on a few occasions when I lived in NYC—at his art shows, which I never missed. Of course, I knew him onstage and on record as a ferocious and intense being. His performances left no doubt of that.

The Alan I met at galleries was kind, engaging, and soft spoken. Charismatic as hell. A barely audible compliment from me was met with a reassuring wisecrack that let me know he sensed my awestruck self.

Some years later, when I found out Alan had made a song called "Kid Congo" on his *Saturn Strip* album, I was floored and left muttering "How can this be happening?" By that time, I was playing with the Cramps; I became convinced that he just liked the syllables in my name. Nonetheless, he was aware of Kid Congo.

This is my largest award in life, to be named in an Alan Vega song.

I followed his music and incarnations until the end, which doesn't seem to have ended at all.

There was a funny moment when I met him, this time as a musician myself, after the release of the song "Kid Congo." Once again, I went to see a gallery show of Alan's wonderful light sculptures. Besieged by friends and well-wishers, I made my way into his inner circle and said, "Hi Alan, I'm Kid Congo." He looked up at me and we both looked at each other with the most shocked faces ever. What seemed like a full minute passed when I finally blurted "Thank you for using my name for your song," to which Alan laughed and said, "Oh yeah, anytime!" We laughed some more as I skulked back to my mega fan world, forever grateful.

Alan was my Elvis Presley. The King.

Although I could mention so many of Alan's works as influential, the song I am continually drawn to is "Diamonds, Fur Coat, Champagne" from the second Suicide album. The mood of the late seventies NYC music and disco scenes are encapsulated so perfectly here. The lyric "A woman, Cadillac, Cocaine" is such a strong visual and symbolic picture of the slumming rich who mixed with downtown bohemian club denizens. Sexy and cold. Physical and disembodied. A snapshot captured. For me this is master storytelling in a few impressionistic words. Alan did this so often. A holy grail of lyric writing. Also, his embracement of characters, "Kung Fu Cowboy," "Mr. Ray," "Frankie Teardrop,"—heroic, tragic, and comic. In his fascination with these characters, I feel a real compassion and love. That's the lesson I learned and strive for from Alan—the ridiculous and the sublime.

Alan Vega. WOW. ∎

∗∗∗

On *Saturn Strip*, Ocasek captured the raw rockabilly vibe of Alan's first two solo albums while weaving in infectious synthpop sensibility coupled with Alan's unique vocal delivery and signature yelps. Ric had a deep understanding of the importance of Alan's process and let him do his thing. He polished Vega's sound without watering it down.

The Cars' Ric Ocasek has lavished unabashed praise on Alan
Vega for years, and now on *Saturn Strip*, Vega's first major-
label release, the rest of us have the chance to find out why. An
Elvis for the apocalypse, Vega cross-pollinates rockabilly and

techno-pop and emerges with a hybrid so flawlessly original
you'd think he was out to re-invent rock and roll altogether.*

During the following summer, Alan traveled to Europe in support of *Saturn Strip*. He was adored there. The single "Jukebox Babe" had made him a star in France and the subsequent *Collision Drive* tour solidified that—the fans were frantic to see him.

In the Eighties, Vega began a . . . solo career with singles like
"Jukebox Babe" and "Saturn Drive," which made him a bona fide
star in Europe, with his souped-up synth-rockabilly sound in the
vein of Billy Idol or Gino Vanelli . . . [and] Vega always displaying
a hilariously unreconstructed don't-give-a-fuck attitude.†

***

Meanwhile, despite his increasing success, his personal relationship with his girlfriend was not going well. Without Alan's knowledge, she had tried to get her own record deal even with her limited musical ability. She also had been having cocaine-fueled altercations with concert goers outside of Alan's gigs that often became violent. One night after a show she was soaked in pepper spray. With eyes watering and coughing, she got into the cramped van with the band and pepper spray seeped everywhere. Everyone started choking as they traveled to the next city on tour. Alan decided that if he didn't want the rest of the band to quit, he couldn't take her on tour again. She was volatile.

After his European tour for *Saturn Strip* wrapped, Alan returned to New York late one night. He was seriously beat from the eight-hour flight after the last tour stop in Paris. He felt drawn and quartered—the exhaustion was wiping him. He went straight home from JFK but when he opened the front door to the loft he shared with his girlfriend, he was thrown into a firestorm of disbelief.

Alan found her naked on the bed with another man.

He stood there, rigid.

The dim lights of dawn started slipping through the windows.

He couldn't comprehend what he was seeing, and his bodily weariness was knocking him down.

He grabbed some clothes from the bedroom closet, turned and left, slamming the door behind him.

---

* Boo Browning, "Alan Vega: Reinventing Rock," *Washington Post*, July 15, 1983, https://www.washingtonpost .com/archive/lifestyle/1983/07/15/alan-vega-reinventing-rock-38/1701715c-aca1-429c-8677-ea4500e09e9d/.

† Rob Sheffield, "Remembering Suicide's Alan Vega: Screamer of Truths, Dreamer of Dreams," *Rolling Stone*, July 17, 2016, https://www.rollingstone.com/music/music-news/remembering-suicides-alan-vega-screamer-of-truths-dreamer-of-dreams-111940/.

He made his way to the Gramercy Park Hotel on Twenty-First Street.

> The Gramercy . . . was where bands went on
> the way up or on the way down.[*]
> —Alan

He got a room and wandered upstairs. He turned the key, opened the door, dumped his bag, and collapsed. He didn't wake up for fifteen hours. He stayed in that very room for the next four years.

***

> He was a twenty-first-century Elvis for me.[†]
> —Bruce Springsteen

---

[*] Max Weissberg, "Inside the Gramercy: The Grit and Glamour of New York's Rock & Roll Hotel," *Rolling Stone*, March 11, 2018, https://www.rollingstone.com/culture/culture-news/inside-the-gramercy-the-grit-and-glamour-of-new-yorks-rock-roll-hotel-203516/.

[†] Interview with Bruce Springsteen, June 2023.

PART TWO

"HEY IT'S A BETTER WORLD

SOMEWHERE ELSE"*

* Alan Vega Notebooks, courtesy of Saturn Strip, Ltd.

Photo by John DiMiceli

12 LIZ

1985 . . .

Love is not just a confrontation with
the absurdity of the world;
it is a refusal to be broken by it.*
—Albert Camus

The city was chilling down. The dank, tenebrous streets pulsed underneath the mounds of excreted scraps and filth littering every street corner with criminal footsteps not far behind. But potholed Fourteenth Street buzzed with excitement. Home to one of the great birthplaces of downtown rock 'n' roll—nearly every rock musician to pass through New York City performed there.

It was October 1985, right before the official release of his most recent recording, *Just a Million Dreams*, when Elektra threw Alan a launch party for the album in the Michael Todd Room at the Palladium.

This party, this evening, this fork in the spirited road—would change Alan's life forever. He meets the woman who fosters, encourages, and stimulates his art and music by giving him a world of acceptance and warmth—bustling with sparkling vitality and inspiration.

Liz: Growing up in a predominantly Irish Catholic town, I attended parochial school for twelve years through high school—this likely accounts for a lot of my rebellious nature. Defying expectations and bending the rules became my favorite form of creative expression. There was the first tattoo at age sixteen combining the planet Saturn, a shooting star, and a lightning bolt—symbols which were eerily prescient of my

---

* Albert Camus, *The Notebooks 1951–1959* (New York: Alfred A. Knopf, 1965).

meeting Alan Vega eleven years later. Around the same time, I pierced my own nose with ice and a needle after seeing women from India on the Boston subway wearing traditional garb and jeweled studs in their noses. I had never seen this on girls living in the pedestrian suburbs. My mom took my newly adorned nose in stride and my dad was fine as long as I kept getting straight As—though he was known to remark to me, "It's the damn inconsistencies I can't stand." It was hard for him to reconcile my eclectic interests.

My father, Robert Kent Lamere, "Bob" or "Butch," was a litigation partner at the major Boston law firm, Sullivan & Worcester, and served for over thirty years as town moderator for the Boston suburb of Milton, where I grew up. My mother, Peggy—"Toots"—was raised in the house next door to her marital home with her three younger siblings and my grandmother, Louise Norris, "Momilou," and Thomas A. Norris, "Grandad."

Peggy studied journalism at Mount Ida college where her favorite professor was William Henry McMasters, who had decades before won the Pulitzer Prize for the Ponzi scheme exposé he wrote for the Boston Globe. *McMasters had been Charles Ponzi's publicist for a short period before realizing what Ponzi was up to. Toots was enthralled by McMasters and excelled in his class, which precipitated her lifelong love of writing. She also became an accomplished equestrian, specializing in dressage and riding five-gaited horses.*

When Peggy met Bob, he had just started practicing law after graduating from Harvard College at the age of eighteen and Columbia Law School by age twenty. One of my dad's favorite professional achievements was also one of his earliest assignments—representing pro boxer Rocky Marciano, who was fighting out of Brockton, Massachusetts, in a contract dispute with his local manager. The firm let young Turk Bob Lamere handle the case on his own. Winning that case meant that Marciano was free to sign with a well-connected New York–based manager who was able to accelerate his career and secure his place in boxing history. This was also prophetic given my future work managing professional boxers.

My dad was a handsome and accomplished young man who swept my mom off her feet. They married and bought the house on Wendell Park right next door to where my mom had grown up. This meant my two older brothers and I grew up with our grandparents living close by. As we got older and learned Dad's two younger brothers called him "Butch," we immediately adopted it as his moniker. Shortly thereafter a friend of my brother's dubbed mom "Toots," which instantly stuck. My mom used to joke that Toots and Butch sounded like a Vaudeville act.

My grandmother, Momilou, had a really strong bond with Alan. He would spend hours and hours talking to her when we visited. One of those times included Marty, who stayed at her house with us when Suicide played at Ground Zero in Boston in the '90s. I can picture Marty and Alan having breakfast with her in deep conversation.

She was tough and had been a rum runner at age sixteen during prohibition. Momilou held down the family fort when Grandad served in WWII as commander of the USS Elkhorn *oil tanker.*

Even though Alan was not naturally comfortable in large family gatherings, for many years he had been coming to Momilou's holiday parties. By the time I met Alan, Grandad had passed away but Momilou still lived next door to the house I grew up in, where my oldest brother Kent was raising his family with his wife Jean and three kids. Alan loved Momilou, and she thought the world of him. My mom had three siblings and by then there were eighteen grandchildren and about ten great-grandchildren. So, there was a full house for holiday gatherings. After the meals, Alan usually sequestered himself up in the attic, where the assorted cousins, aunts, and uncles would go up and spend one-on-one time with him. We used to joke that everyone made sure they had their audience with the pope.

***

When I was in high school, after wearing a uniform all day, I'd throw on my dad's old torn T-shirts, which I wrote on, paired with combat boots. And I started listening to "punk" music—the Dead Boys, Iggy Pop, Patti Smith, Mission of Burma, and sneaking into the rock club, the Rat, in Kenmore Square with my best friend Brian Pike. We had met as young teens at the Blue Hills ski area, which was only ten minutes from home. I was there nonstop during ski season and held every position from lift attendant, national ski patrol, and ultimately ski instructor through college.

When Brian and I decided to start a band, I chose to play the drums. Music's rhythm foundation had always drawn me in and I figured being athletic, drumming would be a natural fit. We called ourselves Backward Flying Indians (BFI). Brian played guitar, wrote most of the lyrics, and sang lead, and we recruited our friend Fred from Blue Hills to play bass. The band set up shop in my family's basement, where we had a separate entrance, so we could have friends over and play loud, especially when Toots and Butch were out on date nights.

After high school, I went to Tufts University, where I studied psychology and played varsity soccer. BFI played at parties in the attic of the house I lived in on campus until the Somerville/Medford police shut us down. We went to many concerts at the Paradise, Channel, the Rat, Middle East Cafe. One night while we were hanging outside the Paradise, smoking a joint before going in to see Nils Lofgren, a long stretch limo pulled up and a huge leathered, bald bodyguard-looking person exited and he was followed by Frank Zappa.

Instead of walking straight into the venue, Zappa suddenly veered over to where we were standing. He stuck out his hand and shook mine and said, "You are a star." Brian's jaw dropped as I said, "Yes I am, thank you."

I never saw Suicide play in Boston but in 1978, Brian saw them open for the Cars at the Paradise. He was blown away by the sound and by Alan, who was unfazed *when the crowd quickly turned hostile. He also noticed Faye Dunaway watching, seemingly enthralled, from the nearby bar area. Little did Brian realize that his girl-friend would meet and fall in love with Vega seven years later.*

The pull of NYC was becoming too strong to ignore. It was a city where you could be whatever you wanted to be. Since I didn't have a set idea for my career path, practicing law seemed like a good way to gain independent financial security while pursuing my creative interests. I was admitted to Columbia School of Law, and I headed to the Upper West Side of Manhattan.

During law school one of my close friends was the incomparable Paula Franz-ese. Together we formed a band consisting of other law students and called ourselves "Moral Turpitude." During my three years at Columbia, I often ventured down to CBGBs, returning alone on the subway at 3:00 a.m. Law school was intense but fun, especially the elective courses in entertainment law. I learned about music contracts and did an internship at Volunteer Lawyers for the Arts. As my dad had also attended Columbia law school, he was very proud that I became a Property Teaching Fellow and a Harlan Fiske Stone scholar.

After graduating, I was offered a job at Cahill Gordon & Reindel, where Floyd Abrams was a rock star in First Amendment law. I envisioned being mentored by Floyd, but soon found out that sitting in the library researching case law was not thrill-ing. The corporate associates were going to meetings and helping to execute deals. That sounded much more engaging. But the lack of flexibility over my time wore me down and I pivoted out of big law practice after six years.

During that time, I became friends with Dori Kuchinsky—another lawyer at my firm. Dori had grown up in Sheepshead Bay, Brooklyn, and was part of the NYC club scene throughout her school years. Her brother Mark, "Kuch," had been a bouncer at Max's Kansas City and played guitar in the Alan Vega band.

After a few months at the law firm, I was boiling. I needed a creative outlet. One day, I answered an ad in the Village Voice from a band looking for a drummer. I was invited to join Bob McCann (guitar), Catherine Cosover (singer), and John Shannon (bass) in their burgeoning band.

Whenever I wasn't chained to my desk I was rehearsing with the band, and we eventually started playing at CBGBs. We called ourselves SSNUB: "Sargent Slaughter's No Underwear Band." Bob and Catherine had seen pro wrestler Sargent Slaughter's vehicle pass them one day and the band name was born.

I was loving this balance of work and play.

Then, on October 23, 1985, Dori stopped by my office and invited me to come out that night. She and Kuch were picking up Alan Vega, who lived at the Gramercy Park Hotel, and bringing him to his record release party at the Palladium. I had never heard Alan's band or Suicide.

I remember my horoscope that day: "You will meet a lamb in wolf's clothing."

Dori and I dressed up for the evening. Dori's club attire tended toward all black, tight and sexy. I was more tough-girl and threw on some Mad Max type getup with combat boots and a sharp spike in my nose—a severe contrast to my lawyer uniform.

We buzzed out of my place on Maiden Lane and Kuch drove us to the Gramercy Park Hotel.

The lobby reminded me of a Grande Dame, with theatrical opulence that had faded with time.

When we got to Room 828, Kuch knocked on the door. Alan flung it open and pulled Kuch and Dori in. I was frozen there for the moment, captivated by the electric energy radiating off Alan. He was lit from behind by three cross-shaped light sculptures on his walls and on the floor was a jumble of wires, cords, and guitar effects pedals strung together like a derailed train. His vigor struck me like a bolt of lightning.

Alan looked into my eyes with fervent intensity.

"Hey," he said to me.

"Hi," I said, and reached my arm out to shake his hand. He stared at me as if I was speaking a foreign language. I leaned back.

"I'm Liz."

Alan pulled me in and immediately launched into his trademark rapid-fire dialog. He had met Dori before but wasn't expecting me, and when Dori introduced me as a fellow Wall Street attorney, his face buckled.

"And she's a drummer in a band too," Dori added.

His intense focus increased. He was peering into my soul.

Kuch broke the spell and said we need to get going. Alan headed into the bathroom where he sprayed the sky-high hair spiking out of his headband. As he came back into the room, I noticed he was wearing a red belt that was encircled with black lettering "wolves, wolves, wolves." Wait—here was the lamb in my horoscope.

We arrived a little later at the Palladium. Alan was the guest of honor, and he was swept into the fray of fans and supporters there celebrating his latest opus. Dori and I hung back on the periphery, sipping cocktails and people-watching. I could feel Alan's dynamism as he surfed through the crowd—each one jockeying for a position to get a word with him. Periodically, he broke away and made a beeline for us.

"So, what's it like being a female Wall Street lawyer??"

"How do you juggle that with being a drummer in a band??"

"Where are you from??"

Each question from him was filtered with his intense, endless stare that transfixed me. But before I could barely utter a word, Dori told Alan: "Go back to your party, she doesn't want to talk with you now!"

After that night, I couldn't get Alan out of my head. I'd spent years adeptly compartmentalizing my life and efficiently focusing on whatever task was at hand.

Now, I was in dreamland.

I couldn't stop fantasizing about this man who moved me unlike anyone I had ever met. As I recounted the night to my friend and former law-school classmate, Paula—who by then had also joined Cahill Gordon and was my office mate—she could see that something life-changing had happened to me. Dori was more cautious and told me the band was soon leaving for a European tour. My gut told me that Alan's interest in me wouldn't disappear.

A few months later, Dori popped into my office on her way to a meeting to say Kuch had just returned from Europe. As soon as she left, Paula looked at me. "Well, you know where Alan lives," she said.

It was late afternoon on a Thursday, and I had a ton of work left to do before I could leave the office. I picked up the phone, called the Gramercy Park Hotel and asked to be put through to Room 828. He picked up the phone with a quick "hello" in that intense breathy tone I'll always remember.

"Hi Alan, it's Liz."

"Where are you?" he quickly replied. "When can I see you?"

About an hour later, we met in the Gramercy Hotel bar. We spent the next six hours talking, talking, talking until the bar started to close. It felt like we were the only two people left on the planet. He wanted me to know everything about him. He openly shared his life story, worldview, and philosophical theories. He asked me profound questions about me and my life. It was the beginning of infinite conversations where I never lost a fascination with whatever he said or thought—ever.

Before I left, he handed me a gift-wrapped package that contained a beautiful black and silver scarf and an African necklace that he had picked out for me while he was on tour.

That night became the next thirty years.

13 "... ain't my song"*

1985 ... 1986 ...

Freedom is what you do with what's been done to you.[†]
—Jean-Paul Sartre

Alan had recorded *Just a Million Dreams* the previous year at Syncro Sound in Boston as well as Broccoli Rabe in New Jersey and Unique recording studios in New York. The record was produced by Ocasek, but he was often pulled away for his own projects with his band.

Elektra's plan for this second Vega album was to take him even further into what they considered to be more "commercial" territory. Along with Ocasek, they enlisted cutting-edge producer, Chris Lord-Alge, to help lead the charge. Howard Thompson oversaw the recording and coproduced the song "Creation."

But instead of a true collaboration, it felt more like a hostile takeover. Elektra held the purse strings and made the decisions on how to spend the budget. They brought in session musicians to replace Alan's band and decided his look needed to be revamped and cleaned up. For the album cover photoshoot, he was made up like matinee idol, Rudolph Valentino.

The end result was a slick pop record that ties in musically with the 1980s soundscape. Yet, it retains Alan's indelible fingerprint due to his distinctive voice and the raw musical elements kept in the mix.

But he felt like a "hired gun" and was even kicked out of some of the recording sessions. No matter how much he tried to bend to the overarching goals of the label, he was perceived as "unmanageable."

---

* "On the Run" by Alan Vega, *Just a Million Dreams*.
† Jean-Paul Sartre, *Essays in Aesthetics*, trans. Wade Baskin (Open Road Media, 2012).

© Bob Gruen/www.bobgruen.com

The problems with Elektra were escalating. For some time, Alan hadn't been happy with the demands of being on a major label despite a supportive A&R team whose job, of course, also depended on facilitating a strong return on the label's investment.

Alan wanted access to greater resources so he could focus exclusively on the creative process, but the requirement to adapt to the vision the label had for him made that difficult. And he refused to comply. It wasn't him.

He was outside the box.

And Elektra found that problematic.

In early 1986, Alan was sent out on a six-week tour to promote *Just a Million Dreams*. However, when he got out on the road, he discovered little or no promotion had been done for the album by Elektra. Local promoters told Alan that the label hadn't set up any interviews and they hadn't stocked the stores with his record.

This was a far cry from the "Jukebox Babe" and *Collision Drive* tours on ZE Records, where posters were plastered everywhere, his records featured in store displays, with loads of press attention. Even though *Just a Million Dreams* was getting early radio play and the fans were coming out to see him, they couldn't buy the record because it wasn't available. Ironically, the little press attention he did get highlighted the album's slick production of the record—definitely not the Vega paradigm.

Elektra was silent on any support for the album—and Alan.

Soon after returning from the tour, it wasn't difficult for Alan to take off the golden handcuffs and part ways with the company.

How the hell did Alan Vega . . . find himself on Elektra? Maybe the fact long time Suicide ally Ric Ocasek and his band the Cars were signed to the label and enjoying no small amount of success almost immediately with their first album. . . . How did it go? Both 1983's *Saturn Strip* and the one we're focused on here, *Just a Million Dreams*, released in 1985, are nothing like Vega did before or after. They are much like those survivor reality programs where the human is dropped into a relatively unfamiliar environment to see how they'll do as the audience watches, or in this case, listens. It wasn't an adversarial environment Vega found himself in, the team around him including Ocasek, Howard Thompson, and Chris Lord-Alge, were doing their best for Vega and Elektra to make *Just a Million Dreams* a hit record. Alan's challenge, if you will, was to be himself (which as a true artist, would be able to do anything but). . . . You might think Alan Vega never had it so good. Here's his way out of the clubs, constant confrontation, stages littered with broken glass and sometimes blood. If Alan Vega was a sellout or remotely commercially minded, he would have seen this as the lifeline he's been working so hard for. However, simply put, that's just not who Alan Vega was. Ever.*

—Henry Rollins

Although Elektra had laid out a sizable advance, much of it had been spent. Before he would make a dime on the back end, the advance would have to be completely recouped out of Alan's measly record royalties.

Since ZE Records had signed Vega to Elektra, he had to look solely to ZE for any accounting. But Alan figured that Elektra would never recoup the advance since the label probably decided to take a loss and wouldn't manufacture enough records to be in the black on his account.

Vega had resisted being locked into a formulaic sound to achieve the sales the company expected from its artists. Alan believed major labels tended to sign artists because of their unique X factor and then proceeded to beat that out of them. Alan's A&R team was aware of his history of artistic exploration and the morphing of his style in both visual art and music and saw him as a pure game changer. But game changers are not the ones who usually enjoy success fueled by the mass marketing machine. Alan was more than happy to unlock the shackles. Being kept under the authority of a major record label didn't fit with his DNA. They truly appreciated his artistry—but that wasn't enough.

***

---

* Liner notes, *Just a Million Dreams*, 1985.

Howard Thompson
Radio Host
Head of A&R, Elektra Records 1984–1993
2023

One day, two albums showed up in the mail when I was at Bronze Records and one of the albums was the first Suicide LP. It looked interesting and I stuck it on the stereo in the office I shared with managing director, David Betteridge. Accidentally, I had put side 2 on first so "Frankie Teardrop" came out of the speakers and it wasn't long before David, who was on the phone, was getting asked by the person at the other end of the line if everything was ok. Alan's shrieks and screams were worrying whoever David was talking to and I was thinking "Wow, I should turn this up."

After a day or two with the record—it only took that long for it to become my favorite album of all time—I asked David if we could license the record and (much to my surprise) he said, "Find out how much it would cost and go and see them live."

Marty Thau's Red Star office was pretty threadbare—three rooms with a table and chair in each—one for Marty (Chairman Thau), one for Roy Trakin (Minister of Information), and one for Miriam Linna, who worked the press. Since then, and to this day, she's the greatest rock & roll chick ever. Red Star was situated in a fancy office building at 200 West Fifty-Seventh Street and there was a Chinese restaurant that featured in some of Thau's propaganda on the ground floor. When I arrived, I was taken into Roy's office by Miriam and immediately was offered a hit on a joint Roy was smoking. We talked for about twenty minutes and then I was ushered into Thau's office, where he was sitting wearing dark glasses. The only art on the walls was a piece by Walter Stedding, a violinist who had some connection to Warhol's Factory.

Alan and Martin Rev wore sunglasses too and, just to add to the effect, Alan was wearing a beret. He looked like a gang member out of *The Wanderers*. I half expected him to pull out a flick-knife and clean his nails with it. Nobody smiled, and there was a hostile vibe of "ok, you limey motherfucker—explain yourself." At this point, Trakin's joint hit me like a ton of bricks and I just wanted to be somewhere else. Somehow I got through the meeting and we agreed to meet up later at Max's. I thought to myself, "no more weed" on this trip.

Before the Elvis Costello and Clash tours, Suicide made their European debut at the International Festival of Science Fiction and Imagination in Metz, France, on June 9, 1978. Bronze Records decided to fly a ten-seater plane loaded with journalists/media types to Metz—a plane that label-owner Gerry Bron flew himself. He had a couple of private planes as a hobby and side business. Included in this party was BBC DJ Alan "Fluff" Freeman, Bronze plugger Roger Bolton, me, and some music journalists. Maybe Kris Needs was one, maybe Giovanni Dadomo was another. The show started late due to Marty's keyboard/drum machine being set up for American voltage and when plugged in the European socket something blew and it took a while to fix and find a transformer. Unfortunately, I don't remember much else, other than the sound was terrible and someone threw a wooden chair onto the stage. The whole thing was kind of a bust as our party of ten, who'd flown all the way from London to Metz to see Suicide's big debut, saw precisely five minutes before we had to leave for the airport because it closed at 11:00 p.m. and most of us had to get back for work the next day.

I can't remember who the booking agent responsible for the UK tours was, but whoever it was, he got them on the Costello and Clash tours. Of course, I was hugely in favor and we came through with the money for tour support.

The album was released through Bronze in Holland, Germany, France, Spain, and Italy. I also have a feeling it might have come out in Australia and New Zealand.

"Cheree"/"I Remember" was a seven-inch and twelve-inch single and John Peel played it once that I know of. The BBC banned the single from daytime play because of the band's name.

The Brussels gig—along with Charles Ball's recording of the first Berlin gig—came out in an edition of 1,000 "official bootlegs," given away by N.M.E. The last time I saw Alan was at Hanover Square in New York. I gave him a numbered copy as a gift.

Working with Alan was a blast. My favorite session with him was when he came to Skyline Studios to add some vocals on Angel Corpus Christi's first record. She'd covered "Cheree" and "Dream Baby Dream," and we thought it would be cool to have Alan on it. He came in, did his parts in two takes, then he added a part to a tune called "Theme from Taxi Driver/NY, NY" which contained the DeNiro monologue and music by Bernard Herrmann. Alan improvised the part of a bum begging for a quarter on the street and nailed it in two takes!

Alan had this New York swagger, like nothing could touch him, which I admired enormously. He was also very funny, quick-witted. I loved just hearing him talk.

Alan took the "riots" in his stride. I think he was a little unnerved by it all, but he didn't show it. I mean, who wants to stand front-of-stage and get spat at throughout your set. Not to mention all the flying missiles. He had this lovely purple sharkskin suit that he wore on the Clash tour and every night when he and Marty left the stage it would be black from all the spit. It was revolting, but it didn't faze him. I think the Clash had people that looked after their clothes who might have taken pity and had it cleaned every night because it always looked good when he walked onstage.

When Suicide opened for the Cars in Los Angeles at the Universal Amphitheater, 95 percent of the audience hated them (as usual) and after everything that wasn't nailed down had been thrown at them, Alan stood at the front of the stage, with his chest out, hands on hips and yelled "Dodgers suck!" through the mic. I was standing at the side of the stage, and I thought "Oh no, this is it," because there were maybe two guys doing security and the stage was low and easy to reach. But the audience of close to 6,000 people who hated Suicide wimped out and let Vega walk. Alan was fearless.

Alan knew a lot about art, music, boxing—all things that interested me, so he'd hold court on the third floor at Danceteria or the Blarney Stone and we'd drink and he'd impart his wisdom and play Lotto, while I listened. I'd ask a question, and he'd talk for fifteen minutes. Some of those conversations I'd tape surreptitiously.

The last time I saw Alan, I came to Hanover Square. He was in good spirits, but the stroke had slowed him down considerably and I found it difficult to make out what he was saying. He'd finished a painting—which looked a bit like Ric Ocasek—and I thought it was beautiful. ∎

Andrew Eldritch, Howard Thompson, and Alan, Gramercy Park Hotel, 1985. *Photo by Kevin Patrick*

***

Then, on November 11, 1986, Alan Vega's father died. After his mother, Tillie, had passed in 1972, Louis had married Laura Liebowitz and moved to Florida. It is there where he continued his life, spending a great deal of time with Robbie, Sue, Amie, and Beth.

> [H]e was happier getting out of Brooklyn.*
> —Amie, Alan's niece

The family picture still didn't include Alan—his unknown, blurred, nebulous self. It is believed he heard about his father's passing from one of his aunts. Robbie had tried frantically to get hold of him so they could all go down to Florida for the funeral, but he was never able to find him.

Alan hadn't seen his father or been in touch in any way for close to fifteen years. The distance was a truth neither one could avoid, and one they both became accustomed to.

As Alan grew beyond childhood it became harder to connect with his dad. Louis was in his own world. He remained aloof.

> I've always felt with him . . . that nothing meant a lot . . .
> he had no emotional attachment to a lot of things.†
> —Sue Bermowitz, Robbie's wife

Alan always experienced his father's austere self as a true injustice against his mother—who Alan watched every day, working herself endlessly to make their home perfect.

> He resented his father for not paying attention to his mother.‡
> —Mariette

However, Louis' lack of attentiveness disappeared into a wealth of outrage when Alan changed his major from astrophysics to art in college. And then when Alan left the Brooklyn fold for downtown Manhattan's art and music scene, his father fumed.

> I know he was not happy at all about what Alan was doing.§
> —Sue Bermowitz

---

* Interview with Amie Bermowitz, February 2023.
† Interview with Sue Bermowitz, October 2021.
‡ Interview with Mariette Bermowitz, September 2021.
§ Interview with Sue Bermowitz, October 2021.

By the time of Louis's death, Alan and Liz were a committed couple and one of the wonderful treats that came along with Liz was her mother, "Toots." Alan became very close with Toots who was only seven years older than he.

When Alan decided not to go to his father's funeral, Toots said to him, "Make sure you're not going to really regret that you don't go. You know what I mean? I don't know your whole background and dynamic . . . but just make sure that you aren't going to feel really badly that you didn't go."*

Alan did not express regret and was OK with his decision. Along with everything else, Alan felt it was disloyal that his father was in a relationship with and ended up marrying Laura, his mother's best friend—so soon after Tillie passed.

Over the years, Alan often thought and spoke about his mother, Robbie, and his cousin Miltie—and he lit candles for them every Yom Kippur. He rarely mentioned his dad.

This surprised Liz. She had always been very close with her family, and it seemed so unfortunate that Alan had little or no relationship with his relatives. She couldn't really make sense of the kind of remoteness he maintained.

It also concerned Toots, as she had come to know Alan's character and values. She knew he was a caring, loving man. When Alan went from calling Toots "man" to "honey man" it was a sign that he felt close to her. Yet, he still wasn't comfortable discussing his family.

I never heard him talk much about the rest of his family.†
—Toots

***

If you can talk with crowds and keep your virtue,
Or walk with Kings—nor lose the common touch,
If neither foes nor loving friends can hurt you,
If all men count with you, but none too much;
If you can fill the unforgiving minute
With sixty seconds' worth of distance run,
Yours is the Earth and everything that's in it,
And—which is more—you'll be a Man, my son!
—Rudyard Kipling, "If"

***

---

* Interview with Toots, October 2022.
† Interview with Toots, May 2022.

Courtesy Jack and Riva Levitt Estate

Toots felt that Alan was the epitome of the traits valued by Rudyard Kipling in his poem "If."

Courtesy Estate of Ric Ocasek

14 Keeper of the Flame

1987 . . . 1992 . . . 1998

> Live, travel, adventure, bless,
> and don't be sorry.*
> —Jack Kerouac

With the Elektra years behind him, Alan was electrified with a renewed sense of purpose about his experimentations in sound. He dove deeper into the "no-notes theory" he was developing with the machines lined up in his room at the Gramercy Park Hotel.

The Gramercy was home. He had been there for a few years and spent a lot of his time manipulating the mass of sound machines he had collected. He shared the space with Liz, who spent weekends there when they went to the Limelight. And Alan visited her at her loft on Hanover Square during the week. Their relationship was growing at a serious pace.

Liz: *When we first met, our chemistry was undeniably intense. But neither of us was looking for a quick hookup. Ironically, I think my friend, Dori (who somehow knew Alan and I would be a great match), was concerned that Alan was a rising "rock star" and could have a different lover as often as he wanted. I wasn't into casual hookups, and Alan made it clear that one-night stands left him cold and, unlike many less secure men, didn't feed his ego.*

We both knew very quickly that we were meant to be life partners. Despite the two-decade age gap, we shared and respected each other's values. I always knew Alan would be 100 percent honest with me. It wasn't in his makeup to tell people what they

---

* Jack Kerouac, *Desolation Angels* (New York: Penguin), 1965.

Photo by Peggy Melgard

wanted to hear to avoid conflict. And he wasn't afraid to show his vulnerability—he wore his emotions on his sleeve. From day one, we always felt we were in this together and could overcome any obstacles. Alan was very romantic, empathetic, and caring. We came to know each other so deeply, the connection we built was very special and never waned over the years.

***

It was the summer of 1987.

"I want to get back into a recording studio to see what other electronic machines are available to work with," said Alan, as he poured some coffee into Liz's mug.

"That sounds like a great idea," said Liz.

"And ya know—music is all about the rhythm," Alan went on. "You're a drummer so you get that."

Liz nodded and sipped her coffee. "Yep."

"Well, that's why when I go back in the studio, I want you with me. I'd like you to play the machines."

Liz laughed.

"What about the no girlfriend rule?"

He smiled, lit his Marlboro, and took a drag. A fire truck screamed outside the window.

"We're so far beyond that!" he blew out.

Liz felt a surge of excitement. She was fascinated by the sounds he was capturing with his makeshift setup.

"My music is all about the movement and placement of sound. You'll be great at it."

Liz got up and gave Alan a hug—she was beyond excited that he was bringing her into the improvisational process of creating his music, into the next stage of his exploration in sound.

When Liz chose drums at age sixteen, she felt what Alan had expressed. His attitude gave her confidence to approach the unknown with a sense of purpose.

***

Alan's "no-notes" theory involved making sound with no discernable notes, keys, chord structure—it was all encompassing: *no notes is all notes, nothing is everything.*

Creating linear soundscapes without traditional song structures also freed him up to deliver his lyrics with freestyle spontaneity and he could layer the sounds in infinite combinations. As he said to Liz many times:

> I sing in the key of V and I make my music to reflect that.
> —Alan

Generating something profoundly minimal was an exacting challenge. Alan believed the simplest things are the most difficult to do well. When there is nothing to hide behind or distract the observer and it's stripped down to the basic elements, you must make sure you stand by each element. Depth was built by layering the minimal elements.

His mantra was "less is more." He lived by the dictum:

KISS: "Keep It Simple Shit."

This adage also applied to his lyrics—every word, every line. Sometimes it was purely literal and other times obscure—always leaving room for the individualized experience and interpretation.

Whenever Alan performed a song live, it became something new. He brought himself, his current state of being and evolution—through the moment, and into it. He also wanted the audience to bring themselves into it—with freedom.

***

Alan and Liz ended up creating a company together—Saturn Strip, Ltd. It would produce and publish Alan's music going forward. Liz had experience in music industry contracts and she and Alan decided he'd be better off financing his own masters and licensing the final product to record labels, maintaining total creative control.

***

It was a sultry late July afternoon in downtown New York. The traffic bumping across Houston Street was frustrated by the endless red lights and towering trucks. The trucks were on their way to the Holland Tunnel to deliver boxes of canned vegetables to the A&P in Hudson, New Jersey, on the other side of the river.

That evening around 8:00 p.m., Alan and Liz ducked through the endless congestion and headed over to the Cable Building at the corner of Broadway and Houston.

Liz: When Alan and I entered the 6/8 Recording Studios in the Cable Building, we had no idea it would be the start of almost thirty years working together alongside engineer and owner Perkin Barnes. My band SSNUB had been rehearsing at the studio's East Village location at East Fifth and Second Avenue and had done some recording with Perkin. He was a cool guy with a laid-back vibe who had played bass in the funk band Konk.

Perkin was very open-minded. His low-key energy was the perfect counterpoint to Alan's intensity. They hit it off instantly. Perkin had just invested in several of the latest effects machines and hadn't much experience using them. He embraced Alan's approach of not consulting the manual when approaching the machines—unlike many engineers, who would not have been happy with someone blindly exploring their equipment. And Perkin was impressed with Alan reaching past the sounds on the machines and manipulating them until they reoriented into something no one else had come across.

***

Perkin Barnes

I am Perkin Barnes, and in 1980 I founded 6/8 Studios in NYC with my partner Ihsan Rashada. The studio remains a staple of NYC.

Well, Liz was the catalyst for my meeting Alan Vega. I had recorded her band at my other studio in '84. Her band was called SSNUB and she played the drums. And Liz thought that Alan and I hooking up would be cool. I had no idea why she thought that. I didn't know what to expect because I read an article about him and Suicide in—I think—a 1977 edition of the *Village Voice*. How long do they think they're going to last with a name like Suicide? But as it turned out, it was a good move.

So, Alan came over. He tried to forewarn me about what to expect and I told him, "I know where you're coming from, I know where you're talking about with this." I respected and appreciated his view of just really going for it. And going into the unknown, if you will, sonically. I was right along with it. So, we clicked pretty much right away.

Let's see, how do I sum up working with Alan Vega for nearly thirty years? Many stories, many experiences. I was Alan's engineer, coproducer, friend, and confidante. What a combo.

We first worked on *Deuce Avenue*. Alan came in and just experimented with sounds and whatnot. And then we started working on the record. We didn't have much of an ego clash at all. I knew what he was there for, and I knew what my role was. And I took that very seriously. We had a great give and take. I was sort of like the audio designated driver.

Alan never wavered. He was extremely disciplined. You know, he would show up to the studio on the dot—8:00 p.m.—not a minute before, not a minute later.

He would tell you in the moment if he likes something or if he doesn't. He didn't sugarcoat it, which was also very cool. We had to make so many decisions all the time because the introduction of one sound would change the whole context of everything else we'd built up.

Yeah, the Vega Vault was comprised of a lot of music that Alan wanted thrown out because he had moved on to the next thing that took him somewhere else. But I never threw anything away. He was throwing away great stuff all the time. And I knew at some point in the future he might want to revisit something.

And when we got to the point when we had unlimited tracks to work with, Alan wanted to keep it in the eight-track context. If we had used sixteen or twenty-four or a hundred tracks, you could put all kinds of garbage in there and clutter it up.

Alan would destroy and re-create. So, there was a process of deconstruction and then reconstruction. I think Alan was always trying to get down to the fractal level of sound. He wanted to just take a sound, totally get into the elements that make up the sound, and then completely change them into something else. He was always searching for something he hadn't heard yet.

I worked with Ric Ocasek and Alan on the song, "Keep It Alive" for the album, *New Raceion*, and Ric was cool. I asked him, "Ric, you're a famous guy. How do you do it?" His answer was, "Just do your thing. Just be you."

There was a process that Alan and I went through. Many people go into the studio and they just start working. But we had to talk it through. We talked about things not related to music. We talked about art, we talked about politics, we talked about race, we talked about racism, we talked about technology, whatever. But then it all came around for some reason—after we talked, we got down to work. Although Alan made it very difficult because he could have easily been a major comedian. He was just so funny. I was in stitches constantly. He could make a joke about anything and point out the absurdities in all aspects of life.

His thoughts could be very heavy duty without being pedantic. Just this common sense, clear sense of things he had. And that went into the music too, because

Perkin, Alan, and Dante at 6/8 Studios, 2007. *Photo by Liz Lamere*

for all the elements and all the cacophony in the music, it was all very simple. It was made of simple ingredients. But it sounds really massive.

It's amazing. Every time I hear it, even though I helped create it—every time I hear it, it sounds new to me, it sounds different. And I hear something in it I didn't notice before. He had such a magical sense of the enormity of tiny fractals.

He was totally brilliant. And he had a real insight into human nature, into how the world was. It was just amazingly refreshing to discuss things with him.

I have so many memories of him because I spent a good part of my life with him. And he helped me through a lot of things as I did him. I mean, there's lots of heavy stuff that happened, really deep stuff.

We're talking about the music, but personally, he was a beautiful person, and he was quite evolved. He had the whole racial thing worked out and understood.

And I altered my sensibility toward music, because I can't listen to just anything anymore after working with him. I love rock and roll—very, very much. But after working with him it's like you have gone somewhere where you've seen things that you can't unsee, you hear things that you can't unhear—because we went so deep sonically. Alan was always searching for the sounds he wasn't hearing.

He was extremely courageous. ■

***

When not in the studio, Alan spent many hours walking the streets, recording the noise of city life—subways pounding down the tracks, the swirling sound of cars streaming across the Brooklyn Bridge—the endless tumult throughout the city.

Both Alan and Liz were also drawn to the sound of cassette mix tapes of local hip-hop artists blasting out of boom boxes on the street.

"That is the future," Alan said. "The sound of the new rock 'n' roll."

Decades later, the vast majority of Grammy award winners and Rock 'n' Roll Hall of Fame inductees confirmed his vision.

Implementing his philosophy of minimalism, Alan wanted to create unique sounds powerful enough to each stand on their own. His approach was to utilize the least amount of traditional musical instruments possible. Rather than using the effects machines—such as the Yamaha SPX90 multi-effects processor to affect keyboard, guitar, or bass tracks, Alan and Liz set about finding sounds generated solely from the machines themselves.

With Liz playing the machines, they often recorded those sounds onto a track and then ran that track back through the processor, bouncing it onto a new track. Sounds were bounced back and forth numerous times, as they continued layering the tracks.

They also brought in those random sounds Alan recorded on the street. They were using analog tape, and the sounds weren't sampled, synced, or looped on a grid. Everything was played live. Although the sounds were produced by machines, the imperfect live playing gave the recordings a warm, human touch.

Those earliest recordings eventually became Alan and Liz's first album together: *Deuce Avenue*. It was released in 1990 on the French label Musidisc, owned by Francois Grandchamp des Raux. Musidisc was founded in the 1920s and known as home to a large selection of classical music. Francois was a music aficionado with a deep appreciation for unique music. They sent the album to him and had their first licensing deal on Saturn Strip, Ltd.

Alan invited Kuch to join him and Liz on guitar when they went on a short European tour to support the album's release.

One night, after a show in Berlin, a sound engineer came backstage and told Alan and Liz he worked with the band U2. He said Bono had brought the CD of *Deuce Avenue* into the studio and he asked how they had achieved some of the sounds on the album. Knowing relatively few people had purchased the album, given the small distribution reach of the label, Alan and Liz were amazed.

***

In 1988, when they were still working on *Deuce Avenue*, Ric Ocasek reached out to Alan and asked if he and Marty would like to record a Suicide album.

Suicide had been on a hiatus through the mid-'80s while the two of them worked on their solo projects. They hadn't performed together in a number of years.

Marty had been busy recording his instrumental work and released another solo album, *Clouds of Glory*. He had done some touring to promote his music but was definitely game to work with Alan again and reignite Suicide.

Marty sent Alan a batch of song sketches; Alan picked his favorites and wrote some scratch lyrics to bring into the studio. Ric financed and produced the album. The album *A Way of Life* was recorded at Electric Lady studios on Eighth Street in Manhattan.

On the first day of recording, Marty and Alan arrived at the studio early. Ric's right-hand man, David Hegelmeier ("Heg"), had already set everything up for the session, so they decided to take a run at the set of songs they had agreed on for the record. Knowing the moment-to-moment energy Alan and Marty worked under and not wanting to miss any gems, Heg recorded the live set.

Heg had become adept at sensing and interpreting Alan's instinctive moves. As Ric's personal engineer, Heg was involved in most of the recordings and live shows Alan did with Ric. And he developed a close friendship with Alan.

***

David Hegelmeier ("Heg")
Ric Ocasek's Sound Engineer
March 2023
I started working for the Cars late in September of 1978. Their first album had already come out. . . . I can't remember where I met Alan or heard the music . . . but when I first did, I couldn't understand what the hell was going on . . . but it was cool. . . .

They opened at the LA Amphitheater gig in '79. It was pretty heavy. They had to get them off the stage 'cause it just got overwhelming. It was aggressive and there was a lot of debris getting thrown up there.

There were also restrictions on the LA Amphitheater in terms of the decibels because of Bob Hope. Behind the amphitheater was a canyon where Bob Hope's house sat up on a cliff. Although it was minuscule, people would point it out—it was the only home there.

They had put an authorized engineer out at the sound console checking volume and decibels. Anything over a hundred, you would get a warning. If you went over a hundred again, the show got shut down.

But some years later, I met Bob Hope at the SVO Hotel in London. The Cars were doing a promo tour for *Heartbeat City*. And we had an interview at the BBC that morning.

I was in the lobby making phone calls trying to get the band to come down. And I had a black and white mohawk and all leather pants, a jacket, and dark glasses.

And Bob Hope came in—I didn't know it was him. He crosses the lobby, which is kind of small and he came in front of me and he stopped. He looked at me and he complimented my haircut. "Some haircut you have," he said. And he just looked at me. So, we talked a couple of minutes. I told him why I was there—he knew who the Cars were. And he even mentioned the volume of that gig outside his house. Right. And I said, I know that when we did play, we got the warning. He kind of chuckled about it. He was a little looser about it than the promoter was.

When it comes to Suicide, I bet Bob Hope would sit through the show and probably really enjoy it. Judging from the kind of person he seemed after talking with him, he would've loved it. And they would've really got along.

Hartford Civic Center in 1980 was first time I had more interaction with Alan and Marty.

Suicide was opening for the Cars and after dinner, the night of the show, I saw Alan and Marty walking in through the loading dock with armfuls of wires, keyboards, etc.

I went over to help them out. We got them set up—checking inputs, a very rough sound check and getting the monitor mix for Alan and Marty together. All this was being done in front of the crowd who were rushing into the center—pretty chaotic.

Alan and Marty were great dealing with all the bullshit. Very kind and patient guys, for sure. So, we get them offstage, take them to their dressing room and relax a bit and we let Ric know they were here, set up and ready to go. Everything was in sync.

Time passes to showtime. House lights go out and the magic begins. Suicide takes the stage with all of us. The Cars' crew were onstage just in case Suicide needed any help during the show. What an amazing start to a show—a wall of driving sound from Martin Rev then Alan singing to the crowd. Things seemed to be rolling along pretty smoothly when a few of us noticed the lighting crew, who were standing offstage, start to run and it looked like they were trying to shield themselves with their hands. They were running for cover.

Looking back at Alan, we see him start to hit himself in the face with the mic. We also see throngs of people rushing up to the barricade, yelling and screaming, giving Alan the finger. It was an unbelievable aggressive posture from the crowd.

Then we start to hear these pinging sounds and see blurs of whatever it was raining down on the stage. It was like a severe thunderstorm raining down nickels and quarters. It seemed like everyone in the audience was throwing coins at Marty and Alan. The throngs of people rushing the barricade intensified, and the security was starting to get outnumbered.

The amount of debris and coins raining down on the stage really accelerated. Anyone onstage was trying to find cover to protect themselves from getting hit.

Then, the word came to get Suicide off the stage. Security thought it was too dangerous—someone could get seriously hurt.

The house lights came on and we got Marty and Alan offstage. With the house lights on, everyone could see the amount of coins, paper cups, bottles, and garbage that had been thrown onstage. A few union crew stagehands started to clean up.

The crew checked amps and Greg's keyboard setup for any damage. When I took the scrim off of the drum kit I noticed a pretty good sized switchblade rammed into the floor of the drum riser. Really scary stuff. Alan and Marty could've been severely hurt.

During the load out, a couple of the stagehands who had helped clean the stage after Suicide said they'd love to have them back again—they had made an extra couple of hundred dollars in all the coins they swept up.

Years later when I was working in Ric's private studio, he bought this digital recorder—Sony Digital all-in-one type deal. The way it would work is if Ric wanted to work in the studio, I would set things up—patch things, set up a vocal mic, set the compressor, all the technical stuff. All Ric had to do was put the machine on "Record" and deal with the performance. And if there was a problem, he would call me. But usually, it was pretty straight ahead.

So, Ric bought this machine and had Alan come over and they did a song on it. And then I asked Ric about the recording, 'cause I was excited—it was the first real digital format. But Ric just kind of passed it off like it was nothing, you know, so I didn't hear the recording they made. He didn't say it wasn't good, he just kind of shrugged his shoulders—like it wasn't any big deal. So, we put the machine in a box and put it in a storage room down in the basement behind the studio. It was there for years. Sometimes, Ric would ask me, what's this?

And he'd say, we could just throw it out. And I'd say, all right. But I didn't and so it was that dynamic for about thirty years. It went to storage in Manhattan and then it did make its way upstate where all of Ric's equipment, art, etc., were kept.

I was upstate this past September with his sons. Eron wanted to know what that machine was and I told him—the whole story about Ric and Alan making this song back then. And he said, let's play it. Let's see if the song is still there. I doubted it would be there after thirty years. So, we play it and it's like they recorded it just yesterday. It was in perfect condition. This song that no one has ever heard. I transferred it, and Ric's sons, Liz, and Dante are collaborating on the song, "Mr. Midnight."

In 1995, I had the pleasure and the honor of working with Alan on the cover of his *Dujang Prang* album.

Ric had a nice graphic set up on his computer on the fourth floor of his house. He, Alan, and I were just up there bouncing ideas around. And we began working on the cover of *Dujang Prang*. I remember expending a lot of time on it. After we got the layout, we were in the font world—of course there were like eight million fonts on his computer. So, we're going through the fonts and Alan's not liking any. I said I could just write the text out and scan it and we could use that if you want. And Alan was like, "Wow. Really? Let's do it."

We put Alan's digital picture into the program and it came out looking a little fuzzy, but he loved that. He said zoom in, zoom in more. I zoomed in until I couldn't anymore. It was like 3,000 times. Ric had a beautiful big monitor, so it was fun, you know. And the whole screen was just pixels and we moved them around until we found like a cool collection of colors and pixels. It just blew Alan away. He loved it.

When Alan was singing, it was pure magic. You have to have been there to know because words would never be able to convey how unbelievable it was. In everything from his performance to his ingenious . . . words, the phrases that he put together, that he came up with were ingenious. Nobody sounded like him. It was such a high quality, deep, beautiful voice. It was hypnotizing. It was cool in the studio because there wasn't any chaos around like there is in a live show, and he was able to concentrate, and it was quiet. So, just silently, I was sitting there thinking to myself, "What a gift this is."

A lot of those times in New York when Alan would come over to Ric's, I'd have time to sit and talk with him before Ric came downstairs. And that's when we would talk about the Mets, the Knicks, and his lotto numbers.

And one time in particular. This is a little sad, but I'm just gonna mention to show you how beautiful Alan was.

He came in, sat down, and he was really bummed and quiet, which is usually not like Alan. I didn't bother him, but then he said that he had just lost one of his cats—Frankie. Alan's energy was really slowed down. We had an amazing conversation just about Frankie, about what he meant to Alan. A lot of the vibe wasn't the words, it was just the emotion you could feel from Alan. He was like— "you gotta understand, he was my family."

You know, when people are reading things about Alan, they should understand that with everything, you know, what a sweet, sweet human being he was.

***

A lot of the fine tuning and fleshing out of the lyrics for *A Way of Life* was done by Alan during the first take. Marty freestyled the music he layered onto the basic tracks.

> Ric wasn't there yet, only the engineers, so Alan and I just started to warm up and . . . started writing some new songs. The engineers decided among themselves to set the recorder rolling and when Ric came in an hour or two later ready to work, he asked the engineers if we had already sound checked. They said, "yeah and they basically recorded the whole album." Ric was amazed and started immediately to listen to what became the first mixes of *A Way of Life*.*
> —Martin Rev

Then Ric worked his magic—refining everything without stripping its rawness. During post-production, it became evident there was one song which Alan felt wasn't quite there yet. The song was *Surrender*, a lovely ballad about falling in love. He wanted to capture a beautiful tone in the chorus section and both he and Ric thought adding female voices would bring out that special quality.

> When you take me
> when you make me
> (I'll fall for you) I'll fall for you
> Tired of goodbyes
> Of never knowing
> About you (About you)
> I surrender
> I surrender
> To you[†]

Ric jumped on that energy and asked Liz if she wanted to sing on the track. She was a little thrown because she didn't feel she was a "real" singer—and Suicide was a duo—they never had another performer on their recordings.

---

* Treble Staff, "Suicide to Reissue *A Way of Life* for its 35th Anniversary," *Treble*, April 5, 2023, https://www.treblezine.com/suicide-a-way-of-life-reissue-announced/.
† "Surrender," *A Way of Life* by Suicide, 1988, Chapter 22 Records, reissued 2023 on BMG/Mute.

Turns out Ric was being a romantic—seeing Alan and Liz had essentially "surrendered" themselves to each other.

But Liz's reply was on point: "I'm not Yoko Ono," she said with a smile.

***

Martin Rev's arrangements were the perfect complement to Alan's lyrics and vocal performance and *A Way of Life* is considered one of their greats.

> If there's one thing *A Way of Life* drives home more than any other,
> it's that Suicide never stopped being ahead of their time, their
> signature big-reverb synth-pop/'50s rock 'n' roll/industrial noise
> mélange . . . too singular to be touched by anyone else.*

Alan's favorite track was "Dominic Christ." It captures the essence of many of the desolate characters in Vega's nightly portrait drawings.

> "Bless you sirs
> The loser Dominic says
> All your gambling dreams
> Reachin' for the stars
> Get ready for the end"†

Courtesy Saturn Strip, Ltd.　　　　　*Courtesy Saturn Strip, Ltd.*

* Joe Tangari, "A Way of Life," *Pitchfork*, January 26, 2004, https://pitchfork.com/reviews/albums/7558-a
-way-of-life/.
† "Dominic Christ" by Alan Vega and Martin Rev, 1988.

Liz: There are so many levels of meaning in Alan's lyrics and he left much to individual interpretation, so the listener could bring their own personal meaning to his words.

***

It was around this time when Liz fell into becoming Suicide and Alan's de facto manager. Being a lawyer, she always reviewed whatever contracts were on the table and having recently joined a small law firm, her workload had lessened. She had also become counsel for the organization Women in Music—giving her more insight into the music business.

However, nothing was agreed to for Suicide without Rev taking a thorough look at it first. He has a lot of business savvy and is very detail oriented. Alan also had a keen understanding of business, but was uninterested in the minutiae of any deal and trusted Liz and Rev to work out the specifics. However, his immediate reaction to any proposal was typically "No!"—if it meant travel and being away from home or out of the studio.

Alan was a true homebody. He felt most comfortable there and nowhere else—particularly if it involved the disruption of his routines. The regularity of a regimen, a pattern gave him serenity and freed him up to stay in the flow of creating.

As one of the most erratic performers in the history of music, he needed the balance of his drawing, writing, studio time, and playful interaction with his family.

Thus, when Liz—in her role as manager—proposed a tour or performing at a venue out of town, Alan would only agree if he felt it was really essential. He was ultimately game—but it took some persuasion. Inevitably, even when he had agreed to do something, and Liz reminded him it was soon time to do it, he'd say "You gotta get me out of this thing."

Alan never sought out opportunities; he wanted to stay focused on creating. Liz became the conduit, fielding inquiries and taking them to him. If whatever was proposed resonated with him, he agreed, especially to collaborate with someone with whom he felt a strong connection, or for a benefit concert. It had to feel special to take him out of his routine.

Added to his discomfort with travel was the fact that whenever they had to go through the border of another country, Alan was inevitably pulled over by security and put through extra scrutiny. Wearing black leather and the ever-present beret and sunglasses was problematic.

Liz: I think he also had a lot of residual anxiety around the holocaust, terrorism, war.

***

After the 1988 release in the UK of *A Way of Life*, Suicide went on a two-week European tour. Their audiences had heard about the riots during Suicide's late '70s tours opening for the Clash and Elvis Costello.

The Jesus & Mary Chain and a young Bobby Gillespie were witness to those riots and mayhem on the Clash tour as well. When Jesus & Mary Chain came backstage one night during the Way of Life tour, they confirmed that Alan wasn't hallucinating when he saw an axe fly by his head. Bobby told Alan he had been at the riot in Glasgow and how that night changed his life. He decided to start a band after seeing Suicide. His band—Primal Scream—became one of the most well-known bands to emerge from Scotland.

At one of the last shows on the *A Way of Life* tour in northern France, Alan was struck in the head by a flying wrench. He suffered a large gash just above his eye. If the wrench had lodged just a hair lower he could have been blinded.

It was more than ten years since those concerts with the Clash and Elvis that were tinged with such hostility. Alan thought that rage was over. Their shows were now well received by most audiences. He believed they were finally being understood and accepted.

He was mistaken.

And shocked.

> You always think that a time will come when you get out of the shit.
> You know it won't happen, but there's a tiny chance, and that's exactly
> why I keep going. I'm a small guy now. I could get even smaller.*
> —Alan

***

> . . . no matter how hard the world pushes against me, within me,
> there's something stronger—something better, pushing right back.†
> —Albert Camus

---

* Alexandre Breton, *Alan Vega: Conversation with an Indian* (Le Texte Vivant, 2017), Kindle.
† Albert Camus, *The Stranger* (New York: Alfred A. Knopf), 1942.

Courtesy Estate of Ric Ocasek

15 Novel

1986 . . . 1990 . . . 1992 . . .

> Be loved, be admired, be necessary; be somebody.*
> —Simone de Beauvoir

Once the tour finished, Alan and Liz decided to live full time at the loft on Hanover Square. Their lives had become deeply intertwined and they spent most of their time there.

Liz: Alan and I had personalities and strengths that truly complemented each other. He was a great listener, advisor, and problem solver and cared about issues I was dealing with at work. And I was happy to handle things he didn't want to deal with. I remember the first tax season we were together, I arrived at the Gramercy one night to find Alan "completing" his tax return. I was completely blown away to see that he had used crayon to complete his return and was attempting to use his sewing kit to stitch the pages together instead of a stapler. When I expressed concern that this may not be acceptable to the IRS, he said he wanted them to believe he was crazy and that would keep them at bay. He described an incident many years prior when he had been audited. Alan showed up at the IRS agent's office in head-to-toe leather, complete with hanging chains and "Suicide" written in studs on the back of his jacket. Knowing Alan, he may have also mumbled in riddles for a short time. The agent then said, "We can finish this over the phone" and sent him away. Alan never heard from the agent again.

Alan mainly left home to go to the studio or the neighborhood pub where he would have his nightcap and chat with the locals before returning to the loft to write in his notebook or work on a sculpture.

---

* Simone de Beauvoir, *Memoirs of a Dutiful Daughter*, trans. J. Kirkup (Harmondsworth: Penguin, 1958).

His notebooks were teeming every night with poetry, lyrics, random thoughts, and portraits he sketched. Creating those pages was a form of catharsis.

He also voraciously followed world events and watched documentaries on every subject imaginable.

Liz: Alan was one of the most intelligent people I've ever known. When I first met him, I was blown away by how well read he was and how much knowledge he had across a broad spectrum of subjects. He had studied all the existential philosophers and read most of the classics—not for classwork, but a pure thirst for knowledge and understanding of the Universe and human nature.

***

The building on Hanover Square, where Alan and Liz now lived, was one of a handful of residential locations in the Financial District in downtown Manhattan. The stately limestone building had been home to the Cotton Exchange, and the neighborhood of Hanover Square was known historically as the publishing district. Adjacent to the building was the India House, a landmarked building with a long tradition as an industry club, first in publishing and later finance.

At that time—1988—the neighborhood hosted only nine-to-fivers commuting into the city for their workday—then commuting right back out of the city at the end of the day. It was a ghost town in the evening.

Alan loved being one of the very few people on those empty streets as the sun went down. He would forage through the industrial garbage and electronic debris thrown out in front of the Stock Market Exchange, the World Trade Center, Federal Hall, or the Bull—seeking supplies for his light sculptures. The loft space had double high walls and Alan mounted his light sculptures up to the twenty-foot-high ceilings. Then he watched them reflect on the ceiling-high windows looking out over the East River.

He also started taking photographs in the desolate streets and of images on the TV. He captured impressions and static shot through colored filters he made himself with plastic sheets. On one long wall he began mounting photos encased in small boxes, lining them up in a linear row.

Liz: These images were featured in a book curated by Edit DeAk. Edit had lined up a Japanese publisher to release a book of Alan's art. Alan had the idea to take photos of the linear wall of photographs and use them as the centerpiece of each page of the book, as the foundation on which to draw and write poetry. The result was Deuce Avenue War: The Warriors V3 97 *released in 1991.*

***

Alan also made a daily excursion to the local deli to purchase multiples of Quick Draw Lottery tickets. Gambling had been a significant part of his father's daily

Lottery Ticket. *Courtesy Saturn Strip, Ltd.*

existence. For Alan it was a passion based on skill, strategy, and the challenge of beating the odds. He loved "playing the numbers." He kept stacks of empty lotto tickets on hand at home and often created art from this piece of life.

Alan's strong math and analytical skills piqued his interest in the game.

***

One late summer weekend early in their relationship, Alan and Liz rented a car to go up to her family's summer cottage in Cape Cod. As they started edging toward the Triboro Bridge, Alan asked Liz to stop the car so he could buy his lottery tickets for the weekend.

Liz looked at him with confusion.

"You can't go a couple of days without playing the lottery?"

"No," Alan replied. "I have a system."

"A system?"

Liz shook her head. Then she stopped the car and he jumped out. Liz laughed as she watched him race into the store.

***

Alan's system involved a complicated statistical analysis of the probabilities of a series of numbers coming in based on previous winning numbers.

Every day, he tracked those numbers and recorded them in a notebook. From these accumulated figures, he calculated his picks.

This day, before they headed out of town, he got his weekend tickets and that Sunday, he won $6,000.

That wasn't serendipity.

That was normal, consistent, fixed.

He played between $10 and $20 in the lottery every day of his life and each year he was up in winnings on an average of over $5,000. Over the years he had many one-off big hits up to $10,000.

Except it wasn't about the money.

It was about the challenge—the game.

> The beauty of the game! In a way, if you don't play, you don't win, but if you do play, there is a chance that you will win, and you can win big!*
> —Alan

Horseracing, however, held a special place in his heart. He thought thoroughbred horses were magnificent animals. Alan and Liz went to the Belmont Stakes a number of times as well as Saratoga to see the Travers Stakes.

Alan's uncanny ability to pick the winners involved studying a combination of the horses' stats, the changing odds, and field conditions. He'd also check the paddocks to see how the horses looked and sense their energy prior to the race.

Against all odds, he picked the winner of the Kentucky Derby every year. He wasn't always sure how—it just came to him.

On May 7, 2016, he picked Nyquist to win the Kentucky Derby. This would be his last Kentucky Derby. Despite his track record for picking the winners of the Derby, he only bet on horses when he was at the track.

In the mid-'70s, when Alan was basically living hand to mouth, he and his close friend, Howie, would go to the racetrack to bet on the horses whenever they

---

* Alexandre Breton, *Alan Vega: Conversation with an Indian* (Le Texte Vivant, 2017), Kindle.

Alan and Marty reviewing their bets. © *Bob Gruen/www.bobgruen.com*

were down to their last bit of cash. Every time, their winnings would be substantial enough to set them up for another few months.

Liz: *And this is a great analogy for his career—reflecting his position as the most non-careerist person I've ever known. The French press delighted in thinking of Alan as the beautiful loser because his music was seemingly not commercially successful. But looking back, whenever Alan needed something to sustain himself, another opportunity would materialize out of thin air. It's like the universe and a higher power was making sure he would carry on creating.*

***

In August 1990, President George Bush deployed American troops into Saudi Arabia in response to Iran's invasion of Kuwait.

Alan and Liz were recording their second album, *Power on to Zero Hour*, at the time and like the abhorrence Alan felt with Vietnam, the Gulf War seeped inside his words with titles of his songs such as "Fear," "Automatic Terror," and "Jungle Justice." They and Alan's fury within them were indicative of the times—and prescient of the future.

Can't close my eyes
This nightmare's everywhere
A gettin' used for nothin'
For the rich man's dream
A fightin' his stupid wars
When are we gonna learn
It's time to do somethin' now*

***

Later thar year, Ric Ocasek went back into the studio with Suicide to record their next album *Why Be Blue*, which was released on Brake Out Records. Alan wrote the lyrics for it during one weekend when he and Liz were in Boston for a Suicide concert at the club, Ground Zero.

Liz drove Marty and Alan up to Boston for the concert. They stayed at her grandmother's—Momilou's—house. Marty stayed in Uncle George's old room and Alan and Liz were in the attic, which was filled with old books and bunk beds along the walls. On the landing at the top of the stairs to the attic was a large statue of Jesus. As a kid, Liz was sure to bless herself whenever she approached that statue.

Alan felt so comfortable and at home in that attic—the space connected with him. They stayed up there whenever they visited, and Alan would bless himself when passing Jesus.

After Momilou passed away in 2000, Alan and Liz inherited the statue, which they placed at the top of the stairs in their home on Hanover Square.

***

When they returned to the city, Marty, Alan, and Ric holed up in One Take Studios to lay down *Why Be Blue*. Recording a Suicide album never took long. Marty would send music sketches, then Alan would select the ideas he liked and meet Marty at the studio with his lyrics to record. Ric took longer on mixing than it took to record the songs.

Why Be Blue was released in July and once again the critics didn't know what to make of it.

> The Ric Ocasek-produced *Why Be Blue* originally released on Break
> Out in 1992, is notable for its upbeat temperament (the title isn't
> ironic) and its display of Alan Vega and Martin Rev at a point in their
> career when they were neither ahead of nor with the times. . . .
> They were somewhere else entirely, if vaguely in line with the groups
> that continued to look to Suicide's past work for guidance.†

---

* "Jungle Justice," by Alan Vega, *Power on to Zero*, 1992.
† Andy Kellman, "*Why Be Blue* Review," *Allmusic*, https://www.allmusic.com/album/why-be-blue--mw0000094178

Suicide played a few shows in support of the album—one of them at the Limelight in New York.

> Suicide doesn't sound like its industrial offspring. . . . Suicide
> still plays on the cusp between parody and sincerity; how much
> can be stripped from a song before it becomes a mockery?
> . . . [T]he answer seemed to be: nearly everything.*

***

By 1992, Alan and Liz began murmuring between themselves about having a baby. They were at a point in their lives where they could envision providing a loving home for a child. Alan felt good about it. Liz never had the "white wedding, picket fence, 2.5 kids" dream. Yet, she felt Alan was so special, she wanted to pass his genes along and share their lives with a child. But approaching her mid-thirties, she knew there was a timeline. And both Liz and Alan felt if they were going to do it—they should get married.

On Sadie Hawkins Day—the day originated in the *Li'l Abner* comic strip in the 1930s with the premise that women ask men out for a date—Liz proposed and Alan said yes. They then set their favorite holiday for the day of the nuptials: Halloween.

But before anything had been set in definitive motion, Liz wanted to look into rebuilding the bridge with Alan's family.

Liz: I always found it so sad for him to not have any relationship with his family.

***

Liz was aware that Robbie and his family lived in the Maryland area where Robbie worked as a meteorologist. She was able to track him down at his office and gave him a call.

"Hi! Robbie?"

"Yes?" he replied.

"My name is Liz Lamere and I'm calling because I will be marrying your brother Alan and—"

"What!? Alan?! Where is he?! How is he?!"

He was nearly breathless. He couldn't believe what he was hearing. Liz sensed from Robbie's urgency that he may have thought something was seriously wrong.

Liz filled Robbie in on Alan's career and assured him he was healthy and fine. Robbie was wildly grateful his brother was happy and following his dreams. He then raised the possibility of seeing Alan.

---

* John Pareles, "Pop and Jazz in Review," July 16, 1992, *New York Times*, https://www.nytimes.com/1992/07/16/arts/pop-and-jazz-in-review-768292.html.

That was very much Liz's plan and she told Robbie they could drive down the following weekend.

Liz hadn't told Alan she was calling Robbie—in case Robbie wasn't accepting of her call. Alan was so thrilled to hear Robbie hadn't disowned him, he readily agreed to go see his brother and his family.

Alan and Liz made the road trip to Robbie's home in Silver Spring, Maryland, where they met his wife, Sue, and Alan's nieces, Amie and Beth.

Alan was exhilarated. When he and Robbie saw each other, they immediately fell into everything sports—Mets, Knicks, Giants. They hugged and laughed and talked without break. Alan was flooded with joy.

Robbie also filled Alan in about his health, exercise, and diet regimen given his heart condition.

They all sat down for a celebratory snack. Sue brought out a low fat, low sugar, egg-free cake, and everyone started eating and catching up. Amie was in college at the University of Maryland. She was studying theatre, which Alan was thrilled to hear.

Before heading to the hotel for the night, they made plans to meet up again the next day to go the local farmer's market where Sue and Robbie loved to get apple cider butter. As Alan and Liz started out the front door, Sue looked curiously at Liz's chunky-heeled, rock 'n' roll black boots.

"You might want to wear some sensible shoes tomorrow," she said.

Liz laughed, "These are my sensible shoes," she replied with a big smile.

When they got in the car, Alan looked around.

"It's a different world out here," he pondered.

Non-Wedding

Liz: Since Halloween was on a Saturday that year, we went to City Hall on Friday. We were both wearing black leather jackets and my friend, Dana, was our witness. When we arrived at the marriage ceremony room, the couple just before us was dressed in full white wedding gown/tux regalia, complete with bridesmaids and flower children. Our black leather was at the opposite end of the "getting married" dress code spectrum.

After the five-minute ceremony, Alan and I went to the Pearl Street Diner a few blocks away—a classic one-story building nestled in the shadows of the towering office buildings surrounding it. We laughed and joked about our non-fancy pomp and circumstance ceremony and practiced saying "my wife" and "my husband":

"My husband is having the scrambled eggs."

"My wife would love a toasted bagel with cream cheese."

Liz and Alan with marriage license outside City Hall, Halloween, 1992. *Photo by Dana Mesh*

Cutting the wedding cake. *Photo by Peggy Melgard*

We then got a rental car and drove to Boston to spend the weekend at the Copley Plaza. The next night—Halloween—we had a small gathering in our room with Chryste Hall, who had brought Suicide to Boston for shows and had become a good friend.

Then on Sunday, my brother Kent and his wife, Jean, hosted a reception for us in their home in Milton. Momilou, Toots, my stepfather, Dick, Butch, my stepmother, Ruth, my brother David, and his wife Sandy, all of my aunts and uncles and cousins came as well as several coworkers who made the trip from NYC. We had invited Robbie and Sue but unfortunately, living in Maryland, they couldn't get up to Boston for the party in good time. It was a lovely gathering.

Alan wore the orange leather motorcycle jacket we had recently found at a vintage store and I wore a purple dress. We ate cake and drank champagne from the cases my dad had bought when I was born and had been stored in the basement all those years.

Alan was always at ease with my family and they all adored him. They shared Alan's love and encyclopedic knowledge of sports and, despite the long-standing Boston/New York sports rivalry, he was immediately embraced. It was great to have none of the stress of making lots of wedding plans.

***

One evening, while Alan and Liz were relaxing at home, Alan started expressing concern about having a baby.

"I'm worried about the state of the world and the uncertainty of what this child will have to face in their lifetime."

Liz looked at him, feeling his concern.

"Well," she said with some thought. "There is something to be said about bringing a child into the world who could eventually make important changes to it, especially if you dedicate yourself to guiding them."

Alan paused. Through the dark steam rising from his coffee, he looked out the window.

"What about adoption?" he asked, turning to Liz. "There are so many children out there with no homes, no food, nothing."

Liz looked at him. She loved this idea but was not yet ready to give up on her dream of perpetuating Alan's genes.

After trying to get pregnant naturally for about six months, Liz consulted with her gynecologist, who recommended IVF.

Unfortunately, Liz had a history of irregular periods and uterine fibroids. She had multiple myomectomy surgeries to remove them.

Despite going through three cycles of IVF, she wasn't able to sustain a pregnancy. She came close once but at work one day when she stood up from her desk, she felt a steady gush of blood down her legs—a miscarriage.

She was immediately taken to the emergency room. Alan raced in to get to her. They both broke down in tears. Alan was so grateful that Liz was OK and as he held her tight, he said, "Losing you would be unbearable." He moved closer and looked in her eyes. "I believe there is another path meant for us."

Liz: *For a long time after that miscarriage, I had dreams that I was pregnant. And I always woke up with a deep feeling of loss.*

At that point, Liz felt a sense of relief they were going forward with the adoption process. It would take at least a year and had its own unpredictable stresses but nothing like going through the IVF process—the daily injections, the hormones causing exhausting symptoms, getting embryos implanted and then learning it didn't work.

And the constant yearning.

She needed to move on.

***

After her freshman year at Tufts University, Liz joined the Amigos de las Americas program. She spent a summer month in the mountains of Guatemala teaching dental hygiene to the natives. She traveled with a small team and local guides through the remote villages where the language spoken was Kekchi, one of the Mayan languages of that region.

Liz fell in love with the beautiful children there. Despite severe poverty, limited plumbing and electricity, and few toys, the children had such a joyful spirit. They found many ways to have fun hiking, swimming in the local watering hole, and kicking or throwing balls. Liz wrote in her diary at the time that she wished she could bring one of these children home with her.

That dream became a reality.

***

The soul is healed by being with children.*
—Fyodor Dostoevsky

---

* Fyodor Dostoevsky, *Poor Folk: The Soul Is Healed by Being with Children*, trans. C. J. Hogarth (New York: Horse's Mouth, 2019).

Photo by Catherine Ceresole

16 Nosedive

1990 . . . 1992 . . . 1996 . . .

> In a world, man must create his own essence.*
> —Jean-Paul Sartre

A seismic shift was about to occur in awareness of the historical relevancy of Suicide.

In 1996, Alan and Liz were approached by Paul Smith, who had been in the music industry for a long time and ran the record label Blast First. He had also worked with Sonic Youth and Psychic TV. He was asked to find a band to open a new performance space located in the prestigious South Bank Centre in London. The space was intended to be the lowbrow counterpart to the very highbrow venue. Paul immediately thought of Suicide as the perfect fit. Paul and his partner, Susan Stenger, then came to NYC to pitch the idea. Marty, Alan, and Liz met them at a restaurant on Bleecker Street, enjoyed a meal together, and had a long talk. It was the beginning of a decades-long relationship that would bring significant awareness to the innovations of both Suicide and Alan Vega.

***

The last time Vega had performed in London was at the end of the *Deuce Avenue* solo tour in November 1990. He was booked for two sold-out nights at the Town & Country Club as "special guest" for "Pop Will Eat Itself." PWEI was very popular and loved Vega.

However, on the first night, 2,000 rowdy kids bombarded Alan, Kuch, and Liz with coins, drinks, cups, and ultimately a large piece of safety glass from a bathroom window. It was intense performing the set while dodging hard objects. After twenty minutes, security shut down the show.

---

* Jean-Paul Sartre, *No Exit* (London: Samuel French, Inc., 1944).

The next night, Alan, Kuch, and Liz showed up dressed for battle. Meanwhile, the club owner called Liz into his office and said it was too risky to let them play. She was not happy with this development and negotiated a slightly larger fee to cancel the set.

There was a lot of press from both London and Paris that night as they had heard about the riot the night before. In place of the show, a party with the hard-core fans and the press ensued backstage. Alan came up with the idea of sitting on the toilet with the large wad of cash he had received to cancel the show.

The next day, the Paris newspaper *"Liberation,"* published a picture of Alan sitting on the toilet, holding the money up to his mouth with the headline: "Paid more not to play; Alan Vega doesn't give a shit."

> I think it's really very funny, but this audience were a streak of piss
> compared with Clash fans. I actually found the crowd reaction
> quite exciting—it's just a shame they couldn't cope with me.
> —Alan

Liz: They thought they were so tough, but when Alan rushed the front of the stage, the audience recoiled in a wave of fear.

***

Back in New York after the release of *Power on to Zero Hour*, Alan ran into Ce Vega, a guitarist living in the East Village—and he had an epiphany. He felt compelled to hear how blending traditional guitar into the evolving experimental music he was creating would sound.

Ce was an awesome player and came into the studio a few times and laid down tracks for what was to become the next Vega studio album, *New Raceion*. The concept for the album was about bringing people of all cultural backgrounds together to create a new race based on shared humanity. Alan was disturbed by the endless divisiveness in the world and increasing acts of terrorism.

Ocasek joined the recording for "Keep It Alive," a track on the new album which featured guitarist Roger Greenawalt. Alan went from having no guitars to four guitarists on that album—including Ce, Roger, Ric, and Kuch. *New Raceion* was released in 1993.

> *New Raceion* is by any measure Alan Vega's most stylistically varied
> album. In addition to the usual chaotic electronic dissonance (*Go Trane
> Go*) and extended poetic rants (*Do the Job*) the album veers all over the
> map musically. It contains the closest Vega has ever come to hard rock
> and metal, complete with thrashing guitars and pummeling rhythms.

The stylistic departures are intriguing, and, for the most part, successful. Vega's songwriting is sharp and focused, so that even the longer tracks sound concise and the production keeps the sound sleek and elegant.*

After *New Raceion* was released, Alan, Ce, Kuch, and Liz did a mini-European tour, and adding to their exposure, they appeared on French TV.

The short tour was a great success with Ce and Kuch blending their guitar styles and adding a unique dynamic to the electronic sounds that had been created for the album.

***

Not long after they returned, Henry Rollins tracked down Alan's phone number. He called and told Alan he was a huge fan, that he was passing through NYC and would love to meet.

Alan knew Rollins had been the lead singer for Black Flag, a hardcore punk band in the early '80s and was a little perplexed as to why Henry would feel a connection to his work.

Liz: *When I pressed Alan for details he said Henry had told him he had to meet him because he had been deeply impacted by the first Suicide album and recently he had found a copy of Vega's solo album* Deuce Avenue *when on tour in Europe. He said that* Deuce Avenue *is incredible and it's crazy that it's not available in the US. He also said no one writes lyrics like you and that he was sure Alan had stacks of notebooks filled with writing piled up somewhere. His description of Alan's work ethic was so dead-on. I said to Alan: "You should get to know this guy."*

Shortly thereafter, Henry arrived at the loft and he was blown away. The explosion of art all over the place—on the walls, the floors, the windows. The light sculptures, the photographs—it was awe inspiring. Alan had been dragging more found objects off the streets with the plan to repurpose them into new and existing sculptures. And of course, there were the predicted piles of notebooks.

Henry stayed for a few hours that day. He was the first person Liz ever met who matched Alan's intensity and enthusiasm in everything ranging from obscure jazz to existential philosophers.

Alan was floored by Henry's knowledge and intelligence.

They were instantly bonded for life.

Over the next couple of years, Henry set up residence in New York in the east village. He founded 2.13.61 Records and opened an office in the Cable Building two floors below 6/8 Recording Studios.

---

* Soundohm, *Alan Vega, New Raceion,* https://www.soundohm.com/product/new-raceion-2lp.

One of the drivers for initiating this new venture was to release Alan's solo records in the United States. Henry already ran a publishing company and planned to release a book of Alan's poetry, portrait drawings, and lyrics.

None of Alan's records with Suicide or his solo work included lyrics. Henry was devoted to getting those lyrics in book form. He felt very strongly that those words were in a class of their own and should be published.

Liz took on the job of listening to all of the records and writing up the lyrics for the project. During a string of Sunday afternoons as the sun stretched across their loft, Henry sat on the couch typing up lyrics and other content for what was to become the publication *Alan Vega: Cripple Nation*.

And on many Sundays when work was finished, Henry, Alan, and Liz hiked across the busy New York streets through Chinatown for a meal at a Thai food restaurant on Pell Street. And after dinner—every time—as they all stood outside the restaurant saying goodbye, Henry exclaimed to Alan as he walked across the street:

"You're the man!"

And Alan came right back.

"No, you're the man!"

***

While working on *Cripple Nation*, Alan and Liz were also in the studio recording the follow-up to *New Raceion*. For this album, they began working in a new studio in Tribeca with Drew Vogelman, sound engineer at Dessau Recording Studios on Murray Street.

This next record, entitled *Dujang Prang*, was released by Henry on his newly formed label. Prior to the release of *Dujang Prang*, Henry launched the label with a beautifully packaged compilation CD containing songs spanning both the Suicide and Vega catalogs.

Rollins made a thousand promo copies and gave them out at concerts and with books sold on his website.

***

Henry Rollins
Singer, Writer
Actor, Artist
April 2023

I met Alan in 1991—think it was in the summer. I had a day off on tour in NYC. I called my agent at the time and asked if he could find the phone number for Alan Vega. I had been a fan since I heard the first Suicide album in the late 1970s. I had been listening to *Deuce Avenue* over and over. I'd wanted to meet him for many years. I thought with this day off in the city, it might be possible. I got the number and cold-called Alan.

I couldn't believe what I was doing but I went for it. He answered. I told him who I was and luckily he knew my name. "You're the Black Flag guy. I know who you are, kid." I asked if I could possibly meet him. He seemed hesitant but said "OK." I taxied to his building and he buzzed me in. I knocked on his door and he opened it, looked me over, and let me in. He asked if I liked coffee. I told him I did. He said, "I'm warning ya, I drink mud," and for some reason at that moment, I knew we were going to get along.

I visited with him for a few hours that afternoon. I had absolutely no idea what he would be like. He blew my mind. We looked through his sketch pads and writing and it was easily the best day of the year for me. I found Alan to be completely fascinating. I think he read people quickly and accurately.

My first introduction to his work was the first Suicide album, which I bought because it looked cool and intense. No record I'd heard in my life up to that point prepared me for it. I didn't know what to do with what the music did to me. It was Ian MacKaye and me, alone in his mother's stifling hot attic, listening. "Frankie Teardrop" shut us down. I don't think I've ever heard anything that intense and committed on vinyl. Nothing to my memory comes close. I didn't understand why a band would want to take the listener "there"—as far as impact.

I think the first Suicide album along with *Fun House* by the Stooges are the two that warped me for life. The stark intensity of the first Suicide album made their second album confusing for me. It didn't seem at all like a follow-up. It was as if the band had morphed completely. It took me awhile to get my head around it. I got Alan's two solo albums to try to understand him better and again, they seemed completely different not only to Suicide but also to each other. I don't think I had ever encountered any artist who seemed to reinvent himself so completely, over and over.

Meeting Alan in 1991, seeing all the work piled up all over the apartment, understanding the man was constantly working, I mean completely living and breathing it—that made me see that no matter what I was doing, I'd have to do it more, with more commitment and intensity. I'm not exactly in short supply on these things but nonetheless, he made me see there was much more to be done.

Working with Alan was great. Finally, someone whose intensity and enthusiasm matched the quality of his work. Also, Alan had vision. He was after something. When we were working on his book *Cripple Nation*, he knew exactly what he wanted to do with it. He didn't need any help that I can remember. I was the one who proposed the idea for the book, which was a sentence or two, a mere suggestion but then the rest of it was all him. I think Alan spent a good deal of his life trying to keep up with what he saw in his head. And it's not like it ever slowed down or that he took a break. As far as people I've ever met, the only other person I'm aware of who is always in constant work mode on an artistic level would

Alan and Henry, 1994. *Photo by Stephanie Chernikowski*

be Raymond Pettibon. To the end of his life, Alan was always working on something.

Working with Alan made me admire him all the more as being around him a bit gave me a slight view into his artistic metabolism. He was completely genuine and friendly but totally intense and attached to his work. It's just my opinion, but I think Alan really understood not only the human state itself, but humans living in the USA. It's like he cracked the code. A lot of what he did, and again, this is just an opinion, was to expose and by doing so, to warn. I think his work, by often being so confrontational, was to urge you not to lose your humanity.

No one experience with Alan stands out as illuminating—as they all were—but perhaps that first encounter, where hours later, I emerged from his apartment and went back to my hotel, all my circuits were blown. Past that, I remember him being very funny and almost immediately upon meeting him, you loved the guy.

I would say that we were friends. I released records for him and did a lot of work in that wheelhouse to get them out and in front of as many people as possible. He was easy to work with as he just wanted to do one thing after another. I'll always remember all the work to get his music over the wall as time well spent. I believed in what he was doing more than what I was trying to do. If you're a creative type, you want to be like Alan: prolific, obsessed, completely in the thrall of what you're doing to where you don't notice your room is on fire. If you work really hard, you might be able to get within a thousand miles of him. ∎

***

Alan was equally impressed with Henry's level of drive. He loved Henry and greatly appreciated all he did for getting Vega exposure and recognition. Yet, notoriety was never Alan's purpose. He was always focused on what new territory he could discover in either his visual art or his music. He went through cycles where his focus was more on the visual and then it would shift to music, but the common thread was always there—his vision.

Liz: *Alan had a childlike and uncanny capacity to see and hear things as if experiencing them for the first time through fresh eyes. He could take a picture of a common everyday object and find a whole other world in the image.*

Alan's artwork and music were counterparts, separated only by the medium and materials used. His music intertwines with the visual.

He literally sculpted sounds.

There was no off button, no "vacation." He lived every waking moment creating with no conscious regard for how to "sell" his work. When Alan left his early conventional life in Brooklyn, he made the conscious decision to jump with no parachute.

***

Dujang Prang was released in 1995. Alan was again cited for his apocalyptic slant.

> Another Vega valentine to urban stress, with industrial-strength beats welded to anxious lyrics (*Hammered*) and jungle images (*Dujang Prang*). Unlike the nervous rockabilly of his earliest albums, the sound here is fully up-to-date, well-produced electronica (*Saturn Drive 2*, Jaxson Gnome) that goes great with Vega's apocalyptic visions. It's an album not relieved by much beauty (even though he's still a romantic at heart) but the sound is hypnotic, and the accompanying art reinforces the music's dark imagery.*

After the release, Alan, Liz, and Kuch were back in Europe, touring in France, Germany, the Netherlands, and Belgium. While in Paris Alan did a series of interviews in the lobby of the Brittanique Hotel, where they were staying, and they spent a lot of time at Pompidou and Notre Dame.

Alan and Liz ran into Henry Rollins at a festival in Copenhagen, where they were all performing. And one afternoon, they went shopping for some rare records. Liz found a Detroit Motor City T-shirt with flames on the sleeves which she brought back to Alan. He wore it onstage during the tour and later ripped it up to add a sleeve for his "Detroit Scree" sculpture. The sculpture would later be purchased at the FIAC art

"Detroit Scree," 1998, collection of Jacques Boissonnas. *Courtesy Galerie Laurent Godin*

festival in Paris in 2012 by Jacques Boissonnas, then president of the Amis du Centre Pompidou, Musée National d'Art Moderne—for his private collection.

---

* Soundohm, *Alan Vega Dujang Prang*, https://www.soundohm.com/product/dujang-prang-2lp.

***

A few years prior, Marc Hurtado—a musician who had collaborated with Alan—introduced Alan and Liz to Hugues Peret, who began filming a documentary about Alan and captured him at the festival in Copenhagen. He continued for several years whenever Alan was back in Europe. The film was titled *Movimento*.

Henry Rollins, Alan, and Hugues Peret. *Photo by Liz Lamere*

Marc, Christophe, and Alan backstage at Le Gaite Lyrique Paris, 2012. *Courtesy Galerie Laurent Godin*

During the *Dujang Prang* tour, Marc arranged for Alan and Liz to meet the beloved French singer Christophe at his studio. It would be the beginning of a long friendship.

After they arrived, Christophe played some of his music. Then Alan tried out the customized chair Christophe had built to record his vocals. The chair had large speakers mounted to hang on each side of the singer's head, in lieu of studio headphones. Alan loved the ingenuity.

Liz: Watching the Movimento *footage of Alan's reaction while singing in that chair is priceless. The joy he experienced from this unusual creation can be heard . . . as he vamped vocals to Christophe's music.*

Alan and Christophe later played a game of poker and their banter was recorded. Christophe put it on his next album, *Les vestiges du Chaos.*

After that exuberant meeting, Marc Hurtado arranged for Christophe to join Alan as a special guest at Vega's and Marc's band Etant Donnés' concerts whenever Alan was in France. Alan's vocal is also featured on Christophe's song "Tangerine," released in 2016. Alan had a deep appreciation for Christophe's artistry and his graceful manner.

***

Marc Hurtado

Christophe was a big fan of Alan's since the time of the first album release of Suicide. They had already collaborated together on the album "Bevilacqua" in 1996. We talked about Alan very often during our night meetings in Paris.

I had already organized the first-ever live collaboration of Alan Vega and Christophe in 2004 at the Centre Pompidou in Paris for the "Blind Speed" night, which brought together Alan, Christophe, and my band Etant Donnés, onstage. This same combination also took place in Nantes at the "IDEAL" festival.

I am very proud to have been able to realize this dream that I had in mind for years. Christophe accompanied me since I was twelve with his fantastic song "Les mots bleus" and Alan Vega had transformed my life since I was fifteen. The two were already united in my heart and being able to bring them together while playing onstage with my own band was an amazing experience.

These nights, Christophe and Alan Vega sang the Suicide song, "I Surrender." It was the beginning of a long-lived collaboration. Each time I played with Alan in France I invited Christophe to come and sing a song or more with us onstage, which he always accepted with great generosity and joy.

I have always felt that these two artists lived on a common planet, certainly Saturn because it's around this planet that their destiny intertwined.

When Alan Vega recorded his voice for "Saturn Drive Duplex" he told me that this song was very special and that it would be important to me. His gifts of clairvoyance have been confirmed. "Tangerine" was remixed two times. I made an alternative version of "Saturn Drive Duplex" named "Saturn Drive Duplex Redux" in 2013 and Laurent Garnier made a new version of "Saturn Drive Duplex" named "Saturn Drive Triplex" in 2023 from which a remix was made the same year. Nine different versions exist of this song.* ∎

***

In 1996, Alan and Liz got a call from Ben Vaughn. Alan had known Ben since the '70s. He mentioned he was coming to the city soon and asked Alan if he would like to go into the recording studio and collaborate on a song with him. Alan was game as he loved the music Ben made and knew he could let loose with his blues-styled vocals.

Alan thought Ben was super talented and was especially happy years later when Ben moved to LA and enjoyed success writing music for TV, including the theme song for *Third Rock from the Sun*.

By the day of the recording session, Ben had spoken with Alex Chilton and mentioned he was going to be making some music with Alan. Alex was keen to join them, and Alan was thrilled to hear it.

Alan was aware of Alex's hits in the '60s with the Box Tops, but he remembered him mostly as the quiet, unassuming guy with whom he smoked cigarettes outside of CBGBs.

They decided to record at Dessau Studio with Drew. Alan went in with sketch lyrics for one song and a copy of that day's *New York Post*.

That was his MO—he had no preconceived notions of what would unfold but knew with Ben and Alex in the room some cool sounds would inevitably emerge.

> [T]his meeting of the minds captures a power on acetate
> that reinforces Ben Vaughn, Alex Chilton and Alan Vega's
> earned spot in the storied canon of American music.†

They started jamming, and Drew, knowing Alan's methodology, made sure to keep the recording going to capture it all. After the first song, they kept going until they had a full album's worth of material. Alan grabbed headlines from the newspaper and freestyled lyrics from there. Alex sat on the floor cross-legged, strumming a guitar. He and Ben also bounced back and forth on multiple instruments.

---

* Interview with Marc Hurtado, March 2023.
† Justin Joffe, "The Bygone, New York Noir of 'Cubist Blues,'" *Observer*, December 2, 2015, https://observer.com/2015/12/the-bygone-new-york-noir-of-cubist-blues/.

After that one-night session, Ben mixed the songs, and *Cubist Blues* was born. It was initially released on Henry Rollins's 2.13.61 Records and reissued on its twentieth anniversary in 2016 on Light in the Attic Records.

With its blues-infused feel, the recording allowed Alan to lean into the nuances of his Elvis-inspired vocals.

> [A] communal spontaneity was part of each player's DNA. . . . These are
> people who are artists before they are anything else. . . . When they did
> anything, they put it all out there. They would come out with something
> totally unrepeatable and the pitch-perfect definition of creation.*
> —Henry Rollins

***

Ben Vaughn
Musician, Songwriter, Producer
April 2023

I was aware of Alan before I met him. Maybe too aware! Late one night in 1977, I heard "Frankie Teardrop" on a Philly college station and was stunned. What IS this? Before it ended the deejay cut in to say that someone called the station and begged him to stop the song, so out of concern he did. Wow. The next day I bought the record. Many stories have been told about that album changing people's lives. Feel free to add my name to that list. I was literally a different person from that point on. My molecular structure was never the same.

A few months later Suicide played at a local club, and I went with a friend who knew the owner. The show was mind-bending. Alan physically attacked the audience, and the sound mix was extremely loud. A lot of people ran outside. When it was over, my friend asked if I wanted to go backstage and meet the band. "No way!" I said. "I hope I *never* meet those guys!"

Fast forward a few years, I'm at the Ritz in NYC and my date went to use the ladies' room. When she returned, she told me Alan was at the bar and that she told him about me and that he wanted to meet me. Before I knew it, she was shoving me in his direction. Alan saw us, smiled, and held out his hand. "You're Ben? Hey man, I'm Alan. Great to meet you." I was truly surprised by how kind and gentle his energy was. Almost like Buddha. We talked for a while and even though I didn't have a career yet, he grilled me about my music. He asked the bartender for a napkin and a pen, wrote down his address and phone number and gave it to me. "Send me a tape of your stuff," he said. We shook hands again and that was that.

---

* Justin Joffe, "The Bygone, New York Noir of 'Cubist Blues,'" *Observer*, December 2, 2015, https://observer .com/2015/12/the-bygone-new-york-noir-of-cubist-blues/.

I sent him a tape the next day and a week later he called me at home to tell me how much he loved it. He said I was onto something original and that he was going to play it for Ric Ocasek and try to get me a record deal. That didn't materialize but it wasn't due to his lack of trying. He also gave me a very important life lesson around that time. I was doing a bit of a Step 'n' Fetchit kind of shuffle saying things like, "Oh man, Alan you don't have to do this for me. You're Alan Vega and I'm just an unknown." He put a stop to that immediately. "Knock it the fuck off. You know your music is great. Now act like it!" He taught me how unattractive false modesty can be. I never forgot it.

I soon got a record deal and started my own journey in the music business, but we stayed in touch through the years. When we spoke, I would always express my desire to produce a record by him as a blues singer, which I always thought he was at heart. Even when surrounded by electronics or modernist rockabilly touches, I always heard the blues in his voice.

Finally, in 1994, I had just received a little bit of money from a piece of music I wrote, and I called Alan and said, "It's time." "The blues?" he asked. "Yes, the blues." We booked time at Dessau Sound in Lower Manhattan and then I asked him how he wanted to approach the recording. I asked what type of band he'd like and he said he trusted me and didn't want to know in advance what type of band I'd assembled. "No expectations," he said. "No expectations."

I had never worked this way before and was a bit wigged out. I was friends with Alex Chilton, and we were talking on the phone and I mentioned Alan's approach and Alex got excited because he was a big fan of "Jukebox Babe." He asked if he could be part of the session. I told him there wasn't enough of a budget to fly him up from New Orleans, but he said he would pay his own way. We agreed it would be cool if the two of us would play all the instruments and follow Alan's voice. Alan knew Alex from the old NYC days so I called to tell him I was bringing Alex up. "That's great but that's almost too much information! Don't tell me anything else!"

When the night of the session arrived, we reintroduced ourselves, chatted a bit and then dug into the process. Two nights later the album was finished and the world looked different to me. You can work like this? Alex said he felt it too. Working with someone like Alan was extremely liberating and intense. A true revelation. He was about pure process and nothing else.

Henry Rollins flipped out over the results and released the recordings as *Cubist Blues*. We performed the album twice, once in NYC and once at a festival in France. Actually, Alex and I performed it. Alan never listened to the record and made up new lyrics onstage which were even better than the first batch.

Traveling with him was great. He was SO funny. Few people know that. We were on a plane with Lemmy from Motorhead and Alex wondered out loud who

Ben Vaughn, Alan, and Alex Chilton, *Cubist Blues* Press Conference, 1996. *Photo by Patrick Mathe. Courtesy Patrick Mathe Estate*

might get top billing if the plane crashed while Alan joked that he would be pissed if Lemmy was in first class. He was also a great storyteller. And a rabble rouser. I witnessed him turn a post-festival press conference into a brawl between himself and the European press. It was wild. Alex and I never got a word in.

I moved to Hollywood soon after *Cubist Blues* and began working in television music. Alan and I would see each other every few years and he expressed concern that I was working too hard. He worried about me and it was touching. That's the way he was. A sweet, caring guy whose art just happened to be terrifying sometimes. He always told me that he loved me when we spoke.

We recorded again after his stroke, and I set things up exactly like *Cubist Blues.* This time I brought in Palmyra Delran on drums and Barb Dwyer on bass. Not that I told him beforehand! I learned that lesson a long time ago. We pressed the record button and let it rip and he did it again—improvised lyrics with yelps, groans, and moans. Alan the blues singer with no signs of a stroke while the recording light was on.

He passed away about a year after that and it's still hard to grasp. I still feel his spirit so strongly. How could he be gone? My approach to art was forever changed by him and every time I'm in a creative situation and feel tempted to play it safe, I feel a tap on my shoulder. I know it's Alan telling me to stay pure and go deeper. In other words, "Knock it the fuck off." I am forever indebted to him for that.

As Alan said: "We just show up, turn on the machine, and see what happens." ∎

***

As Alan finished work with Ben and Alex, he and Liz were back in the studio twice per week creating tracks of sounds with Perkin at 6/8 Studios that would ultimately result in their next studio album release in 1999 titled *2007*. Alan was feeling great working on his love of music with the love of his life. On top of that he had time to watch the Mets on TV—perfect.

***

> One's life has value so long as one attributes value to the life of others.*
> —Simone de Beauvoir

---

* As quoted in Eric Pfeiffer, *Successful Aging: A Conference Report* (Durham, NC: Duke University Press, 1974).

17 Root

1999 . . .

Alan loved cats. He adopted many when he was living alone and then with Liz. His first cats were Toughie and Rowdie when he lived on Greene Street in SoHo and then his famous black cat, Frankie, who is pictured with Alan on the first Suicide record.

Frankie lived to age nineteen and by 1995 when Alan and Liz were finishing the album *Dujang Prang*, he died, which took some work to recover from. They decided later to adopt a kitten. They found a tiny black and gray tiger-striped tabby from a pet store in Harlem. They called him Dujang.

When they were in Paris later in the year, they came across a pet store along the Seine, and fell in love with a little Birman kitten in the window.

Liz: I had never seen such a beautiful breed of cat and was told Birmans were the national cat of France. It felt like kismet. Unfortunately, if we brought the kitty back to the US, he would have to be put in an eighteen-month quarantine. Once back in the city, I tracked down a local Birman breeder. Shadow joined our family and Dujang later that year.

***

During the mid-'90s, Alan spent a lot of time at Ric's place on East Nineteenth Street. All these years working together, they had remained super close. Alan considered him a brother.

---
* Jean-Paul Sartre, *The Flies* (New York: Alfred A. Knopf, 1943).

Photo by Dante Vega Lamere

Shadow and Dujang, 1996. *Photo by Alan Vega*

Ric would call late at night and the two of them had long talks about every-thing from the mundane to the profound. Liz could always tell it was Ric on the phone when she heard Alan belly-laughing in the living room.

Photo © Marcia Resnick

Ric had a state-of-the-art recording studio in his basement and he and Alan always had a productive, fun, inspirational time recording music together.

In 1996, their collaborations resulted in two albums, one titled *Ti Stadt*, which Ric continued to revisit over the years, and the other was a collaboration with Gillian McCain titled *Getchertiktz* which was released on Sooj Records.

The record label hosted a release party at the Whitney Museum and then Alan, Ric, and Gillian performed at the Knitting Factory. But the show time coincided with a crucial MLB playoff game. Alan insisted on having a couch and TV set on the stage.

He performed while sitting on the couch—mic in one hand, TV remote in the other—watching the game in between bursts of vocals. Ric was in front playing guitar and singing his parts in traditional style while Gillian recited poetry. It looked like avant-garde performance art. Yet, it was staged that way primarily so Alan wouldn't miss the game.

***

The creative dynamic between Ric and Alan was an unusual one as they were very different in some ways, yet very much in sync. Alan thought Ric was extremely clever, in tune with pop culture, technically brilliant and astute. Ric admired Alan's raw creativity and freedom to follow his vision wherever it led him.

When Ric was recording his solo records, he'd invite Alan into the studio, often when his manager or record label A&R reps were coming in to hear what he had in order to decide which tracks should be singles.

Liz: Alan would tell me Ric's A&R people asked him which were his favorite songs so they would then know not to pick those as the singles.

***

Meanwhile, in 1998 Finland, Paul Smith had been working with a duo of musicians called Pan Sonic. The duo was comprised of Ilpo Väisänen and Mika Vainio—two brilliant innovators who built their own synthesizers.

Alan was intrigued when Paul described Mika and Ilpo's creative process. Paul told Alan they were inspired by his work and wanted to collaborate.

The plan was for Pan Sonic to come to New York and record with Alan at 6/8 Recording Studios, with Perkin engineering. Mika and Ilpo arrived for the first session, rolling in large cases housing their homemade machines.

Alan was fascinated as they unpacked the machines they had put together on their own—piece by piece—and plugged them in. The sounds the machines created were transformative. Alan had a visceral reaction. The low end was so deep, he felt pulsations resonating in his gut.

Alan had some scratch lyrics prepared and he was so inspired by what he was hearing that he went right into the booth and started freestyling his vocals.

After three recording sessions over the next few days, the album *Endless* was realized.

Mika was an intense and meticulous artist. He spent more time honing the mixes, but the performances were all captured in the moment. The chemistry and creative output were transformative for all of them and it was clear this was the beginning of a long artistic relationship. Alan, Mika, and Ilpo dubbed themselves "VVV" in recognition of each of their surnames as each began with a V.

The album was released on Blast First in 1998, Then in 2005, VVV recorded and released their second album, *Resurrection River*.

When Mika and Ilpo arrived at 6/8 Studios to record this album, they brought a young filmmaker, Ed Quist, now known as Embryoroom.

***

Edward Quist (aka Embryoroom)
Artist/Filmmaker/Musician
July 2023
I first encountered Alan Vega in 1998 at Coney Island High, the night before Halloween. He performed an aggressive and forward-leaning set along with his wife and manager, Liz Lamere. Also on the bill were the Finnish duo Pan Sonic, who at the time performed as Panasonic. They and Alan already had a remarkable

collaborative album called *Endless*, and it captured the early days of Suicide's atmospherics combined with Panasonic's minimalist techno experiments. The results were absolutely unique. That night, as I documented Panasonic's brutalist set on video, Alan suddenly appeared on stage. We were about to see VVV live for the first and last time. From his MPC 2000, Mika launched the beat to VVV's "Incredible Criminals." It sounded like a new electronic genre was being born before our very eyes. There was a glitch when Alan stepped on the main line out; a quick repair followed, and the set continued with ferocity. It became clear that night that these three artists seemed destined to collaborate. Something was in the air.

Later, I spoke to Alan, He asked where I was from, and I replied, "Brooklyn, like you." Alan smiled, nodding. "I thought I could hear a slight Brooklyn accent." From there, Alan and I got along well, and he humored some of my more crazy ideas as I went on to document Suicide shows in the early 2000s.

In 2002, I received a call from Mika, asking if I wanted to see Alan record vocals. He and Ilpo were in New York and recording with Alan for the second VVV record. Of course I did. Could I bring my camera? "No camera," Mika replied. "Just you!" I arrived at 6/8 Studios on Broadway, where Perkin Barnes, Alan's longtime recording engineer, nodded me into the small recording space. Mika, more tense than usual, was at the computer, tracking waveforms to manually affect Alan's voice. Alan, dressed darkly, with a beret and sunglasses, was behind the glass in the small vocal room like something out of a Francis Bacon painting. He was in full Vega ominous mode. I could see Alan rewriting the words, holding sheets of paper to the light, scribbling bleeding lyrics through the back of the page against the window. Perkin reminded Mika that time was of the essence, who in turn wanted me to tell Alan they had to "end this session soon," exclaiming that Alan "keeps changing everything." I walked into the vocal room, greeting Alan, who looked away from the lyrics. I noticed the title of the song was "Monkeys." "Ed, man, I almost have what I want." "What's he saying?" Alan asked, pointing to Mika. "The session is almost over," I said. "Let him know I'm almost done." Mika is such a perfectionist!

Suddenly, Alan belted out, "I'm selling my monkeys to the junkies!"

Everyone sensed that line would be the missing hook in Alan's rewrites. The second VVV album, *Resurrection River*, was being born. Later, Mika and I met Ilpo; Perkin had burned the day's rough mixes to a CD. Ilpo, smoking a large blunt, exclaimed, "Put it on, man!" We started listening. Alan's vocals were powerful, matching Pan Sonic's sound nearly perfectly. Ilpo yelled, "This sounds proper! "So so good, man!" Mika looked at Ilpo and said, "Everything sounds good on that shit you are smoking." Mika had to admit, "It does sound good. Better than expected." We arrived at the track that became known as "Sellin' My Monkeys."

Alan and Pan Sonic. *Photo by Liz Lamere*

Alan's voice echoed, "Sellin' my monkeys to the junkies! I'm sellin' my monkeys to the flunkies!" Mika turned to me and asked, "Ed, what is a flunky?" I smiled, realizing how lucky I was to have experienced that day.

Years later, and six months after Alan passed, Mika was bringing back VVV with Alan's voice for a memorial show in Alan's honor in New York. Sadly, it would never come to be. Mika himself tragically died nine months after Alan, in April 2017. Mika and Alan are truly missed, and it seems destiny eventually takes what it has given. We still have the art. Maybe that is enough in the end. Their work is Endless as they both cross the Resurrection River. ∎

***

Mika was a man of few words and fewer facial expressions—beyond solemn.

Rarely, Alan managed to get Mika to crack a smile. Over the years Mika called Alan whenever he needed to hear Alan's voice and talk. Alan thought the world of Mika. Unfortunately, he left this realm much too young.

***

Shortly after the first VVV collaboration, Steve Lironi came to NYC to record with Alan as the Revolutionary Corps of Teenage Jesus. The album they created, *Righteous Lite*, was completed in one session, released in 1999 and reissued in 2021 on Creeping Bent Records.

Suicide's self-titled debut album in 1977 was so out-there and so
confrontational that it out-punked the punks . . . and it still sounds
way ahead of its time all these years later. It's impossible to listen
to [*Righteous Lite*] without being reminded of it, because Vega's
vocals sound the same and the music is underpinned by the same
basso continuo ultra-minimal keyboards and drum machines.
But also into the mix come rather nineties dance influences . . .
and interesting samples of what sound like religious rallies.*

***

Douglas MacIntyre
The Creeping Bent Organisation
July 2023
Righteous Lite: It was late 1994 when the fax machine in my Mount Florida flat
slowly stuttered and juddered into life. The fax was coming through to Glasgow
live and direct from New York, sent by former New York Dolls and Suicide man-
agerial figure, Marty Thau. He'd heard a techno version of a Suicide track from
their debut album that he'd released on Red Star, the track in question was the
epochal and terrifying saga of Frankie Teardrop. The techno deconstruction of
Suicide was by Revolutionary Corps of Teenage Jesus aka Stephen Lironi, former
drummer with Glasgow post-punk era groups Article 58, Restricted Code, and
Altered Images.

RCTJ had sampled the Suicide track and put it to a ferocious beat, Marty
loved it and wanted to do a deal. The track was released as a twelve-inch single
on Creeping Bent and quickly was awarded the coveted Single of the Week in the
NME, the most influential UK music paper. Marty got in touch again to inform
us that Alan Vega loved the track and wanted to join the Revolutionary Corps of
Teenage Jesus. This was mind-blowing, Vega was a legend in Glasgow after his
incendiary performance during the punk period when Suicide opened for the
Clash at the Glasgow Apollo (getting booed/bottled off in the process).

And so it came to pass that Stephen Lironi and Alan Vega teamed up in a
studio in Brooklyn to write and record an album—*Righteous Lite*. The album is
an incredible piece of work, Alan's lyrics are right up there among his best and
Stephen's production created the perfect backdrop. Dystopian blues. I met Alan
in Brooklyn, he was a groover—erudite and charming. We went to his apartment
and he showed me some of his art pieces, which were inspiring (one of which was
featured on the *Righteous Lite* cover art).

---

* See https://www.godisinthetvzine.co.uk/2015/05/05/alan-vega-revolutionary-corps-of-teenage-jesus
-righteous-lite-re-issue-creeping-bent/.

The combination of Alan and Stephen on the album created a certain unique magic that is even more prescient today than it was on its release in 1999. Alan's lyrics foresaw where society seems to be now, with corporate government utilizing mass media to control the mass market and populace. Stephen's production and music echo the analogue vibrations of the debut Suicide album, and in tandem with Alan's primal scream, created an album that works as a raw conceptual piece.

It was a pleasure to meet Alan and to release *Righteous Lite* on Creeping Bent. He was a gentleman. ■

***

It was early 1999 and the snow was relentless as it slid down and coated the city streets. Alan continued slogging through the wet and blizzard-filled streets to 6/8 Studios to finish the sound recordings he and Liz had been laying down.

But Liz had stopped going into the studio. She needed time to prepare for the arrival of their baby.

***

Real generosity toward the future lies in giving all to the present.*
—Albert Camus

---

* Albert Camus, *The Notebooks 1935–1942* (New York: Paragon House, 1991).

18 Dante's Homecoming

1999 . . .

Taking a new step, uttering a new word, is what people fear most.*
—Fyodor Dostoevsky

Alan and Liz were shocked but not surprised by the amount of paperwork and vetting that went into the adoption process. Alan would joke about how no one needed the government's permission and proof of ability to financially support and care for an infant before getting pregnant, but to bring a child in need into this country, you need to be inspected by social workers and submit financial statements.

All the paperwork had been submitted many weeks before and the waiting period was indefinite. One night, Liz sat up in bed out of a deep sleep and turned to Alan saying, "It's a boy and his name is Michael." The next day the adoption agency called and said, "Congratulations. You have a son and his name is Miguel Angel."

The birthmother's name was Alba Isbeth, which they found remarkable as the child's father and mother would be Alan and Elizabeth.

Alba was in her early twenties and had two boys and a girl all under age three who lived with her, her mom, and her grandmother in the village, La Democracia, south of Guatemala City. Alba was a bright young woman who was working her way through college in the city and got pregnant by the same man—Miguel Angel Figeroa—several times. Each time she discovered she was pregnant, she returned home to give birth then leave the child with her family so she could return to college. Once Alba's daughter was born, she had decided any additional children would be given up for adoption in the hopes of finding a better life for them.

---

* Fyodor Dostoevsky, *Crime and Punishment* (New York: Random House, 1956).

***

Liz: *Alan and I were beside ourselves with excitement once we finally had a court date set for January 19, 1999, to finalize the adoption at the courthouse in Guatemala. We immediately made plans to go and bring Miguel Angel home.*

There had been two instances of moratoriums being placed on adoptions out of Guatemala while we waited for the adoption to go through. Alan and I hadn't yet discussed a name. One day, sitting in my office, I decided to make a list. The first name I wrote was Dante. My paternal grandfather was Italian and I loved Dante Alighieri. Almost immediately, the phone rang and it was Alan. He launched into "I have a name for the kid and I hope you like it!" Simultaneously we said "Dante!"

We decided that my mother, Toots, and I would travel to Guatemala as I spoke Spanish and she had lots of experience with kids having three children and six grand-children. And Alan would stay home.

Alan was concerned about all the political unrest south of the Mexican border, and the fact that he didn't look the part of "clean-cut" dad. His long black hair, ever-present beret, sunglasses, and leather jacket made him look like Khadafi—or at least that's how some press had referred to him lately. He was afraid he'd make us more vulnerable in an uncertain cultural situation.

Toots lived outside of Orlando, so we met in Miami and flew together from there to Guatemala City. The plan was on the night before the court date, the foster mother would bring Dante to our hotel with the attorney, who had prepared all the paperwork.

Our flight was scheduled so we'd get to the hotel at approximately 7:00 p.m., but due to bad weather, the flight was delayed by two hours. We were so nervous that Dante wouldn't still be at the hotel. This was before cell phones became popular and we had no way of letting the attorney know we were delayed.

I'll never forget arriving and seeing the foster mother still sitting in the hotel lobby at almost 10:00 p.m. and well past Dante's bedtime—with the most adorable six-month-old baby boy in the world. The lawyer was by her side. Toots and I were elated.

I started crying and exclaimed, "Oh my gosh, he is so beautiful!"

The foster mom lifted Dante up toward me. He smiled and reached out his arms to me. I was overcome.

We had been told by the adoption agency to be prepared that it may take some time for the baby to bond with us. But it didn't seem to be turning out like that with Dante. He had a big smile on his face from the first moment I held him.

The hotel was near the courthouse and routinely had adoptive parents coming to bring home their babies. Our room was set up with a crib between two twin beds. Toots and I had no idea what to expect once Dante realized these two strangers were now the only ones with him. Since it was so late, we changed his diaper, put on his pajamas, and laid him in the crib. He was asleep within minutes. Toots said, "He'll probably wake up in a couple hours and don't worry if he is confused and crying."

But that's not what happened. He slept through the night and woke up in the morning just after we did. I was the one who woke up every hour or so—to gaze at him while he slept.

When we brought him down to the dining room for breakfast, he sat in my lap drinking his bottle and then in the high chair while I ate—as if this was his normal routine.

Toots and I looked surreptitiously around the room at the other parents and babies, many of whom were crying.

We both thought—wow, not only is he the cutest, but he's the easiest!

After breakfast, we went to the courthouse, where we sat for two hours with many other families and babies waiting to be summoned in front of the judge. When we were finally called up, we handed in all the paperwork including the US permanent resident card and confirmed this was the baby in the photo.

The entire time, Dante was looking all around the room at the other babies and people. He was very excited but he was also content. We kept whispering to each other how this baby was a dream.

The next day we flew back to Miami and then to Orlando. Dante happily bounced along in my Bjorn carrier on my chest as I sang walking through the terminal, "I want to be in America, plenty to see in America!"

We had planned a two-day layover with Toots and my stepdad Dick for Dante to meet his extended family—my brother David, his wife Sandy, and Dante's new cousins, Katie, Caroline, and Rachel. This time gave me a chance to firm up the basics of "baby-care" with my mother's guidance. She kept saying how unusually easy a baby he was. Over the next eighteen years it would often feel like Dante was raising us.

I called Alan several times a day to give him the play-by-play. He was getting so excited. When the time came to fly to NYC from Orlando, there was a winter storm raging up the East Coast. Despite the turbulence, Dante was happy during the whole flight. I had just enough formula and extra diapers on hand to keep him fed and clean.

We were about to touch down at JFK Airport when the plane suddenly lurched back up into the sky. There were audible gasps throughout the cabin. The captain announced we were no longer cleared for landing because of visibility issues and were being diverted to Syracuse.

We sat on the runway in Syracuse for over two hours with no way to contact Alan. Dante charmed all the flight attendants, who heated up his formula and kept him entertained.

Meanwhile, Kuch had driven Alan through the storm to JFK and they were looking at the arrival board when my flight information suddenly disappeared.

Alan was a wreck trying to find out what happened, and the airline wasn't giving any information other than most of the airport runways had been temporarily closed.

Alan and Dante on Day One. *Photo by Liz Lamere*

They decided to go back home in case I tried to call. After waiting at home for a couple of hours, Kuch suggested they go to LaGuardia, as the flight may have been diverted there.

Incredibly, that is where our flight ultimately landed and just as Dante and I were exiting the gate, Alan and Kuch walked up to us. The timing was miraculous. I'll never forget the look on Alan's face when he first laid eyes on Dante. Priceless.

Alan had brought the car seat we bought before I left. We secured Dante in the seat. Alan sat in the back with him, repeatedly kissing his cheek and holding his hand while Dante proceeded to fall asleep.

The next day was the first time Alan was left alone with Dante while I ran out to stock up on more diapers and formula.

I was nervous leaving Alan home alone with Dante for the first time. Before I left, I went through a list of what to do in an emergency. I rushed through the errands and raced home. When I opened the front door, the first thing I saw was both Alan and Dante asleep on the couch—so much for Alan being the nervous dad.

***

In 1994, Alan's niece, Amie, had moved to New York to pursue an acting and singing career on off-Broadway. Alan was so excited to have her in the city near him.

Not long after she arrived, Liz and Alan had dinner with her in Chinatown.

Amie was thrilled to be connecting with Alan. She had been in awe of him and his music since she was a young girl.

Alan and Amie, 1994. *Photo by Liz Lamere*

> We have a store near me called Joe's Record Paradise. When
> Amie was in high school, she thought it was the coolest thing ever
> that her uncle was Alan Vega. So, she went over one day to Joe's
> Records and looked around. I think the guy said, "Can I help you?"
> And she said, "Do you have anything by Alan Vega?" And sure
> enough, they did. And very proudly Amie said, "He's my uncle!"*
> —Sue, Amie's mother

Amie couldn't stop asking Alan questions about his work and his music and
her grandparents. He was so sweet and giving. The only thing that jumped out at
her was—Alan couldn't keep still.

> He was always antsy. He was never idle. Just sitting there, he wasn't idle.[†]
> —Amie

A few months after they brought Dante home, Robbie and Sue came up to
visit and meet him. Amie came by as well to see Dante and her parents.

They spent the afternoon together catching up and playing with the
baby—laughing and cavorting. Alan was thrilled to have his family meet
Dante—who was such a sweet and happy baby.

---

* Interview with Sue Bermowitz, October 2021.
† Interview with Amie Bermowitz, February 2023.

Pan Sonic, 1998. *Photo by Liz Lamere*

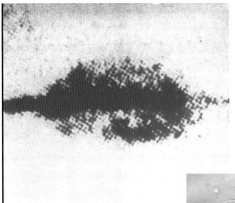

Endless, 1998. *Courtesy Saturn Strip, Ltd.*

Resurrection River, 2005. *Courtesy Saturn Strip, Ltd.*

Righteous Lite, 1999. Courtesy Saturn Strip, Ltd.

100,000 Watts of Fat City, 1998. Courtesy Saturn Strip, Ltd.

Sombre, 1998. Courtesy Saturn Strip, Ltd.

Sculpture purchased by Swiss collector at Collision Drive Show, 2002. *Courtesy Deitch Projects*

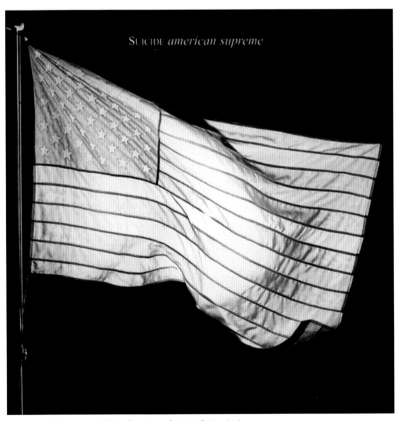

American Supreme, 2002. Courtesy Saturn Strip, Ltd.

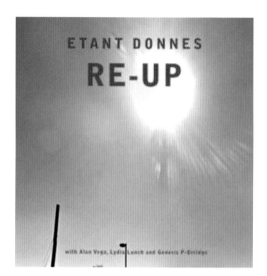

Re-Up, 1999. Courtesy Saturn Strip, Ltd.

2007, 1999. Courtesy Saturn Strip, Ltd.

Station, 2007. Courtesy Saturn Strip, Ltd.

Sniper, 2010. *Courtesy Saturn Strip, Ltd.*

Alan with Eric and Marc Hurtado (Étant Donnés)/Le Glob-Lyon, France, 1993. *Photo by Frédéric Brugnot*

"Untitled," Alan Vega, 1983, Infinite Mercy Show, 2009, Private collection of Julian Schnabel. *Courtesy Museé d'art Contemporain de Lyon*

"Untitled (boxer)," 2008, Infinite Mercy Show, 2009. *Courtesy Museé d'art Contemporain de Lyon*

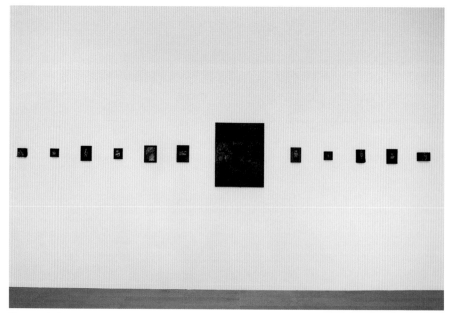

Boxer paintings and Black painting, Alan Vega exhibition, Infinite Mercy Show, 2009. © *Blaise Adilon, Courtesy MAC Lyon*

"Infinite Mercy," 2009, Alan Vega, Infinite Mercy Show. © *Blaise Adilon, Courtesy MAC Lyon*

FIAC show, 2012. *Courtesy Galerie Laurent Godin*

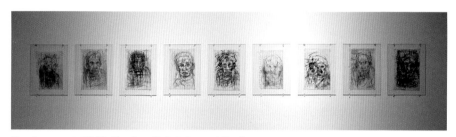

Drawings, FIAC, 2012. *Courtesy Galerie Laurent Godin*

"Mike," Alan Vega, 1983, FIAC, 2012. *Courtesy Galerie Laurent Godin*

Boxer Paintings and "Al's Bar," Alan Vega, Armory Show, 2015. *Courtesy Galerie Laurent Godin*

ALAN VEGA:
JUST A MILLION
DREAMS

© *Marie Losier,* NYC

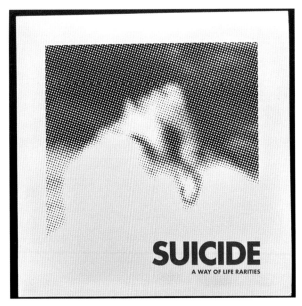

A Way of Life Rarities, 2023.
Photo by Jared Artaud

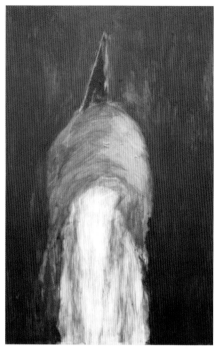

Alan and Johnny Thunders. *Photo ©Marcia Resnick*

"Prophesy," Alan Vega, 2016, Collection of Joel Yoss. *Courtesy Benjamin Tischer,* INVISIBLE-EXPORTS, *New Discretions*

The Spirit Paintings, Alan Vega, 2016. *Courtesy Benjamin Tischer,* INVISIBLE-EXPORTS, *New Discretions*

Photo by Liz Lamere

Photo by Liz Lamere

Photo by Viviani Vilas Boas

Vega Jacket and *Saturn* sculpture at Trinity Boxing Club, Alan's eighty-fifth birthday celebration, 2023. *Amy Verdon, FANCY! Partners Media Arts*

"Duke's God Bar," Alan Vega, 2016, Private collection of Beth Rudin DeWoody. *Courtesy Benjamin Tischer, INVISIBLE-EXPORTS, New Discretions*

Alan Vega reissued albums designed by Jared Artaud and Michael Handis, 2019. *Photo by Jared Artaud*

Twelve-inch release, 2022. *Photo by Jared Artaud*

Mutator, 2021. *Courtesy Saturn Strip, Ltd.*

Alan Vega After Dark, 2021. *Courtesy Saturn Strip, Ltd.*

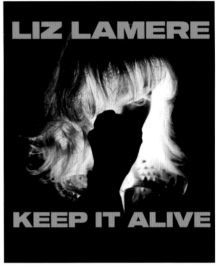

Cheap Soul Crash, poems and drawings by Alan Vega, Heartworm Press, 2021. *Courtesy Saturn Strip, Ltd.*

Keep It Alive, 2022. *Photo by Jared Artaud*

Lydia Lunch and Liz, 2022. *Photo by Sébastien Greppo*

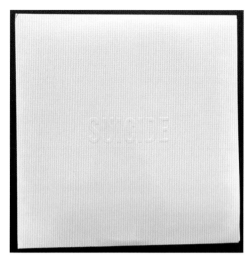

Surrender, 2022. *Photo by Michael Handis*

Insurrection, 2024. *Courtesy Saturn Strip, Ltd.*

American Dreamer Collection, Midnight Studios, 2019. *Photo by Liz Lamere*

"Invasion b/w Murder One" by Agnes b, 2022. *Photo by Liz Lamere*

"Dream Baby Dream" by Dries Van Noten, 2022. *Photo by Liz Lamere*

Celine Hoodie, Alan Vega Collage, 2023. *Photo by Jared Artaud*

Alan, Amie, and Dante, 1999. *Photo by Robert Bermowitz. Courtesy Robert Bermowitz Estate*

Dante and Robbie, 1999. *Photo by Amie Bermowitz*

And Alan felt at peace, complete, when Robbie was around. It was family.

***

Dante's Christening, 1999. *Photo by Liz Lamere*

The next month, Alan and Liz brought Dante to Milton—Liz's hometown—where he was christened in the Catholic church. Alan received a special dispensation from the priest to wear his beret and sunglasses during the ceremony.

After taking three months of maternity leave, Liz went back to work. Alan was now Dante's primary caregiver. It was a big adjustment as Alan was accustomed to staying up all night and sleeping on and off throughout the day. But he immediately adjusted his sleep cycle and routine to include Dante. Whenever Dante slept, they played classical music for him, and

Dante and Alan in the Financial District, 1999. © *Bob Gruen/www.bobgruen.com*

Alan taught Dante to play chess. By the time he started kindergarten, Dante could hold his own with Alan.

Liz: *One Saturday, when Dante was a first-grader at PS234 in Tribeca, we attended the Tribeca Film Festival Family Day Fair. Our attention was drawn to a large platform with three-foot-tall chess pieces. We stopped to watch. There was a teenage girl on a winning streak. Dante urged me to sign him up.*

"How will you be able to see the board when the pieces are almost as tall as you are?" I asked him with a smile.

Unrelenting, he said "I can do it" so I put his name down. Soon it was his turn and the crowd let out an audible murmur when they saw this tiny kid mount the stage. He proceeded to beat the young teenager in short order.

Harvey Keitel had been standing next to us and turned to me.

"That your kid?"

"Yep. His dad taught him well."

Alan loved taking Dante for walks—often without a stroller—to nearby Battery Park and along the East River esplanade. As they walked side by side, holding hands, Alan played "numbers games" with him. He'd call out equations for Dante to solve using addition, subtraction, multiplication, and division in his head. They quickly

Alan and Dante, in front of White Cube Gallery, London, 2006. *Photo by Howard Thompson*

graduated from two- to three-digit numbers. . . . Dante was truly his father's son as Alan had always had a remarkable facility with numbers.

***

In 2000, Liz made plans to bring Dante to visit Toots, her stepdad Dick, brother David, and his family in Florida for Thanksgiving. She and Alan had decided that he would stay home since he was planning to go to Milton with her and Dante to spend Christmas with Kent and Jean and Dante's cousins Kelsey, Dan, and Kevin. Alan was happy to have a much-needed break before the Christmas trip.

Liz: *On the night before Thanksgiving, Toots came into my room and said Alan was on the phone and sounded upset. It was a surprise because it was late, and we had already spoken earlier in the evening when he called to say goodnight to Dante. When I got on the phone, Alan sounded awful—barely audible, his voice shaking.*

He told me Sue had just called to tell him that Robbie had passed away from a massive heart attack. He started to cry—uncontrollably. I told him I would get a flight home right away. But he said no—he was leaving first thing in the morning to take the Amtrak train to Silver Springs, Maryland, to sit shiva with Sue and the family. Robbie was to be buried over the weekend per the Jewish tradition. He said he would be fine going by himself and wanted me to stay with my family for Thanksgiving with Dante in Florida.

I was destroyed that I couldn't be there with Alan as I know how deeply painful it was for him to lose Robbie. Since they had reconnected, Robbie would call Alan and they'd watch sports games together, especially the Mets and the Knicks. I'd hear Alan laughing through the play-by-plays as they'd watch the games.

Alan often reminisced about growing up with Robbie. Robbie was very conscientious and studious, whereas Alan was more of a free spirit and schoolwork came easier to him. He'd be outside playing stickball while Robbie studied inside. He said that they were a bit like the Odd Couple, Felix and Oscar, with Robbie taking five minutes to fluff his pillow up just right before laying his head down and Alan impatiently exclaiming "Enough already!!" But it was always clear Alan deeply loved his brother.

***

In 2002, when Alan recorded the song "Misery Train" for the Suicide album *American Supreme*, the lyrics for the song had been written for Robbie on Alan's Amtrak trip to his funeral.

> Train, train
> Train, train
> Misery train
> Misery train
> Destiny's train
> Destiny's train
> Gray train
> Gray train
> Sulfur sky, sulfur sky
> I buried my brother today
> Today, today
> Forever
> Today
> Rain rain, rain, rain
> Rain, gray rain,
> Gray rain
> Rain rain
> Pyro domes, pyro domes
> I'm burying my brother today*

Liz: *Life had reimagined itself in 1999 for us. The gift was Dante, who saved our meaning in the journey. The death of Robbie was hard.*

***

---

* "Misery Train" by Alan Vega and Martin Rev, 2002.

Robbie, 1982. *Photo by Amie Bermowitz*

Blessed are the hearts that can bend; they shall never be broken.*
—Albert Camus

---

* Albert Camus, *A Happy Death* (New York: Alfred A. Knopf, 1971).

PART THREE

"... [THE] ELEGANCE OF HE WHO DEFINITIVELY EMBODIED THE FLIPSIDE OF ROCK 'N' ROLL"*

———
* Alexandre Breton, *Alan Vega: Conversation with an Indian* (Le Texte Vivant, 2017), Kindle.

Photo by Alan Tannenbaum/Sohoblues.com

19 Consonant

1998 . . . 2001 . . . 2002 . . .

To make living itself an art, that is the goal.*
—Henry Miller

Even though Alan hadn't shown his light sculptures at any gallery since the last Barbara Gladstone exhibition in 1983, he never stopped making art. He was constantly finding and collecting materials for his sculptures, which he continued to construct without any conscious intention of showing them. And drawing portraits was part of his nightly ritual.

While he had included his artwork in the books he created with Edit DeAk (*Deuce Avenue Warriors*) and Henry Rollins (*Cripple Nation*) there hadn't yet been a book published focusing entirely on his light sculptures.

In 1998, Alan was approached by photographer Anna Polerica and journalist Jean Marc, from Paris. It was arranged for them to go to the loft, interview Alan, and take photos of the sculptures hanging on all the walls of his home.

They ended up spending two weeks in the city and each day with Alan. Jean Marc sat with him and talked about his art and creative process while Anna meticulously photographed each sculpture.

The first day they arrived, it was a chilly October day and Alan hadn't slept well. When Anna took hours to set up the lighting to shoot the first sculpture, Alan became impatient. It could take weeks at that rate to photograph all of them.

"This is gonna take forever!" he squawked.

Liz calmed Anna, telling her, "His bark is worse than his bite." She told her not to worry and do whatever she needed to capture the images she envisioned. Anna

---

* Henry Miller, *Big Sur and the Oranges of Hieronymus Bosch* (New York: New Directions, 1957).

Courtesy Galerie Laurent Godin

was a brilliant photographer and created new works of art in the beautiful images she captured of the sculptures.

While talking with Jean Marc about the book, Alan found himself quite intrigued. His questions were fortuitously deep and insightful. Alan believed the meaning of his art should be left open to the interpretation of the viewer—to what their experience was in observing it.

"You should write my answers," Alan said, as he lit a cigarette. "I love how you describe the work. Your explanations and perceptions are better than anything I could say about them," he said.

The book resulting from their meticulous two-week project was *100,000 Watts of Fat City* with a foreword by Julian Schnabel.

After it was published in '98, Anna sent a half-dozen large prints of the photos to Alan and Liz. They framed and hung half of them at home and the rest in Liz's office.

***

Alan left much of the meaning of his artistic expression to the subjective interpretation of the viewer and listener. He tapped into universal and relatable themes which were relevant enough to the audience that they could find their own personal meaning. He lamented when MTV emerged, and music videos became prolific. In his mind, seeing the video of a song tended to limit the listeners' imagination as experienced by purely listening to it.

***

Not long after the publication of *100,000 Watts of Fat City*, the French film director Philippe Grandieux approached Alan. He was shooting a film about a serial killer, Jean, who was on a road trip following the tour de France and murdering female prostitutes until he meets a disturbed woman who falls in love with him.

Philippe told Alan that he was playing Alan's solo music on set to create the mood and motivation for Jean's character and wanted to license it for the film.

Alan was thrilled and told Philippe he felt the effect of his music created soundscapes which have cinematic overtones. Philippe agreed and he suggested Alan create the soundtrack for the film.

This became one of the most personally fulfilling projects Alan ever worked on. When the time came for the premiere of the film—*Sombre*—at Lincoln Center, he was excited to see the movie poster with his name credited for the soundtrack. He was blown away sitting in the theater watching the movie and hearing his music helping propel the unfolding story. It was truly one of his most cherished accomplishments.

***

And then a true-life story unfolded that was beyond any of Alan's vehement premonitions.

Liz: *On the morning of Sept. 11, 2001, Alan was home with Dante, who was due to start preschool in a week. I was at my office at Fifty-Third and Sixth Avenue when the office manager came in to say a plane had hit one of the twin towers at the World Trade Center. At the same time Ric was calling Alan to make sure he was* OK. *Our home on Hanover Square was just south of Wall Street by the East River but a short walk to the Twin Towers. Ric told Alan to turn on the* TV *and was still on the phone with him as the second plane hit. By this time, I had put on my sneakers and started running home, heading south from midtown to the Financial District. The streets were* *filled with people heading north and fighter planes could be heard overhead buzzing up and down the island. Just prior to leaving my office, I was able to get Alan on the phone and told him I was coming home. He said he and Dante were safe and weren't going anywhere. By the time I was just north of Canal Street I saw the second tower fall and a huge plume of black smoke cross the sky from west to east. Armed National Guardsmen were on almost every corner steering the mass exodus north. I was stopped several times and told no one was allowed into the area below Canal. Everyone living and working downtown was being evacuated.*

The guardsmen weren't accepting my explanation that I lived in the Financial District with my husband and son who were still home and expecting me. So, I started walking backward to blend in with the crowd.

The courtyard in front of my building was covered in shredded paper and a dusting of white powder—debris from the collapsed Twin Towers.

It was a warm day and Alan had the windows shut with the air conditioning on. The apartment was sealed. We hadn't lost electricity.

Arriving at our building, I met our neighbor, her husband, their two young kids, a parrot and two cats all packed up and on their way to stay with friends in the West Village. They feared gas leaks and additional attacks on historic sites in the district. Meanwhile, I was covered with white dust and suggested to them they shouldn't venture outside. They were afraid to stay. Half the residents in the building chose to evacuate.

When I got inside, Alan said there was no way he was taking Dante outside to breathe that air and felt that the worst was over for now. We were able to follow developments on TV of what was happening right outside our home. The phone rang nonstop with friends and family checking on us.

It was surreal.

In the weeks to come we had to go to Chinatown to get basic supplies and show our I.D. to the National Guard still stationed all over the area. The burning site emitted an unforgettable noxious odor that took many weeks to subside.

We lost our innocence that day. Alan had been predicting this type of attack for years. After the bombing in the World Trade Center parking garage in 1993, he said we should expect more to come for that target.

Two days after the attack, Alan and I walked to Ground Zero at sunset. We were struck by the image of the remaining metal structure of the fallen South Tower. It looked eerily majestic.

Was it wrong to find beauty in the devastation?

***

Courtesy Saturn Strip, Ltd.

> I was always fascinated by the war and all the stories I heard. I was sick
> a lot as a child so I would read all these books on WWII at home. The
> Nazis, it was the uniforms, the atrocities, the concentration camps. It
> was partly fascination, partly horror. It's like when I saw the World Trade
> Center a couple of days after it happened, only the structure was left.
> No artist, no human being, could make a sculpture like that. It looked
> like it had been done from God's hand and yet it was a site of death.
> A sculpture fashioned out of insanity turned into something beautiful.
> The most beautiful and also the most horrific thing I'd ever seen.*
>   —Alan

***

An increased interest in seeing Suicide play live was evolving due in part to Paul Smith's reissuing of Suicide's music on Mute/Blast First after having brought Suicide to London to play three sold-out nights at the Garage in early 1998.

***

Paul Smith
Founder Blast First
And Blast First (petite)
Record Companies
May 2023

I first saw Suicide on their opening night joining The Clash's UK tour in July 1978. In my mind it was at the Top Rank in Sheffield, but better scholars than I list them as joining the tour the night after the gig in Leicester.

I had been to punk gigs but that night, unprecedented *waves* of phlegm were washing over the stage. Vega resolutely stood on the lip of the stage while normally thrifty British punters RAN to the bar to buy pints of beer to hurl at him.

This band had no guitars AND no drummer—what kind o' punks could they possibly be!!?

I had gone specifically to see Suicide and happily left after a couple of Clash "punk-by-the-numbers" songs were done for the adoring crowd.

My partner an I were the ONLY people on Suicide's guest list. It was facilitated by our kindly EMI rep who serviced the mining town record store where I worked, having slipped me an advance copy of the first album. This performance changed my life, not only their innovative sound, but a greater vision, the possibility of a world beyond the flat, gray, low skies of the city, the mining towns bereft of unimagined art not referenced in the small public library I haunted as a callow youth.

Sometime in early 1996, David Sefton, Head of Contemporary Music at the prestigious, traditionally classical music London Southbank Centre, started to

---

* Mathieu Copeland, *Alan Suicide Vega, Infinite Mercy* (Museé d'art Contemporain de Lyon, 2009), 39.

shake things up by programming contemporary *rock* based musicians in these august halls that had in the late '60s hosted performances by the likes of Pink Floyd (the Syd Barrett fronted version), The Incredible String Band and one of those hen's teeth gigs by Mr. Nick Drake.

David had convinced the Southbank board of directors to give over a set of the under-used adjoining Hungerford Bridge railway arches they sublet for commercial service for additional artistic use—a small club perfect for rock based and electronic "dance" music.

David and I had similar musical taste and I was thrilled to see someone like him hold this esteemed position while espousing the cultural views he was so passionate about.

"Of all the band's you've seen, what would you most like to see again to launch the new space?" inquired David over dinner. Immediately, I said, "Without a doubt it would be Suicide."

"OK, go get 'em."

Lower Manhattan on a Sunday evening in April, I sit down at the modern looking Spring Street Natural, a bar/restaurant I occasionally used for meetings. With me were friends and intrigued fans, Susan Stenger and Robert Poss from Band of Susans—both engaging conversationalists and drinkers of hard liquor cocktails.

The "boys" arrive within minutes of each other. They greet us and then roll into a catch-up conversation about kids, cats, and partners, making it clear it has been several years since they have actually seen each other at all.

I attempt to interject what I thought was the point of our meeting—to reconfirm the business details—but I am brushed aside with a friendly "Yeah, yeah. All good."

We talked among ourselves while I regrouped my thoughts to raise issues of technical and personal preferences and necessities: "Perhaps we should arrange some rehearsals beforehand? Here in New York or if you prefer when you arrive in London?"

"Nah, we're good." And they go back to their chatting.

After about an hour they stand, shake our hands, and head off in their separate directions without either one glancing back.

Ladies and Gentlemen. . . . Alan Vega and Marty Rev!

A boardroom power struggle had blocked and eventually ousted the plan for the Southbank club. But I still had Suicide patiently primed to play live again, an opportunity not to be wasted, so we reluctantly pivoted into three nights at Highbury Corner's the Garage club. It was by then May of 1998.

The opening act for all three nights were my Finnish 'tronic sound terrorists then called Panasonic (until the Japanese corporation of the same name insisted they change it "to avoid confusion"). Like myself, Mika Vainio had a similar life-changing experience seeing Suicide live—his in a far committed pilgrimage as he hitchhiked from Turku, Finland, to Rome alone just to see Suicide play.

After Vega's first-night nerves resulting in his turning up so drunk he pleaded to Rev to "play only the slow ones," they redeemed themselves on night two by playing a blistering high velocity set AND Vega checking out the opening act to better assess the audience's general vibe and demeanor. Alan fell hard for the Finns' brand of beat blasted harsh instrumental electronics which began a lively mutual love affair between Alan and Panasonic and serial collaborations.

Alan was bemused by the change in audience reaction—Suicide were now adored legends. Post-gig, while waiting on their transport back the hotel, I over-heard Alan say to Rev: "We're fucked maaan. They're actually listening to our music now."

Liz told me that Alan had taken to calling me "The Sledge" (as in hammer) due to my continued bashing away at both artist and cultural structures.

True enough—we'd been able to lift Suicide from occasional footnote to a subjective paragraph, to "Godfather" status in several music categories.

They could now command headline concert hall bookings and the occasional "Special Guests" status at large outdoor festivals. They released a new album *American Supreme* to supportive reviews and spoke to a multi-generational audience well beyond the balding carnival of punk survivors.

Through the resurrection of the band, in 2002, Alan got his first invitation to exhibit his visual art again (his first in some twenty-plus years) via the sharp ears of cartoon character art dealer Jeffrey Deitch. It was followed in 2009 by a major retrospective solo show in Lyon Museum of Contemporary Art in France—a beautifully presented curation by Mathieu Copeland. As Alan and I walked around the gallery right before the opening night, Alan thoughtfully noted "Ain't this the kind of show they give you after yer dead?"

"It is," I said, "I just thought YOU might like to see it too!"

He smiled and made a short bow of appreciation.

Art dealers began to take note and prices of his works rose, not least because Alan had thrown away or cannibalized many of his works. "They mostly came from street trash and then went back to being street trash," he matter-of-factly stated, without the slightest regret.

June 2008 was Alan's sixtieth birthday, I know because I had a copy of his passport. Liz laughed out loud, 'You've missed that one by a good while!" She explained that Vega had somehow renewed his current passport by fax and had shaved ten years off his birth date—so he actually would be seventy that year! I was determined to mark this event and show the influence and love out there for him. But first, I had to convince him.

He was not pleased by the sudden age leap yet over a lengthy phone call, I pointed out EVERY other major art form—painting, writing, poetry, jazz, blues classical—this was the age of assuming the role of an "established artist." Only "pop stars"—those disposable entertainers—were held inside their youth. Be you sixty or seventy years old, the days of young dalliance were well behind him—a point he took well. "Gives me even more time to make my drawings rather than travel," he replied, knowing I was about to give him a list of obligations.

Bruce Springsteen, a long, longtime fan of Suicide and Vega's solo works, easily cleared the way for us to release his epic elegiac live version of "Dream Baby Dream"—a huge uptick in celebrating Vega's standing as a writer. It guaranteed sellout pressing. But the middle management henchmen at Blast First said, "I don't see the point of it." Thus, the record company Blast First (petite), was born, screaming into the world.

Before these sad times Mute Records (not Blast First mind you, as Marty Thau and I never really got along) bought the rights to Suicide's first album once Thau decided to settle into his Floridian retirement. CEO Daniel Miller immediately upped the band's royalty rate to a more respectful percentage rate. Blast First had licensed Vega's solo back catalog for a healthy sum tho' only one record was ever actually released.

Vega put his Blast First windfall to very good use and continued his weekly recording sessions with long-standing compadre Perkin Barnes at his 6/8 Studios in the famous music hub building at 611 Broadway.

Vega crafted what I consider to be his finest ever album, which became known as *IT*. Multiple versions ensued, as he honed it down to a precision tooled monster while he patiently waited for me to find it a suitable home for release. So mesmerized was I by these recordings I was convinced it required a bigger machine to release it than I had available.

The downturn in record sales while labels and audiences grappled with the new problems of online music consumption led to a welter of changes and problems within the record industry. I was never able to find *IT* the home I believed it deserved.

In 2010, we ticked off another line on the invisible bucket list when uber music-fan promoters All Tomorrow's Parties had Suicide open for Iggy and the Stooges in London's legendary venue, Hammersmith (no relation!) Odeon. Seeing the Stooges in 1969 was Vega's own epiphany, that first turned his mind to try his hand at his own music making and thus alter the course of his life from purely visual arts. A circle closed.

When Alan died in 2016, it was not a surprise—his health had been poor for some time and the arts vultures were already circling. When Liz called from the hospital to say he had just passed, I was just not able to muster the spirit to rise to the occasion with the help she needed with the inevitable press. Ever the friend and always a preternaturally organized artist, and to my great relief, Henry Rollins stepped up and marshaled his own team to manage the news flow.

Time zones became waves of grief as people woke to hear the news.

All hail Alan Vega—the biggest star in my night sky. ■

Susan Stenger
Sound Artist
Band of Susans/Big Bottom
May 2023

I encountered Alan for the first time in spring of '96 with Paul Smith and Robert Poss (my bandmate in Band of Susans, who subsequently mixed live sound for Suicide several times). Paul had arranged a meeting in New York with Alan and Marty Rev to talk about them coming to play in the UK. . . . Robert and I were just tagging along to say hi and have a drink. I'd already met Rev the year before when he'd come to London to play Paul's tiny but radical and influential Disobey Club. Rev had massively out-hipped the hip audience (which had included Jarvis Cocker and Nick Cave), bashing his keyboard and shaking his booty in an ultra-sleek jumpsuit. Afterwards I told him "You're the coolest guy in the universe" and he replied, "Thanks for confirming my suspicions." I guess I should've expected nothing less from a guy who traveled with a flight case for his sunglasses collection! I anticipated Alan being even cooler and more intimidating, given all the stories I'd heard about performances involving broken glass and swinging bicycle chains, but he was as sweet as could be. When Marty sauntered in, we moved down to the end of the table to just let them talk. They hadn't spoken in ten years, I think, but they fell right into it. Paul sorted the performance questions in a few minutes but the rest of it was "So how's it going? How are the kids? How's the cat?"

Of course, when they did finally come to London they blew everyone away. They stormed through three nights at the Garage in '98, each show magnificent in its own way. Paul had paired them with Finnish electronic duo Pan Sonic for all the shows, which was a genius matchup. They pushed one another to ever greater heights and bonded backstage over the free-flowing vodka. Alan, Mika, and Ilpo eventually recorded together as VVV. Mika was famously stone-faced, but Alan could always get him to smile.

I was living with Paul Smith in London by then, so had many opportunities to experience Alan's electrifying presence onstage and his "hang out" personality backstage. It became kind of a family thing, as his whip-smart and beautiful wife Liz and young son Dante were often along on tour. Alan and Liz had their own "Honeymooners" vibe going sometimes, but it was crystal clear how much he respected and adored her (and she knew exactly how to handle his moods).

I was also touched by how tender and attentive he was with Dante (who is now an accomplished performer and producer in his own right). I spent a lot of time backstage playing "Hangman" with Dante. My proudest moment was when his secret message was revealed to be "I wish Susan could come to live with us in New York." When Suicide played at All Tomorrow's Parties in 2005, Dante developed a little crush on Peaches, so he spent all one morning making an elaborate drawing for her, which he presented with pride and she accepted with great grace. Vincent Gallo was there too, who was amused to find out Alan was a Buffalo Bills fan.

I became really close to Alan when I was working on *Soundtrack for an Exhibition*, a project conceived by curator Mathieu Copeland and staged at the Museum of Contemporary Art in Lyon in 2006. In line with his objective of engaging multiple perspectives of time in film, painting, and sound, Mathieu had asked me to make music that would last the entire length of the exhibition. I chose to frame it using classic pop song structure "blown up" to fill ninety-six days, so the bridge ("the middle eight") would be eight days long rather than eight bars, the intro and outro four days each, the choruses eight days and verses sixteen. Each of the three verse sections abstracted and collaged tropes of a different genre type (easy listening, folk/blues, and rock/heavy metal) but was grounded with a slow-moving drone chord progression. For instance, the easy listening section played out the chord progression of "The Girl from Ipanema," with a chord change every two days, but was layered with processed scraps of stock instrumental patterns and ghostly imprints of everything from Nelson Riddle and Chet Baker to the Carpenters.

To expand the library of raw material, I enlisted a group of contributors to respond to little scores or sets of instructions. After Robert Poss, my primary collaborator, Alan was first on my list. He was such a "magpie" in the way he made his visual art, compiled lyrics, and synthesized aspects of old and new in his songs; I couldn't wait to hear what he'd do over the various atmospheres I'd assembled of slide guitar, samba shakers, mournful horn figures, and hand claps. I also wanted to "magpie" his signature grunts, groans, and exhortations.

We started one session with a little Mississippi John Hurt–style loop and gave him a few phrases to riff off of. I was astonished when, after a couple of warm-up takes, he came out with a fully formed blues that seemed to be called "Epiphany Way!" It was amazing, but for other parts I asked him to do less. One time he just recorded various moans over a "D" drone. I had separately asked Kim Gordon to improvise some vocals using a few phrases ("come on," "shake it, shake it now," "meet me at the crossroads") and I later put those together in various ways to make some great duets. I did the same with Alan (vocals), Nick Cave (piano), and my own flute for another project—we recorded our parts completely independently but in the same key. Kind of inspired by Exquisite Corpse, the surrealist drawing game in which each person makes a different part without knowing what the others have done, except that I would combine chance and choice by ultimately deciding how it would all fit together.

One night I played Alan a repeated bass and finger snap clip from "Fever," and he did an entire take using just that one word. Another time I lowered the lights and put on a dreamy, romantic loop and a set of phrases extracted from various Sinatra songs. I'd made it long, so he had plenty of time to get into the mood. He'd been sexily whispering and crooning over it for quite a while, when he suddenly blurted out "when is this fucking thing ever going to end?"—needless to say, I kept that line in! It was so Alan.

Alan and Liz were able to come over to Lyon during *Soundtrack for an Exhibition* and I was thrilled when MOCA Lyon director Thierry Raspail and Mathieu spoke to Alan about exhibiting his visual art. The resulting retrospective in 2009, *Infinite Mercy*, was beautifully installed with a reverential nod to Alan's recycling techniques. Mathieu had ingeniously adapted many of the structural materials from the museum's previous show. Alan also made a huge new cross-shaped triptych that involved "shopping" for castoff bits of detritus in the museum workshops and repurposing the plastic drop cloth splotched with scarlet paint from the preparation of the exhibition entrance as draping for the first panel. It was extremely powerful to experience so many facets of Alan's creativity manifested in one place—paintings, drawings, light sculptures, collages—and very emotional for me to realize that our song-form experiments for *Soundtrack* had led to this, thanks to the commitment and dedication of Mathieu and Thierry Raspail.

Some of my most precious memories of Alan are of the time spent after recording sessions at 6/8 Studios on lower Broadway, when we would repair to his regular late-night haunt, the Blarney Stone on Trinity Place in the far west of New York's Financial District. This was a sacred place for him, a kind of third-shift *Cheers*, where everybody knew his name, but it was not "Alan Vega." There were two regular bartenders, Aiden (Irish) and Claude (Haitian); they always greeted him with a "hey Al, how ya doin'?" and the first of many straight Smirnoffs. (I drank mine diluted with cranberry juice so I could attempt to keep up.) He fit right in with the sparse assortment of off-duty firemen, Staten Island ferry crew, and bleary-eyed office workers as he multitasked drinking, bantering, playing Keno (often coming out ahead at the end of the night), and drawing on any available surface, usually napkins and Keno cards. Sometimes he scribbled bits of lyrics that would come to him, but mostly he drew self-portraits, over and over, haunted and Artaud-inflected, all while cracking jokes and musing on things like "why was Buffalo [which was my hometown] called Buffalo, if there weren't any buffalo there?"

On any given night, our conversation might encompass the poetry of baseball, our childhood TV hero Fess Parker having played both Daniel Boone *and* Davy Crockett, the original Roebling suspension bridge over the Delaware River, the nearby Zane Grey Museum, how many Westerns were based on Zane Grey novels, and the possibility of retiring in Wyoming and becoming cowboys.

One night we discovered a mutual love of prime numbers. I remarked that our birthdates were both primes; mine was based on fives and his (23) was considered an especially significant one (Illuminati iconography, conspiracy theories, KLF lore, William Burroughs). Also, Alban Berg, one of my favorite composers, was obsessed with 23 and used it in constructing several pieces. Alan was excited by this, as it turned out he also loved Berg and Webern and how they combined the constraints of defined structure (twelve-tone) with lyrical expression and the occasional reference to previous popular forms (sounds familiar!).

Attributes of a 23 birthday:

Emotional sensitivity and creativity. Also restlessness. Versatile and a quick thinker, with a mind full of inventive ideas. Can learn new subjects easily but may prefer practice to theory.

Huh.

His mind could range from John Wayne to Wozzeck at lightning speed. He never seemed to get tired, whereas these sessions left me equal parts energized, exhilarated, and utterly exhausted. I'd get back to where I was staying, having bought a couple of slices and some Haagen Daz to offset the booze, and wake up later with half-eaten pizza and melted ice cream on my chest but fizzing with new ideas. I miss him immensely. ∎

> *Come with me baby, I'll show ya the stars*
> *Down the dirt road to Epiphany, baby*
> *To the holy, the holy cross*
> *Take my hand, come with me baby*
> *I'll show ya the real life*
> *Come on now, I'll show ya the real life*
> *Down Epiphany Way . . .*
> —Alan Vega, *Soundtrack for an Exhibition*

***

In late 1998, Paul arranged for Suicide to perform at the Barbican Centre, London's premier emporium of the arts, as part of its yearlong exhibition dubbed the world's largest celebration of American culture. It showcased art, music, dance, theater, film, and literature. Suicide's performance centered on an exhibition—Cycles of Culture—with over thirty Harley Davidson motorcycles. New audiences were discovering the classic first Suicide album.

Suicide then did some short tours in Europe and played local venues in NYC including a New Year's Eve performance at the Knitting Factory in Tribeca in the years 2000 and 2001.

Curiously, these shows were packed not only with Suicide's fans from the '70s and '80s, but also younger kids who weren't even alive when the band first played.

Two of these fans were Brain McPeck and Matt McAuley of the band A.R.E. Weapons.

***

Brain McPeck
Cofounder, A.R.E. Weapons
May 2023

I don't exactly recall how it all started, but I ended up with Alan Vega's phone number.

This was a big deal for me as he was the artist I most respected, whose vision had profoundly shaped my own. Our band, A.R.E. Weapons, had a bunch of influences, but none larger or more direct than Suicide. The first time I heard their first album in high school, a switch clicked. I still get chills thirty years later. Seeing them live at the Knitting Factory in the early 2000s was revelatory. It wasn't just his work with Suicide. Tattered copies of his solo albums *Collision Drive* and *Deuce Avenue*, to name a few, traveled with me through my early years in New York—prized possessions.

And now, I had his phone number and was supposed to call him.

In 2007, our friends Dan Colen and Dash Snow were having an art show at the Deitch gallery on Broome Street. I gathered Jeffrey Deitch and the guys thought it would be interesting to have us play with Alan for the closing. Like minds or something. Jeffrey had been a champion of Alan and Suicide for a long time. When asked if we were down, of course we were.

I called him. I was a little bit nervous—meeting your hero and everything. He was—no surprise in retrospect—exceedingly cool. I think we decided to play "Ghost Rider" and take it from there. We were all comfortable improvisers. I don't think anyone was worried.

The show was called NEST. It was a re-creation of something Dan and Dash would do at hotel rooms, where they filled the place with shredded paper, like a hamster cage, and acted like—maniacs. For the Deitch show, they covered the floor with knee-high shredded paper and they and our friends covered the walls with graffiti.

We met Alan out front and shot the breeze a bit. We had programmed some suicide-esque tracks with an Akain MPC and some synthesizers. We played "Ghost Rider" and I think we played "Rock and Roll Is Killing My Life," which we'd been covering for years, and could thoroughly relate to. I think we sprung some stuff of ours on Alan. Having him vamp on our song "Saigon Disco" was surreal. I sang along with him on some of the Suicide songs. It felt easy and familiar. It felt great.

This led to another show the next year, at the bigger Deitch gallery around the corner. For this one, strictly among ourselves, we'd decided to call the act Silky Al and the Vegabonds—like a doo-wop group. Alan really laid into the crooner thing. I think this is actually how I always saw him. Larger than life, like a deranged Elvis, but one singing about the outcasts, the misfits. Matt and I were proud to be vagabond acolytes in sharkskin suits. I think the audience liked it. By this point, Al and Liz felt like old friends. We talked about getting together to work at Perkin's studio. ■

Matt McAuley
Cofounder, A.R.E. Weapons
Bass
May 2023
Shortly after getting together with Alan for the NEST closing and the other Deitch gig, we started regular weekly sessions on Tuesday nights in the studio of Perkin Barnes on lower Broadway. Perkin and Al went way back, and their working relationship was so strong and sweet. The whole thing was as much about just hanging out as it was producing music.

Brain and I would go back and forth between Alan in the vocal booth and Perkin in the control room. One of us would work on music with Perk for a while, using stuff we brought in—little sounds, beats, or just an idea, while the other one would sit in the booth and crack up and tell stories with Alan. There was a lot of sports talk and tales of New York. Al would tell us about his days betting on the ponies and stuff like that.

Of course, the subject always came back around to music. He was mainly listening to new southern hip-hop at the time. He was always looking for something that was coming from street level but sounded like the future. It would go on like that for hours, then suddenly he would hear something that got his attention from what was being worked on in the other room and we'd all get in there and mess around with it together. Ideas would get thrown around until it got to a point where the track was good and weird, then Al would say, "OK, I'm ready." He'd go into the booth with whatever notes he had with him, mostly shit that he had written either late at night at home or at his favorite bar, the Killarney Rose—stuff from notebooks, the back of napkins, Keno slips, and who knows what else. Perkin would dim the lights and Alan would step up to the mic and sing. Man, that voice. It was always—the voice. We'd be in the other room listening, entranced. It was like watching new commandments being etched in stone, to witness this man—who had so thoroughly informed our own way of thinking—bring out

Alan and A.R.E. Weapons performance at NEST exhibition, Deitch Projects, 2007. *Courtesy Deitch Projects*

something alive from the darkness on an ordinary weeknight. Then he'd get to the end and be like, "Oh I don't know. What do you think about that?" and we'd all laugh and say yeah, you got it. I still laugh and shake my head every time I think about it—the casualness with which he would toss off things that were so genuinely powerful.

That's how we did everything that came out of that studio together; talking shit about the Mets or Giants, making weird noises, and listening to Al do his thing. We kept that Tuesday night date for a few months. In addition to the hanging, talking, experimenting, we actually managed to finish a few tracks. There were two songs for a twelve-inch that came out—a cover of Edwin Starr's "War (what is it good for?)" which was someone else's idea, but came out well and an original, "See Tha Light."

"See Tha Light" was one of those moments Alan just went in the booth and dazzled. Brain and I brought in a Gun Club sample that we had looped and tweaked until it sounded like there was a jet engine running back and forth on it and he just went in and poured out this deep riff, barely looking at his notes. The whole thing was a joy. We also recorded an epic cover of Bruce Springsteen's "State Trooper" that is still unreleased. I hope it's unearthed someday because we are really proud of that one. It's haunting. I listen to it often to remember Alan and that time we spent together. ∎

***

A few of those younger fans at those Suicide gigs were gallery assistants for Jeffrey Deitch at his SoHo gallery, Deitch Projects.

After seeing Suicide, they were talking about it at the gallery, noting how intense Suicide was and how they blow away acts half their age. Jeffrey overheard them and asked if they were talking about Alan Vega. He had never forgotten seeing Alan Suicide's (Vega) art exhibition at OK Harris gallery in the early '70s. At the time he thought it was the most radical art he had ever seen.

Jeffrey was intrigued to hear Alan was still performing with such vitality and wondered if he was still making sculptures. He asked one of his assistants, Erin Krause, to track Alan down.

Not much later, Erin and Alan connected, and it was arranged for Jeffrey to go to Hanover Square and catch up.

When Jeffrey walked into Alan's loft in early 2001, he was ecstatic that Alan never stopped making art. There were numerous cross-shaped light sculptures on the walls and his latest creations—long vertical hanging pieces streaming down the twenty-foot-high walls.

Jeffrey immediately said he wanted to do a one-man show of Alan's work—as soon as possible.

Although the show at Deitch Projects had originally been scheduled for the fall of 2001, 9/11 changed that. It was rescheduled for February 2002 and titled *Collision Drive*, after Alan's second solo album.

The exhibited works included his classic cross light sculptures, floor pieces in the vintage '70s style, and a number of the new hanging pieces.

Courtesy Deitch Projects

The opening was packed. Some notable attendees included Moby, Bjork, Ric Ocasek, Martin Rev, Agnes b (who flew in from Paris), as well as popular local artists Dash Snow and Dan Colen, and Brain McPeck and Matt McAuley.

One of the floor pieces Jeffrey sold was to a Swiss collector. It included piles of lights and wires strung along the floor together with cigarette butts and a small black-and-white TV set broadcasting a basketball game during the opening.

To celebrate the closing of the show, Jeffrey organized a Suicide concert at the Wooster Street annex space around the corner, which had the capacity for about six hundred.

Always on the cutting edge of trends, Jeffrey was an early proponent of the cross-marketing of art, music, and fashion. Through his promotions and word of mouth about the night of the show, the space was filled to the walls. Hundreds of additional fans were in the street trying to get in. The police eventually showed up to disperse the crowd, although by then the show had ended.

It was an incredible and intense set. The downstairs of the exhibition space became a makeshift backstage. Glenn O'Brien from *Rolling Stone* came down after the show asking to talk with Alan.

Alan was deep in conversation with someone. When he was told that Glenn wanted to interview him, he said in a very loud voice "Fuck *Rolling Stone!*" Alan hadn't forgotten that after the first Suicide album was released in 1977, *Rolling Stone* published a review calling the music "sophomoric and puerile."

During the period that Alan was preparing for his Deitch show, he and Marty began organizing to record another studio album. They planned to produce it themselves with Perkin engineering. Marty sent Alan about twenty song sketches and Alan picked eleven that he connected with. It was titled *American Supreme* and was met with "complicated" reviews.

Displaying a sense of timing that's eluded them in the past, Suicide is releasing American Supreme, *their first album in over a decade, this week. With Vega's choppy, Beat-inspired lyrics and Rev's often crude sense of sonics,* American Supreme *is remarkably similar to the group's seventies work. But that doesn't mean the album isn't challenging. In fact,* American Supreme *proves that Suicide can reach backward and still remain ahead of the pack.*[*]
***

He wrote the lyrics of "Death Machine" for the album after September 11:

I am
The death machine

---

* Ethan Brown, "In Brief: American Supreme," *New York*, October 28, 2002, https://nymag.com/nymetro/arts/music/pop/reviews/n_7876/.

I am
A war machine
I am
Your God machine
I am
The scheme machine
Count, count
Body count.*

And he wrote a song to Dante—"Child It's a New World"—about what he was growing up into.

Child, oh Child
You gotta understand, understand
it's a new world, it's a new world
we're livin in
today
There's gonna be changes
changes around here
life will never be the same
I know, I know
it's gonna be sad, it's gonna be sad
for awhile, awhile.†

***

On this album Vega and Rev don't come up with anything as instantly memorable as "Cheree" . . . or as disturbing as "Frankie Teardrop" (possibly rock's scariest song) but it's still an accomplished release that attests to their enduringly unique sound and vision. *American Supreme* is a soundtrack to a world on the brink (again). Let's hope we're still around in ten years for Suicide's follow-up.‡

***

I was too enamored of truth ever to mourn lost illusions.§
—Simone de Beauvoir

---

* "Death Machine" by Alan Vega and Martin Rev, *American Supreme*, 2002.
† By Alan Vega and Martin Rev, *American Supreme*, 2002.
‡ Wilson Neate, "The Return of the Ghost Riders of the Apocalypse," *Dusted* Reviews, November 24, 2002, http://www.dustedmagazine.com/reviews/483.
§ Simone de Beauvoir, *The Prime of Life* (Paris: Gallimard, 1960).

Collège Des Bernardins. © Dom Garcia, 2013

20 Confrère

2001 . . . 2007 . . . 2010

> It is better to be unhappy and know the worst,
> than to be happy in a fool's paradise.*
> —Fyodor Dostoevsky

It was Lyon. 1990. North of the French Alps—the city was stunning. The snow dropped a seductive blanket along the historic cobbled streets.

Alan, Liz, and Kuch were finishing their tour for *Deuce Avenue*. Alan and Liz were heading out to meet with Marc Hurtado and his brother, Eric. Marc had been in the group Etant Donnés with his brother since the late '70s.

Marc and Eric were very striking in appearance—handsome and dressed head to toe in black leather. They invited Alan and Liz to dinner with friends at Brasserie Le Sud on Place Bellecour. The group was welcoming and lively and it was a fun evening.

Over the next few years, Alan would cross paths with Marc at concerts in Europe. He was struck by Marc's deep understanding of his artistry. Whenever he spoke about Alan's music, and his art, his words were very poetic and genuine. "He really gets it," Alan would say to Liz.

Alan could see that Marc had the same level of commitment to his own artistry. They each created work true to their ideologies.

He ended up suggesting a collaboration with Marc. Alan rarely pursued collaborative projects—they were always proposed to him. This was unusual.

Marc was thrilled. Their first project was the album *Re-Up* in 1999 which also featured Lydia Lunch and Genesis P-Orridge. Alan contributed vocals.

---

* Fyodor Dostoevsky, *The Idiot*, trans. Taylor McDuff (New York: Penguin Classics, 2004).

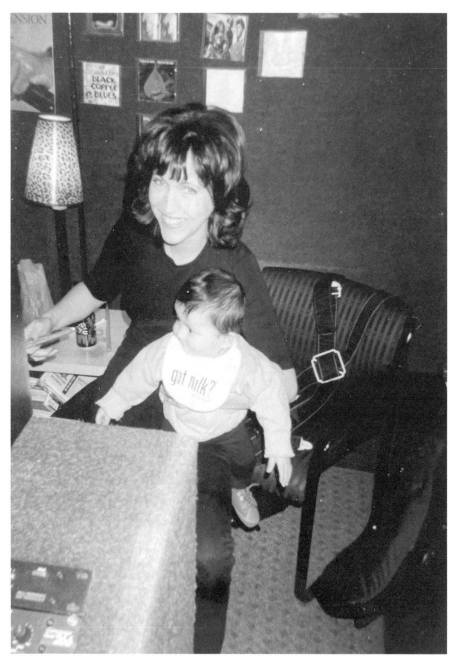

Liz and Dante, 6/8 Recording Studios, 1999. *Photo by Alan Vega. Courtesy Saturn Strip, Ltd.*

Also in 1999, Alan released his latest solo album titled *2007*. Although he and Liz continued going into the studio with Dante in tow, they wouldn't release the next album for eight years given the amount of time and attention necessary for raising their young son.

Starting in 2004, Marc began arranging a few shows combining Vega solo, Alan and Liz, and Etant Donnés on the same bill. French singer Christophe often joined for an encore.

After the *Station* album release and tour in 2007, Marc joined shows in Paris in 2008 and 2010 with Alan, Liz, and Dante, who was now performing with his parents. These Vega shows consisted of tracks of whatever new material he had cooked up in the studio. Marc would add synth and background vocal.

Marc was moved to suggest collaborating on another album, and *Sniper* was recorded and released in 2010.

Liz, Dante, Alan, and Marc, Collège Des Bernardins, Paris, 2013. *Collège Des Bernardins.* © *Dom Garcia, 2013*

Alan, Marc, Liz, and Dante, Collège Des Bernardins, 2013. *Collège Des Bernardins.* © *Dom Garcia, 2013*

After the album's release, Marc continued to join Vega, Liz, and Dante in concert. These shows combined new Vega songs with songs from *Sniper*.

Their last concert together in 2013 was very special and held at the Collège Des Bernadin. A thirteenth-century Gothic building, it had been home to a Catholic religious order of monks and nuns. The concert was held on Maundy Thursday and Marc had an ornate throne on the stage for Alan, whose balance had been impaired after his stroke in 2012.

Hurtado was also a highly regarded filmmaker, and he had the opportunity to follow Alan and Suicide for a number of years, filming them. The result was a DVD collection, "Alan Vega • Martin Rev • Suicide: Five Films."

Alan was always amazed with Marc's care, commitment, profound discernment, and appreciation of what Alan was doing. Marc understood Alan. It added fuel to his desire to keep pushing forward. And Alan appreciated Marc's artistry as well, encouraging him to keep creating on all fronts.

***

Marc Hurtado
Musician, Filmmaker
March 2023

I became a fan of the work of Alan Vega at the first listen. I was fifteen in 1977 when I discovered the first album of Suicide. Their music was so revolutionary, new, wild, and free. I felt in total communion with their work. Discovering such free and innovative artists helps you grow and create.

I had started making music and founded the Etant Donnés duo with my brother Eric that same year in 1977. The portrait of Alan Vega sat above my bed with photos of Arthur Rimbaud, Fédérico Garcia Lorca, Maïakovski, Antonin Artaud, Edgar Alan Poe, Lautréamont, Raymond Roussel, Iggy Pop, Sky Saxon, James Brown, and Lou Reed.

In 1990, the day after a concert in Gothenburg with my band Etant Donnés, we went to a concert of Alan's. He was playing in an almost empty venue in front of about thirty spectators with the same determination as if he was in front of a crowd of two thousand people.

To me, he was an iconic figure—out of reach—but when we went backstage to meet him and give him a copy of our album *Aurora*, he greeted us as if we'd known each other for years. He hugged us, joked with us, complained about his new diet, and told us about his solitary visit to the Stendhal Museum in Grenoble in 1982—where I was living at that time.

He told us he loved our album and suggested we work on a collaboration together. I thought it was a joke because I could not imagine that one of my greatest living heroes wanted to work with me.

I went to New York with my girlfriend to record his voice at 6/8 Studios with Perkin Barnes, who had worked with Alan for many years.

The recording was an unforgettable moment. When he arrived, he smoked a cigarette or two, joked with me, then asked Perkin to start recording, letting the four tracks play without pausing in order to record these four songs in one go.

I pointed out to him that in the title song, "Brutal Piss Rods," his voice must be very tense and very spatial like in Suicide's new version of "Ghost Rider."

The music started, then he went to sit down quietly, took a packet of biscuits out of his pocket, a pack of cigarettes, heaps of little papers, and some drawings, which he placed all around him on the floor.

When he started to sing, it was like lightning struck. The music had been playing for a while and his ultra-relaxed demeanor did not hint that he was going to attack the song like a lion that leapt on a gazelle—with absolutely incredible pinpoint precision to the tempo of the music.

He finished each track with screams as if he had timed them and practiced on them for hours when it was entirely improvised. It was recorded in one go.

That day, I realized the incredible genius of Alan Vega. I had witnessed a moment of pure magic.

What had struck me the most during my first meeting with him after years of admiring him was his simplicity, his kindness, his humor, his tenderness, and the immediate complicity he established during our discussions. It was quite in opposition with the tormented, violent, and hard character that he was onstage.

I had heard about the visual artwork of Alan Vega in the early '80s but I only discovered these works in 1990 thanks to the book *Deuce Avenue War: The Warriors V3 97*, edited by Edit DeAk. This book is composed of photos made by Alan Vega, very often of a television screen glued horizontally and surrounded by hand-drawn words. The first part of the book is a kind of portrait of America and the second part contains many photos of Nazi death camps.

His photos looked like his music—portraits of America, poverty, sex, violence, capitalism, drugs, capturing the pinnacle of horror with the corpses piled up from the camps in the last pages. In 1994, I discovered his poems, the lyrics of songs, and his magnificent portraits.

When I discovered this side of Alan, I was immediately struck by the great depth of his visual artwork. We immediately realized that we had not been dealing with a musician who is getting into visual art but rather exactly the opposite.

Discovering the art made me feel possessed by a strange magic spell in an alchemy of lights and colors, like a chemical wedding surrounded by mysterious, poetic, intense, and liberating energy—a kind of hallucinatory dark fire.

I must say that throughout my artistic career I have only collaborated with artists whom I adored for a long time and with whom I felt a deep artistic and human communion. This was the case with Alan.

He was the first person to want to collaborate with me after sixteen years of working only with my brother in Etant Donnés.

When Alan invited me to work with him, I put my entire creation system into a kind of revolution.

Alan and I shared the same determination of the confrontation of man facing the world, the one that produces this violent experience of tearing apart space inside the body of the public.

I was literally sucked up by the chaos, the grace, and volcanic emotional charge of Alan's work. He helped me touch the impalpable and make the invisible visible, feeding off a force of infinite life from 1998 to 2016.

Alan and Marc, *Expo Galerie Laurent Godin 10.* © *Dom Garcia, 2012*

For me, Alan was above all a poet and when I interviewed him for my film *The Infinite Mercy Film* on his luminous sculptures, drawings, and paintings and for the feature film *Infinite Dreamers*—he had simple, hard-hitting, flamboyant words, carried away by his limitless passion.

In 2016, the singer, Christophe asked me to go to New York to film Alan Vega. The idea was to release a video that would be screened from a jukebox during the performances of songs Christophe and Alan made together.

I had arranged a shooting with Alan in New York on May 21, but the day I went to his apartment to start filming, Liz told me Alan had broken his hip.

Just before leaving for the hospital to see him, Liz showed me a series of paintings that he had just painted. They all represented men with absent faces. It struck me deeply coming from an artist who had been drawing faces for years. In my eyes, these portraits represented as many strangers as self-portraits of him—they were a sort of ultimate representation of man on Earth. These new painted works, these absent faces, immediately made me think of a farewell to the Earth—a big "Goodbye."

I will always remember his last words in the hallway of the hospital:

"Marc! I love you! I love you man!"

When I heard these resound in this sad hallway, I did not want to turn around because I immediately felt in his voice that it was the last time I would see my friend—and unfortunately, that was the case.

Lydia Lunch
Singer, Poet
Actress
2015

To come full circle like the noose we attempted to cut free of by severing the connective tissue from a life we were forced into living, a life that felt like it was living us, we turned the beating around and struck back and attacked not only the enemy within, but the ever-present enemy surround . . . with sound.

We used music as an assaultive weapon that furthered the divide between those who were built for abuse, because not only could we take it, not only could we fucking dish it out—but like a hysterical manifestation of preverted/perverted archetypes, we were created to fully inhabit—we bore the burden in our bloodline of all of history's misguided lovers, hate fuckers, witches, wretches, and wastrel minstrels who troubadoured through the trenches in search of other extreme out-siders that even a coven was too restrictive to contain.

There are certain tribes that stand completely outside of everything and every-one else and in that isolation there is a sense of freedom, desolation, and longing.

This was not a caterwaul for the collective, but a personal exorcism of the most gloriously murderous romantics, whose blood longed for blood as our bones were broken and shattered once more as if fated upon the breaking wheel.

Where what has been done shall be done and done again until you sever the chains and decode the secret language which reverses the repetition of the endless cycle from which only an agonized scream of merciless negation into the darkest and most lonely of all those dark and lonely nights might actually rip a new black hole into your personal cosmos. And when upon hitting that most excruciating and soul-shattering, god-forsaking pitiless howl, can the soul truly be set free to reclaim and reconfigure the damage already done to our battered psyches which bear the pain of all man's inhumanity done in the name of a terribly addictive love, an unquenchable greed or an obsessive and forever unsatisfied lust.

Suicide . . . all this . . . and the inverse too. How fucking beautiful.

True contrarians. For as terrifying as they could be—"Frankie Teardrop," "Harlem," etc., they also composed outlandishly tender psycho-saccharine love songs—"Sweetheart," "Dream Baby Dream," "Cheree"—psychobilly grindcore "Jukebox Baby," "Johnny," "Ghost Rider"—driving, post trance ranters I Don't Know . . . and half a dozen other genre defying reconfigurations highlighting which would help me to define my own coming musical schizophrenia.

I met Suicide in 1976 at Max's Kansas City. I crawled out of my bedroom window in Rochester, New York, jumped on a greyhound bus and ended up staying in a loft that Lenny Bruce's daughter Kitty had just evacuated in Chelsea. I went to New York searching for like-minded miscreants whose sense of true romance meant blood-soaked sheets and long slow screams that would shatter what remained of the night I never wanted to end. Suicide was the first show I saw, Alan and Marty were the first people I met (other than the flock of hippies I connived into taking me in) and to a violent seventeen-year-old hate-fueled art terrorist in training, their performance was one of the most inspiring events of my life. Suicide. I thank you. ■

***

In 2003, Alan and Liz ran into James Murphy of LCD Soundsystem at Meredith Danluck's downtown studio. Alan was there for a promo shoot after collaborating with DJ Hell on the tracks "Listen to the Hiss" and "Meet the Heat." In 2009, James covered Alan's song "Bye Bye Bayou." Alan loved the way James reimagined the song with his own vision and style.

***

James Murphy
Musician, Producer
LCD Soundsystem
May 2023

Liz: Do you remember when you met Alan and me—Meredith Danluck was filming Alan for a video? I remember Alan saying, "That guy was really nice." He really liked you.

I think I probably had such an adrenaline dump that I can barely remember . . . I spent three years looking for the first Suicide record. I heard that record on tour in the early '90's. And I was like, "OK, I need to get that." And then I just spent three years trying to find it until I finally got a store on the Lower East Side to track one down, and I had to give them a whole bunch of money.

Alan is one of the most important performers and writers to me. When meeting people that I really admire, I kind of shut down. My self-consciousness goes into overdrive. . . . I don't process anything. And I think he probably could have punched me in the throat, and I would have been like, "He was great. It was great to meet him."

The things that I admire about Suicide is that as I'm sitting there, and I'm listening, I'm like, "At some point, while this craziness was coming out of the speakers, somebody that is the creator of this turned to somebody else and said, 'Yep, we're done. This is it.'" They weren't like, "Is it too crazy? Is it too long? Should we polish this up?"

And I love that there's always a confrontational challenging thing. But it's a generosity of confrontational challenge. If it's ever, "Fuck you people," it's the "Fuck you people," you need to have right now. It's not like disdain.

That's a really hard thing to maintain because it's like you're walking into judgment and dismissal. You're walking into potentially just being written off. . . . It's kind of beautiful. And then doing "Body Bop Jive" stuff. . . . Just being willing to be like, "Oh, yeah, we're going to do this. This is cool. I like this. Let's do this."

I have this policy since I was a child that if I love a record by a band or a series of records by a band and one comes out that I do not like, I always buy it. And I live with it for a year before I pass judgment on it. Because I'm like, "Well, if they made these other things then—" And before I use my "twelve-year-old from a farm town in New Jersey brain" to say if this is good or not, I live inside of it for a while and see if I'm just wrong. And this is a teaching moment. This is a moment where my taste changes.

The first Suicide record was so perfect to me. Like literally so absolutely fearless, and perfect, and without ornamentation. The songs feel like action poems or something. At first, when I heard the second record, I was like, "I don't know about this. This isn't that thing—the whole process seemed filtered in a way through like Ric Ocasek's ear. It feels like there's . . . somebody who also loves them but it's coming from someplace else like, "Let me make this. Everyone is going to love this. Let me make this."

I'm projecting onto what I hear in the music, but I think the Stooges and Suicide are the two examples I use all the time. It's like bands used to be way weirder and way more self-possessed, and ambitious. There's nothing in any of that music that says, "We're not going to be huge." There's like an ambition in it. And they wanted to be outsiders. Real outsiders typically want to impact the world.

It's not a cynical quest for success or for popularity. It is instead like, again . . . the word is generous. When I found Suicide, it was the early '90s. Probably '90, '91. And I'm twenty-one years old. And the idea of this band listening to the kind of shit that's being said by independent bands today. . . . Like, "Oh, you can't use reverb. You got to record everything live." All this kind of self-imposed sets of weird self-flagellating rules about how you're allowed to do things. And you can't even have choruses or whatever. It just felt so weird to me, and it was such a relief to hear Suicide and the music then. . . . There's a series of things that always gave me hope—The Fall, Throbbing Gristle, Suicide, Stooges. These things that were like, "No, there's people who just fucking believe in what they're doing and believe it should be shared with the world."

I think Alan's way of singing, and way of writing lyrics, and way of presenting that was like, "Hey, this is who I am. Let's see what you're about." And the weird range of people that love his work. . . . Most people think "Dream Baby Dream" is a Bruce Springsteen song.

I saw Suicide once—at the Knitting Factory. The Old Knitting Factory. And I was filled with Joy, and I kept yelling, "Play the hits." And there were all these indie rockers around that were like being very serious, and they had their arms folded. They thought it was the weirdest thing to yell that at a Suicide show. It was unbelievable. People were like, "You don't understand Suicide if you're asking them to play their hits." I was very boisterous and fueled by them.

I never saw him solo. And it's happened to me all the time. Sometimes I'd get the luckiest break. Like the Suicide show at the Knitting Factory, that was so well announced that even my idiotic brain got it. I just lived on an inflatable mattress in my recording studio in a basement. So, like I didn't go out.

When they go do their separate things, I felt like when you look at it and say, "This is Martin's work," and, "This is Alan's work," they are those two people without the other and then filling in the shape of . . . and if you think of the first Suicide record, the second Suicide record, and then the other one would be like "Misery Train"—wow.

And I think when you look at like Alan's solo records and . . . You don't even have to find out where you overlap with somebody in some ways. Although they all often feel really collaborative . . . they feel like there's always space for whoever is playing guitar. The people that are getting involved, know who they're getting involved with, and . . . making an Alan Vega record. But it always feels like there's freedom in the playing. And minimalism in space and . . . and I think that sense. . . . These are not programmed loops. This is playing the machines. Polish is not the goal. Like kind of warts and all. Like, "This is what it is."

When you've created an X in the cultural timeline. . . . When you are an X . . . like Kraftwork or Suicide, people will be like, "Oh, it's like Suicide meets—" You become one of the X's used to describe lines to find intersections with. Like Bad Brains and Suicide. You know what I mean? People will just say these things to help you understand and contextualize what's happening. . . . And when you create something that a lot of people do not want to veer from, that they want you to repeat—but if you're a real artist, like Alan or Lou Reed . . . you don't—

And you never drive away from yourself. Like Alan's always going to be himself. The things he loves are the things he loves. There's going to be a way of singing, a way of presenting, you know what I mean, that's like, "This is how I'm projecting myself to the world." And what would possess anyone to believe that he would want to repeat it.

There's a great Miles Davis quote where he was sitting on his stoop at his apartment building in New York, and some guy came by who was a big jazz fan. And he's like, "Oh, I love you. I'm a big fan. All this work. . . . Blah, blah, blah.

So amazing. And then you did this that was incredible. But a lot of the new stuff, this fusion-ie stuff, I'm just not into." And Miles Davis said, "Should I wait for you, mother fucker?"

The thing you love. . . . If you're like, "Oh, that first Suicide record—" Do you think the mind that made that is concerned about what you want them to do now? Do you think the personality that made this thing. . . . "They didn't give a fuck. They did what they wanted. . . . But now you would like to ask them to do something else." It's insanity.

I play Alan's song, "Ice Drummer" all the time because I think it's one of the most perfect and beautiful heartbreaking songs. It is not a perfect song for the whole world because it wasn't made polished. . . . It wasn't made palatable. Not because making something palatable is bad. But because it was made by somebody who made it palatable to himself and to the people that he understood, and that was all it was. Like the original "Dream Baby Dream," and then there's a Bruce Springsteen "Dream Baby Dream," and I love the Bruce Springsteen "Dream Baby Dream." It's very honest to himself. But he also communicates to large masses of people in a very different way. So, that song is part of like the collective unconscious. Because he was able to say, "Hey, this is how I see it." And the way I see things and the way large masses of people see things is more aligned sometimes than the way Suicide made it. . . . But I also see it the way Suicide made it.

One time, Pat (from LCD) and I were listening to the first solo record, and "Bye Bye Bayou" came on. And I was like, "Oh, man—" We didn't have a band together yet. We didn't have LCD Soundsystem. And I was like, "I really want to cover this song. I loved the different kind of drone than a Suicide song." It was just something else. It just . . . this floating, sort of unchanging blues.

I think there are just people that have developed a thing that's . . . it isn't about notes. It's something else. It's a gesture that is not about melody, even though there's melodies in there.

And I think someone like Alan had self-possession that didn't need to bother with that, and his charisma and power came from that self. . . . Alan was just like, "I'm going into the fear. The fear is a tunnel, and I'm going to live in this thing." Like, "I'm going to go in. . . . I'm not concerned about how the world sees me."

I wish I had the self-possession and confidence to have talked to Alan more or to do something with him, and I regret that. Thank you for asking me to be a part of this and thank you for this reminder that I should work with the people I admire so much.

And if you don't know, there's a verse in a song on our last record called *American Dream*, and the song is called "American Dream." The whole song is like an homage to Alan. Like the way it's recorded, the way it's sung. The way I think of the melody. That is meant to be an Alan song. And there's a verse in there about him.

He's somebody really important to me. It was a very meaningful loss to me, and I'm really sorry for your loss. I'm really thankful for you bothering to talk to me. It means a lot to me.

Seeing him that day at the film studio—it was a brush with one of my heroes. ■

***

In 2007, the *Mojo* Awards were presented in London. The list of awardees included Suicide, Iggy Pop, Ron Ashton, Amy Winehouse, Bjork, Alice Cooper, Ike Turner, Ozzy Osbourne, the Doors (Ray Manzarek), Slash, and Duff McKee. Suicide was given the Innovation in Sound Award.

At the event, Alan introduced nine-year-old Dante to Iggy Pop. For the occasion, Dante had twelve-inch black extensions in his hair and had painted his nails black. Liz's brother, David, joined them for the trip and at the ceremony, Sharon Osbourne flirted with him.

Before gathering for the photo shoot of the awardees with the photographer, Ross Haflin, they were given strict instructions that no managers were to accompany the artists. So, Liz and Paul watched through the window and cringed when Sharon Osbourne yelled at Alan because he was sitting in front of Ozzy and his beret was apparently blocking him.

Liz: *When Amy Winehouse was called to accept her award, she hadn't yet arrived at the ceremony. About ten minutes later I went to the bathroom and she stumbled in behind me. She had apparently just arrived at the venue and seemed very spaced out. I told her she had been called up to accept her award and I think she said "oh, bloody hell" and went into the stall. I was pretty shocked that there was no "handler" there with her and apparently no one outside the door waiting for her. I waited outside, prepared to go back in if she didn't come out soon. She quickly emerged and was immediately swept into the crowd. She made it to the stage on her second call and mumbled a brief thank you.*

Paul Smith
Finally, some recognition from the mainstream to put in their unused trophy cabinet.

Originally selected for the Classic Album Award, we collective of "award show virgins" were bumped out of that slot by Island Records promising a ferocious and extensive ad-buying campaign as long as "and the award goes to Bob Marley & the Wailers for 'Exodus.'"

Thus, *Mojo*'s first (and quite possibly last) ever "Innovation in Sound Award" came to Suicide. Presented by longtime admirer and then label mate, Nick Cave, who amped up the situation by describing them "as one of the greatest bands that ever lived" to slight and polite applause. Nick once told me it was the first Suicide album he'd force people to play at parties in Australia 'cos only the cool people would stay to listen to it.

Nick was particularly gracious as some years earlier when he was the guest curator of London's Southbank Centre's highly prestigious "Meltdown Festival," he invited Suicide to open for Dr. Nina Simone. The show with Suicide never happened but it was Nick's dream gig pairing.

Sarah Lowe as head of Mute Records Press Office was far more *au fait* with award ceremony shenanigans and timed our awardees' commemorative group photo shoot, to which we were decidedly NOT invited. Vega, bless him, went straight to the front row center, earning a sharp reprimand from the redoubtable Sharon Osbourne—"Oi! YOU, Red Hat, get down you are blocking Ozzy," followed by Osborne moaning, "Oh Sharon you're making me look a cunt in front of all these people." Rev slipped easily to the side of the fray next to Ray Manzarek of the Doors—chatting easily across the generational keyboard divide.

A well-earned great night out for the Biggest Star—and Nick, Iggy, and Alice Cooper all came over to say hi and praise Suicide! ∎

***

[H]e was a visual artist working in sound. . . .
Alan was an architect of sound.*
—Jared Artaud

***

Without music, life would be a mistake.†
—Friedrich Nietzsche

---

* Interview Jared Artaud, September 2021.
† Friedrich Nietzsche, *Twilight of the Idols*, trans. Anthony M. Ludovici (London: T. N. Foulis, 1911).

Photo by Iarla Liath (aka Paul Smith)

21 Kill the Fatted Calf

1999 . . . 2007 . . . 2010 . . .

> The absurd is born of this confrontation between the human
> need and the unreasonable silence of the world.*
> —Albert Camus

Alan's album *2007*, released in 1999 and dedicated to Dante, is decidedly his most intense and at times ominous record to date.

> Alan's darkest solo work yet, which seemed like a grim warning of
> some kind. The black clouds of aural ectoplasm and mutant electro
> beats on tracks such as "Meth 13 Psychodreem" and "This Is City"
> crystallize a fathomless essence beyond anything else going on around
> that time; techno, industrial or otherwise. Although "King" manages
> to take its dismembered heavenly chorale on an opium trip, by the
> closing "End" Alan has just let the pulsing machines take over.†
> —Kris Needs

Dante's presence in his life was at once a dream and vision of hope, but brought significant, frightening realities to Alan. They ate at him.

---

* Albert Camus, *The Myth of Sisyphus and Other Essays* (London: Hamish Hamilton, 1942).
† Kris Needs, *Dream Baby Dream: Suicide: A New York City Story* (Omnibus Press, 2017), 342, Kindle.

Liz: Alan was very reflective during the making of 2007. He was having premonitions. He was sensing something really significant was going to happen soon in Dante's lifetime. It was really scary because he was foreshadowing what ended up being the attacks on 9/11.

In 1999, when work finished on *2007*, Alan and Liz centered themselves at home, rebuilding themselves into parents and caregivers.

From the time Dante was five years old through high school, Liz was very active in the downtown youth sports leagues, coaching soccer and serving on the board of directors of the Little League, which led to her appointment to the Community Board in Lower Manhattan ("CB1").

Throughout this time, Alan maintained his focus on his art while staying involved in these activities. He was a great sounding board and was kept apprised of the issues facing the quality of life and access to resources in their community. The initial impetus for Liz joining CB1 was to advocate for more sports fields for their growing residential community post-9/11. When Liz joined the Trinity Boxing Club in 2006 and began managing pro boxers, Alan was especially supportive as he understood the grave sacrifices made by the fighters.

Alan always had an interesting perspective on everything from the early days of Liz's life on Wall Street (and

Dante, Downtown Soccer League Team, 2004.
Photo courtesy of Liz Lamere

the Drexel Burnham "junk bond" offerings) to landmark preservation to soccer rosters and the business dynamics of A-side versus B-side boxing matches. And he was always "all in" when it came to Dante.

***

Dante Vega Lamere
Audio engineer/Producer
May 2023

Growing up with my dad was unique because he would be a regular stay-at-home dad and then at night, he would turn to his art and his music. The sun went down and his creativity came out. It was fascinating to watch as a kid because I didn't really understand how much effort he was putting in around the clock. When I look back on it, I realize how dedicated he was to both me and his art.

Before he had the stroke, he was very unfiltered. I always called it rapid-fire dialogue. He would speak his mind no matter what it would be. And that's one of the double-edged sword great things about him. He was as honest as you could be. And he was one of the most caring people I ever knew. He would never shy away from anything, and he would tell you everything without sugarcoating it at all.

He was also extremely fun. He was one of the most hands-on dads I knew. As a kid, he would show me what he was doing with his light sculptures and try to teach me how he put them together. He wired his own lighting. He would splice his own cords onto the sculptures to create the lights for it. Once he scared me when he tested the spliced cord in the wall outlet and sparks flew out, leaving a char mark on the wall! It was really amazing to see, even though I didn't comprehend the reasoning behind it at the time.

My dad first introduced me to chess before elementary school—when I was about four years old. After that I got into the chess club at elementary school and that's where I really honed my skills. I continued through middle and high school. I still play regularly online.

One of the things I admired most about my dad was that he would give 100 percent to whatever he was doing. Even though he was older, he was very clever at adapting to becoming a parent and creating a strong bond with me. When he walked me to preschool, he quizzed me on math, a subject he loved. He called it the "numbers games." While dad pushed me in the stroller initially, neither of us liked using it (for different reasons), so he let me out and I pushed the stroller and walked alongside him to preschool.

As I got older and got into sports—that was something I shared a passion for with my dad. He loved all sports and knew so much. He believed athletes were artists. My dad was invested in everything I did in baseball, basketball, soccer, table tennis, and boxing. Dad came to most of my games at the downtown sports field near Battery Park City. I knew he must've loved watching me play more than he hated the pain of walking, as his knees got worse with age.

Over the years, Dad showed me his side of art and music, but he didn't try to persuade me to go down the same path. He just tried to enlighten me and help me make my own choices. He wasn't pushy at all about my career or anything. He just wanted to see me succeed at whatever I wanted to do, which was really amazing.

When I got into college, he was very proud of me. I didn't really know what direction I would take. I knew I wanted to do something with music, but I didn't know exactly what yet.

I had been singing in the Trinity Wall Street youth choir since second grade (through high school) and then began playing the trombone in fourth grade. The first time I brought the trombone home, I got off the bus struggling to carry this big case and my dad said, "You couldn't have picked the recorder?"

But as it turned out I grew to love the trombone and I was extremely lucky with my teachers. My middle school music director played the trombone and then my high school music director at Eleanor Roosevelt played the trombone and the piano.

From a very young age I spent school vacations on tour with mom and dad. Some of the most iconic places I remember going to were Red Square in Moscow, the Frank Gehry Museum in Bilbao, Notre Dame, the Pompidou Museum in Paris, Piazza San Marco in Venice, and the Gaudi churches in Barcelona.

As I got older, I was able to appreciate and take away more from each journey. One of the last overseas trips with Dad was to Marseille, which was beautiful. Suicide played on an island off the coast in front of ancient ruins.

We took a ferry over, but on the way back the ferry wasn't running and Uncle Marty, Marc, Dad, Mom, and I had to hitch a ride on a small fishing vessel during a bad storm. The waves were so choppy we almost fell off the front of the boat. And I'm pretty sure the captain was drunk, though as a seasoned veteran he got us back ashore!

Dante playing the trombone, 2007. *Photo by Liz Lamere*

Liz and Dante in front of Gehry Museum, July 2005. *Photo by Alan Vega, Courtesy Saturn Strip, Ltd.*

Liz and Dante in Moscow, July 2005. *Photo by Alan Vega, Courtesy Saturn Strip, Ltd.*

And for some reason, early on, I became the tour manager—the navigator. I liked reviewing the itinerary and reading the signs along the way, to help make sure we got to our next destination seamlessly. Dad's focus was elsewhere, and it felt good to help. I remember once when I was about seven, we had flown into Paris and needed to take a train to Limoge. We waited at the station for hours and when we showed our tickets to an agent, he put us on the wrong train. I had seen the track listing and knew this wasn't the right track. The train was about

Suicide onstage, Marseille, 2014. *Photo by Liz Lamere*

to pull out when I told Mom and Dad our train was on the next track over and we needed to get off this train right now. Good thing they believed me because we jumped off just in time. If we hadn't, we would've gone in the exact wrong direction!

One of the first times that I went out onstage with Dad was by accident. I was maybe five years old. I was just coming out from behind the curtains to put out a cigarette he threw behind him because I thought it was gonna start a fire. When I ran out, the whole crowd started cheering like crazy. And then I ran back. It was kinda exhilarating. I didn't really realize at the time that the cheering was for me. And neither did Dad. He thought, "Oh, they really liked that song!"

Liz: That was at the Roskilde Festival in Denmark. And there were tens of thousands of people in front of the big stage. You could hear the waves of cheering. And then after the set when we were heading to the trailers in the back—hundreds of people rushed to the fence, clamoring for autographs.

They were literally covering the entire length of the fence—completely packed, pressed up against it trying to get to Dad and Marty. Dad went over and started autographing whatever they were passing through. The only other time I saw that many people was at the ATP festival.

One of the most special things I learned from my dad was his mindset about his creative process. By middle school I was learning about the theory behind jazz vocal improv and that gave me insight into my dad. He wouldn't even do a sound check and just be present in the moment at every performance, which was astounding. There aren't many people who would do that. But it was going to be OK no matter what because there was no rule book. That was really eye-opening because it made me realize that Dad's process was much like the jazz legends from the '50s. Being in the moment and utilizing negative space were key.

Photo by Liz Lamere

After high school, I started producing music and studying audio engineering. I realized this brought me more joy than performing as a singer or musician. One reason I fell in love with engineering is because it is the universal language of music, regardless of the genre. I didn't realize it at the time, but seeing Perkin engineering my dad's music from a young age had a subconscious effect on me. While the music being created was unique, the process of capturing the sound was the same as it would be for any type of music. That was enlightening. Producing music is like making a canvas and engineering is the paintbrush used to translate the artist's vision.

Alan and Dante, 2012. *Photo by Liz Lamere*

After my dad passed away it was very difficult. I miss him very much, but he is still with me. He gave me so many life lessons and still guides me as I remember how he thought about things. ∎

Dante and his father, Webster Hall, 2015. © *GODLIS*

***

After Dante's homecoming in 1999, Alan had scaled back studio work to one night a week, with Liz and Dante often joining him. From 1999 on, Alan and Liz worked on tracks for *Station*, released eight years later.

Alan, Liz, and Dante followed up the release of *Station* with a two-week European tour in 2007. One of the highlights was Vega playing at All Tomorrow's Parties (ATP) festival at Butlins Holiday Camp in Minehead, England. It was curated by the Dirty Three with Grinderman/Nick Cave on the bill.

Nine-year-old Dante joined Alan and Liz onstage for portions of the concerts. He primarily played the mouth harp. Dante had been coming into the studio with them regularly most of his life and he had been singing with the Trinity Church youth choir and playing trombone for years. Music was built into his soul.

Dante's school vacations almost always consisted of going overseas to do shows either with Alan Vega solo or Suicide. And throughout these years of touring overseas, Toots would meet up with them.

From 2008 to 2010, there was great interest in having Suicide perform shows consisting of their classic first album. Highlights of these shows include the 2009 All Tomorrow's Parties festival curated by the Flaming Lips held at the Kutcher's Holiday Camp in the Catskills, and the Sonar Ray Ban festival in 2010 in Barcelona where Alan and Liz hung out and partied with Big Boi and his entourage. There was also a short Suicide tour of Copenhagen, Bologna, and Venice in August 2010.

The Venice show, however, ended up canceled when the promoters failed to get a liquor license for the festival on an island off the coast of the city. The island had formerly housed an insane asylum.

The Suicide touring group ended up spending two days off in Venice before going to Bologna for the next show.

Meanwhile, Toots and Liz had planned to surprise Alan by flying Toots to Venice to meet the Suicide party out on the Island. But Liz wasn't able to reach Toots in time to tell her the show had been canceled.

Toots traveled from Orlando to Venice by herself—at age seventy-nine—and took the ferry to the island. She went to the hotel lobby restroom and changed into a wig, beret, sunglasses, and a Roy Orbison T-shirt with a pack of cigarettes rolled up in the sleeve for her Alan Vega impersonation.

When Liz didn't show up to meet her, Toots went to reception and asked if the "Suicide" party had checked in yet. There was no such reservation and the agent looked at her like she was crazy.

Soon, Liz was able to reach Toots on her mobile and let her know she needed to ferry back to Venice. Dante and Liz met her when she got off the ferry and brought her to the hotel where she completely floored Alan, Marty, Sue Stenger, Paul Smith, and Robert Poss, who didn't recognize her in the Vega ensemble and had no idea she was coming.

***

Alan had long been thought to be ten years younger than his chronological age, having been married for a decade before coming into his own as an artist in his early thirties. Rev was in his early twenties when they met back in the '70s. Everyone assumed they were about the same age.

Liz: *When I met Alan at the age of twenty-seven, I thought he was perhaps in his early to mid-thirties. I had known him for about six months when I learned he was forty-seven. I was blown away. The partners I worked with at the law firm who were in their thirties seemed old compared to Alan. When* Station *came out in 2007, there were several reviews highlighting how intense and brutal Vega's music was despite his age of almost sixty. It was not widely known that he would turn seventy the next year. So, in 2008, as the milestone date approached, Paul Smith had the idea to commemorate the occasion with a party and a limited-edition EP featuring artists covering Vega and Suicide songs.*

The party was held at Alan's local hang, the Blarney Stone on Trinity Place near Battery Park and was attended by many close friends, including Ric, Marty, Howard, Kevin, Jesse, Paul, and Susan, who flew in from the UK and Mika, who came in from Barcelona. It was apropos that the celebration was held at the pub and not a trendy venue.

Kevin Patrick, Duane Sherwood, Liz, Dante, Alan, Mika, Howard Thompson, and Marty Rev, 2008.
Photo by Peggy Melgard

First EP, "Dream Baby Dream," 2008. *Courtesy Saturn Strip, Ltd.*

An outcome from the celebration was an EP Series with a number of songs by artists paying tribute to Alan and Suicide. Among the fourteen artists were Springsteen, Primal Scream, Peaches, Lydia Lunch, Pan Sonic, and the Horrors. The EPs were released on the Blast First (petite) label between 2008 and 2010. The first EP included a live version of "Dream Baby Dream" by Bruce Springsteen from his Devils & Dust tour.

Alan was flattered by the party and the recordings that came out of it.

> I'm knocked out by these new versions; they just keep on coming and coming and [they're] like whole new worlds to me . . . so completely different . . . and some of these new upcoming bands man, they've really got into it. It's really great. It's like a soap opera you know, what's gonna happen in the next episode!*
> —Alan

> Happiness consists in realizing it is all a great strange dream.†
> —Jack Kerouac

---

* Luke Turner, "Klaxons to Release Suicide Cover (It's Ace)," September 10, 2009, https://thequietus.com/articles/02717-klaxons-to-release-suicide-cover-it-s-ace.
† Jack Kerouac, *Lonesome Traveler* (New York: Penguin, 2006).

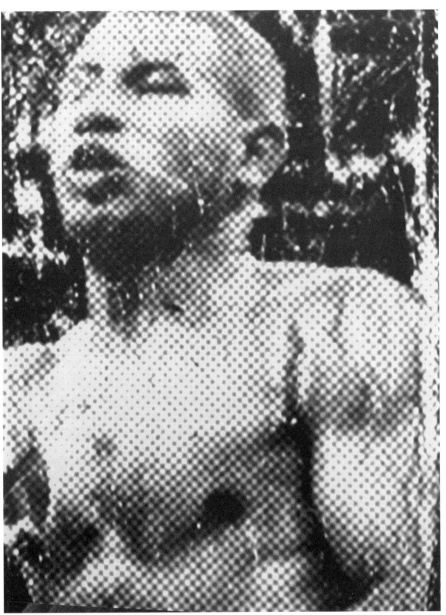

Details of "Untitled" (boxer), 2008; Infinite Mercy Show, 2009. *Courtesy Museé d'art Contemporain de Lyon*

22 Infinite Mercy

1999 . . . 2007 . . . 2010 . . .

We have art in order to not die from the truth.*
—Friedrich Nietzsche

Not long after the birthday celebration in 2008, Paul Smith and art curator Mathieu Copeland reached out to Alan about mounting a major retrospective of his artwork. They planned to show it at the Museum of Contemporary Art (MOCA) in Lyon, France under the auspices of Thierry Raspail, the director of the museum.

Over the course of about a year, Mathieu meticulously tracked down many of the vintage light sculptures that had been sold, including the Marilyn Monroe sculpture from Ric Ocasek and a large cross sculpture belonging to Julian Schnabel.

When Mathieu came to New York to meet with Alan for the first time, he was blown away by his portrait drawings and ninety-four of them ended up in the exhibition. It was the first time these drawings were ever exhibited.

Alan had long been a huge fan of boxing and appreciated the art form and the grave sacrifices made by the athletes who forged this path.

He included Mike Tyson in one of his earliest cross light sculptures well before Mike was a heavyweight world champion and a household name.

Just months prior to Mathieu's visit, Alan started painting small canvases with pictures of boxers torn from *The Ring* magazine. He would select the most disturbing images, where the boxer's face had been damaged during a fight and paste it on the canvas. He then added a base of black paint and distressed the images by scratching them. The final portraits looked like Old Master's paintings.

---

* Friedrich Nietzsche, *The Will to Power*, ed. Walter Kaufman (New York: Vintage, 1968).

As with the portrait drawings, the Lyon retrospective, titled "Infinite Mercy" would be the first time the boxer paintings were shown. They were very special to Alan. As he finished each one, he hung it up with the others on one of the walls in the loft. It became a shrine.

For the "Infinite Mercy" retrospective, there was a long row of boxer paintings on one wall with a black-on-black painting in the center. The painting was in honor of his mentor, Ad Reinhardt. The overall effect created the form of a cross.

On the wall facing the boxers was the largest light piece Alan had ever done—sixty-five feet long and titled *Infinite Mercy*. It was Mathieu's idea to have Alan create a light sculpture on-site at the museum, and plans were made for Alan to arrive ten days prior to the exhibition's opening to execute the piece.

***

Alan had left for Lyon with a handful of photographs he had taken of images off the TV and a small statue of the crucifixion of Jesus. The photos included Nazi soldiers, boxers with bloodied faces, and aliens.

When he arrived, Alan was greeted by Paul Smith, Susan Stenger, Mathieu Copeland, and a crew of about six museum workers. Alan had the photos blown up far larger than life size, including a photo he had taken of the statue of Jesus nailed to the cross. That image was blown up to ten feet high and was the centerpiece of the sculpture.

A large TV was set at the feet of Jesus. Alan, Mathieu, Paul, Susan, and the crew spent a few days foraging for materials to use in the piece. They pulled discarded tarps, wires, and wooden frames from the last exhibition and sourced florescent lights and wires.

Alan then set to work configuring the piece. A large opaque tarp with red paint splattered on it became a bloody body on one end of the piece and the eerie images of soldiers, aliens, and boxers populated the remainder, wrapped in wire and glowing light.

> Blowing up those TV photographs of boxers was beautiful because of what it becomes. It changes reality, and changes everything around you.*
> —Alan

Alan was excited and grateful to have the resources and equipment to execute such a large piece; it was a creative highlight for him.

***

---

* Mathieu Copeland, *Alan Suicide Vega, Infinite Mercy* (Museé d'art Contemporain de Lyon, 2009).

Mathieu Copeland
Curator and Editor, "Alan Vega Infinite Mercy"
at the Museé d'art Contemporain de Lyon, 2009
January 2023

I was such an admirer of Suicide, and Alan's solo albums. Growing up in France, "Jukebox Baby" was a fixture of our sonic landscape! I first met Alan through Susan Stenger. I invited Susan to contribute to "Soundtrack for an Exhibition," a major exhibition that I was curating at the Museum of Contemporary Art in Lyon in 2006. Susan composed, wrote, and recorded an outstanding piece of continuous music that lasted ninety-six days. For this, Susan assembled a stellar ensemble of collaborators that included Robert Poss, Alexander Hacke, F. M. Einheit, Kim Gordon, Mika Vainio, Bruce Gilbert, Ulrich Krieger, Warren Ellis, Jim White, Jennifer Hoyston, Andria Degens (Pantaleimon), Spider Stacy, and Alan.

Susan recorded with Alan and Robert in New York, and we organized a photo shoot for the publicity of the exhibition. During "Soundtrack for an Exhibition," Alan came to Lyon. That was when we all finally met over a memorable dinner. It was then that the desire to curate a major exhibition of Alan's art became clear to myself and to Thierry Raspail, the director of the MAC Lyon and an avid Alan fan.

From then on, I had the joy and privilege of working closely with Alan, especially in curating his first retrospective at the Musée d'Art Contemporain in Lyon in 2009, and editing the first comprehensive monograph of his work, bridging his entire body of work—from the light sculptures through to his drawings and paintings.

I was immediately struck by the power of Alan's art. His light sculptures were—and remain—revolutionary. His drawings present us with humanity within its most challenging truth. When he was a student of Ad Reinhardt at Brooklyn College, Alan's artistic journey began with the death of painting. Reinhardt's black paintings are often referred to as the end of painting. Alan was also a student of Kurt Seligmann, the Swiss surrealist painter, who came to New York at the onset of World War II.

Alan Vega's art grew from the ashes of art and the inner sanctum of the unconscious.

It is impossible for me to look at Alan's drawings without immediately calling up Antonin Artaud's own drawings and his philosophy of the Theatre of Cruelty. Both Artaud's and Vega's art and writing offer an eternal journey into the human mind, with all its glorious beauty and tragic darkness. And yet, Alan's art is very much of our time—an art of the now and the necessary—with consideration of the ecological urgency and need for sustainability.

A striking characteristic of Alan Vega's art is its use of recycling. Alan went into the streets to gather the raw materials for his works and presented them in the gallery. For a solo show at OK Harris gallery in New York in 1975 he used trashed TVs and junk and turned them into artworks for the exhibition. When the show was over, he returned them to their primary reality—back on the streets. Somehow the same can be said about Suicide's music—it recycles the city streets' pure energy. In Alan's own words: "from dust to dust, from creation to death, the whole cycle."

Alan Vega embodies the ultimate artist who achieved what only a few ever did—as a musician he revolutionized music, and as a sculptor he produced uncompromising and radical art that resonates to this day. Alan is the incarnation of an "artist's artist"—one who constantly affects all those who experience their art.

Art-Rite, the journal founded in 1973 by Edit DeAk, Mike Robinson, and Joshua Cohn, covered Alan's work under the headline "Alan Suicide: Prophet of the Little Guys' Apocalypse." In 1977, *Art-Rite* invited Alan to curate issue #13. This issue was to encapsulate all that created Alan's personal universe, from horse racing (Alan's passion) through to Elvis and Iggy and a critical vision of the Americana. Yet it is also striking to find in these pages a celebration of life, of popular culture (the Ghost Rider), sex, and crucifixion, as we can see in Joseph Catuccio's painting. Mortality plays an important part in the making of this piece, as seen in the double-spread of a picture taken inside a morgue by Donald Greenhaus.

When I came to prepare the catalog, my desire was to reproduce in its entirety the issue of *Art-Rite* that had become a rare and collectible item. As an echo to this striking piece from 1977, I invited Alan to realize "Let U$ Pray," a sixteen-page booklet that concluded the publication. This piece revealed once more Alan's up-front and uncompromising reading of our contemporary world. The manner in which Alan approached the making of this second journal was outstanding. He recycled his obsessions and made use of second-hand imagery—graphic news clips, NYPD, sci-fi movies, World War II, religious iconography, consumerism, boxing, daytime TV, porn—time paired with his own drawings and handwritings. It created a narrative of both the second half of the twentieth century and the artist's very own inner cosmology.

Working with Alan on the retrospective was a lesson in radicality. It was a curatorial experimentation, and an array into twentieth- and twenty-first-century art of the avant-garde, from surrealism through to minimal art, protest art, and of course, punk. Alan brought all this into his work, and in the making of the exhibition. As we prepared for the retrospective and later the catalog, Alan would sit down with me for hours at his home looking at his archive and his art and answering my endless questions. I was so thankful to him for indulging me in all the series of conversations that I needed to conduct for the book, including the memorable three-way conversation with Edit DeAk—and not having seen Edit for years.

His generosity was boundless, and I am forever grateful to him for trusting me and allowing me to work the exhibition. Very much inspired by his art and his concern to constantly recycle to make his pieces, I decided to recycle all the materials from the museum's previous exhibition for Alan's exhibition. The fragmented temporary walls became sculpture plinths, the metal structures became the site for the wall sculptures, a small room became the storage for the crates, and large recycled protection glass sheets became a temporary display for Alan's extensive selection of drawings.

I would say that these experiences did not change my conception of him, but rather confirmed and enhanced it. Alan was bigger than the sum of its parts: musician, singer, punk icon, rock star, painter, draughtsman, sculptor, filmmaker, writer, man, father, husband, friend, idol, fan—he simply was a true revolutionary artist.

Of all the memories that I have with Alan, if I am to choose one today, it would be the poignant experience of watching him draw. For the exhibition *A Mental Mandala*, which I curated at the Museum of Contemporary Art (MUAC) in Mexico City in 2013, I invited Alan to realize a series of drawings, and record him in a studio in New York, while reading a selection of Antonin Artaud poems. Together with artist Philippe Decrauzat, we made a 16mm film of Alan creating those drawings, closely following his hand. To experience Alan's mastery with the pen on the paper remains to this day a lesson in making art. His assurance with the pen and his precision was mesmerizing as he gradually revealed a standing figure and the striking presence of a human face that is uncannily similar to both that of Vega and Artaud.

I would like to recall stories today that reflect Alan's true dedication to his art. The first is a story that reminds me of Gustav Metzger. Both Vega and Metzger lived their lives by their words. Radicality prevailed and this was uncompromising. Both lived in extreme hardship at times for their art and beliefs. Both moved around extensively. How can you safely keep anything living such a life? During one of our working sessions at his apartment, Alan showed me one of the few memories he had kept from his time as a student at Brooklyn College in the '50s. Alan had been close to his teacher, Kurt Seligmann, who invited him to his farm in Orange County, New York. During our conversation, Alan shared strong memories of Seligmann, who retired from Brooklyn College in 1958, and died of an accidental self-inflicted gunshot in 1962. It was then that Alan showed me a framed print by Seligmann that the artist had given him. I kept wondering, of the few objects that one would keep while living such a tumultuous life as Alan had, and to choose to keep this print for so long—it was truly telling of Alan's commitment to art.

Another story has to do with how Alan created some of his early light sculptures. To realize his anti-form and anti-aesthetic loose wire sculptures, Alan went down into the NYC subway to steal as many light bulbs as he could. For me, this story encapsulates the artist's ultimate desire to make art—nothing shall get in one's way to realize one's work—may this be hardship, lack of means or access to material—art is all that must prevail!

Alan came up with the title for the retrospective—*Infinite Mercy*. When I asked him how he would like to title the exhibition, his answer seemed obvious to me. It was, after all, the only—and unfortunately, ended up being the

Museé d'art Contemporain de Lyon Catalogue, 2009. Author's Collection

only—retrospective exhibition dedicated to his art in a major museum in his lifetime. This title seemed to me to be both a sign of acknowledgment of an artist grateful for the show, and very satirical, in that it was indeed *long* overdue. I absolutely loved when I learned that it had nothing to do with that. It was a line he immediately liked and jotted down from a science fiction movie he saw the night before. It was so perfect that once more, Alan would appropriate something from the popular culture he lived in and recycled—as a title for his own retrospective exhibition. ∎

***

A work of art which isn't based on feeling isn't art at all.
—Paul Cézanne

***

Photo by Liz Lamere

23 Aftershock

2012 . . . 2014 . . .

I have nothing to offer anyone except my own confusion.*
—Jack Kerouac

Time has a way of breaking down the body no matter how sharp the spirit. It was 2012, and Alan was walking home from the Blarney Stone one evening after his nightly vodka rendezvous and as he crossed by the Bull, north of Battery Park, he was attacked.

Across the street one of three young men had called out to him. Alan raised his fist in a show of solidarity and responded, "Power to the people!" He walked toward the building they were leaning against.

Suddenly, one of them rushed up to Alan, grabbed him by the shoulders and slammed him into the side of the building, cracking open the back of his skull. He then threw Alan into the street where his face hit the pavement, resulting in a gash above his right eye.

He turned Alan over and took his wallet and his watch. When he got closer to Alan, he looked at him.

"Shit, it's an old dude!" he screamed.

The three of them then bolted. Given Alan's appearance with the motorcycle jacket, beret, sunglasses, and black hair he was easily mistaken for significantly younger.

He was seventy-three and his advanced age made this attack an automatic felony assault.

---

* Jack Kerouac, *On the Road: The Original Scroll* (New York: Penguin Classics, 2008, originally pub. 1957).

Liz: I was asleep at home when I got the call from our doorman at 1:00 a.m. telling me Alan was on the steps out front, that he'd been assaulted, and an ambulance was on the way. The EMTs saw the blood gushing from his forehead; then I noticed blood pouring down the back of his neck. It was amazing that after such a brutal attack he was able to get up and walk about four blocks home.

At the NYU Downtown Hospital, Alan received twelve stitches above his eyebrow, which was minor compared to the twenty-five staples it took to close the back of his skull. After a CT scan he was to be kept for forty-eight hours' observation, but Alan insisted on being released the next day—against medical advice. Alan hated hospitals and was anxious to get home.

The police detectives interviewed him extensively both in the hospital and then during two follow-up visits to our home. The detectives seemed fascinated by Alan and did a fair amount of follow-up. They brought a book of suspect photos for him to review. He described the men as white and approximately in their forties and they acted as if they were hopped up on drugs. In time, they came up with some leads but were never able to find the men involved.

Alan put the incident behind him and didn't tell many people what had happened. He alludes to that night in the song "Prophesy" on the album *IT*.

I get knocked down,
but I get up
I will survive
I will go on and on
so fuck you killers
this is my prophesy*

***

Not much later, Laurent Godin from the Godin Gallery in Paris reached out to Alan to mount a one-man show of his art at the gallery for the fall of 2012. Despite the timing and still in recovery mode, Alan didn't hesitate to agree.

Paris had long held a special place in Alan's heart. Not only had the enormous attention "Jukebox Babe" received in France been inspiring but after Alan's solo tours in the early '80s, he spent extra time in Paris, including a month living at the family-run Hotel Champagne.

The matriarch of the hotel would have afternoon tea with Alan and speak with him only in French. He always had a strong ear and he picked up enough conversational vocabulary to be accepted by the locals. For the next several decades, Paris would always honor and support Alan as an artist.

---

* "Prophesy," *IT*, words and music by Alan Vega.

Thus, when the opportunity was presented to go to Paris in support of this important art exhibition, even with his uncertain health, Alan accepted. Then, in addition to the Godin Gallery show, Laurent secured a booth at the FIAC (Foire Internationale d'Art Contemporain) international art fair. The organizers told Laurent if the Godin booth was exclusively works of Alan Vega, they would give him a prime location.

On October 17, 2012, when Alan, Liz, Dante, and Liz's niece, Kelsey, arrived in Paris on the VIP day at FIAC, the Alan Vega booth was the first booth by the VIP entrance.

FIAC, Alan's booth, 2012. *Courtesy Galerie Laurent Godin*

Alan sat for hours in a comfortable chair in that booth and proceeded to talk with numerous collectors. As a result, Godin was able to place many of the sculptures, drawings, and boxer paintings in significant collections.

Alan and Liz also decided to do a concert with Marc Hurtado at La Locomotive and Laurent arranged a party at David Lynch's private club, Silencio. During the event at Silencio, the 16mm film shot by Mel Auston documenting his and Alan's 1973 road trip to Gallery Marc was shown.

It was an ambitious schedule even for a young healthy person.

***

Laurent Godin
Godin Gallery, Paris
March 2023
Dream baby dream.

I was a little too young, a little too provincial when in 1979 Martin Rev and Alan Vega's record "Dream Baby Dream" came out. At the time, I was crazy about the Sex Pistols and Mötorhead, but Suicide. . . .

I had to wait until 1981 when, like out of space, "Jukebox Babe" started to be played everywhere in France. The guy was strange, the voice deep and fragile at the same time. From then on, that song and so many others from Alan and Suicide entered my personal Rock 'n' Roll Hall of Fame!

It was several years later, in 2009 at the occasion of the large survey of Alan's work at the Museum of Contemporary Art of Lyon organized by Thierry Raspail (director) and Matthieu Copeland (curator) that I realized Alan was not only this genius singer and writer but also an amazing and unique visual artist. The show was a shock!

A few weeks later, in the strange neighborhood of Wall Street in NYC, I entered a building lobby and asked the doorman for the floor of Alan Vega's apartment. He called Alan upstairs with a big smile!

From there, I met Alan, Liz, his wife and "sparring partner," and Dante, their son. I was so impressed, and at the same time I felt like I was entering into a family. Alan was the kindest and most delicate man I met. I always thought he was like crystal—very strong and extremely fragile.

We start showing his work as an incredible solo at FIAC in Paris, at the Armory in New York, and a couple of shows at the gallery in Paris. He was a unique artist, absolutely global, he was a pioneer and all his practice reflected ambivalence between violence and refinement.

We really miss him. Once Liz said to me: "That's funny, usually Alan always says, 'No, not interested.'"

Suicide, no compromise! ∎

***

In early 2012, Artists Space, a nonprofit art organization founded in 1972 in SoHo, contacted Alan and Liz to let them know Alan had been chosen Artist of the Year for 2012. Their annual award dinner, held in April, honors artists who have had a significant positive impact on the art community.

Alan was surprised to be chosen—at that point he didn't feel visible to the art world.

"Did I die and not realize it?"

"Isn't this the type of thing that happens once you're gone?"

It made him a bit nervous to be spotlighted like this. However, the event was very beautiful, and he felt humbled to be honored.

There were several long banquet tables with a formal dinner and a lovely performance by Emily Sundblad and a laudation by Diego Cortez. Several other people, including Jeffrey Deitch and Kim Gordon, also addressed the assembled guests and spoke about Alan's art and its historic impact on them and the art world.

Alan said it felt like a "this is your life" moment as many near and dear to him were gathered to celebrate him—Ric, Paulina, and their son Oliver, Martin Rev, Jesse Malin, Perkin, Howard T., Kevin Patrick, Michael Alago, Jeffrey Deitch, Laurent Godin, Mathieu Copeland, Brain McPeck and Bob Gruen, as well as friends and family.

Alan was stressed and uncomfortable leading up to the event as he didn't welcome this type of attention, but he was very gracious to the organizers and those who came out to celebrate him.

Marty, Ric, and Alan, Artists Space Award Dinner, 2012. © *Bob Gruen/www.bobgruen.com*

Near the end of the evening, however, he started having stomach problems. Alan was rarely sick with cold, flu, or other ailments, so it was unusual when he had to leave early but he was feeling awful.

During the next week, he also had to leave 6/8 Studios early as he continued feeling sick to his stomach.

A number of days later, on May 16, 2012, Alan woke up at about 4:00 a.m. He had fallen asleep on the couch downstairs, which he often did after hours of writing and drawing. But when he tried to sit upright, he kept falling over. Dante heard him cry out for help. It looked like Alan was in serious trouble. Liz immediately called 911 and told the dispatcher she suspected he was having a stroke. It turned out to be both a stroke and a heart attack.

The doctors at Weill Cornell hospital diagnosed him with congestive heart failure. He had substantial plaque in every artery, including both of his carotid arteries, which were over 90 percent blocked. He ended up staying in the hospital for over three weeks.

In addition to Liz's daily visits, he had regular visits from Kevin, Howard, Michael, and his niece, Amie.

Dante visited a few times, but it was hard.

He was nearing his fourteenth birthday and until this time, he and Alan were together whenever Dante was at home.

He stayed busy with school, choir, sports, and the family of one of his best friends who lived upstairs. They made sure he was never alone. The trauma of almost losing his dad was breaking his spirit.

Liz: And was nearly breaking me. But I had to stay strong.

At times, Alan was a very uncooperative and agitated patient. After a procedure to scope his arteries, the specialist, Dr. Wong, met me in the hall shaking his head. My immediate thought was that we had lost him. I almost fainted on the spot.

But Dr. Wong just said:

"He's a very difficult patient. I had to tell him if he didn't stop moving, he would die on my table."

Then the doctor showed me the films—they were dismal. The team was not optimistic, but Dr. Wong was the stent guru and he felt that he had a good shot at snaking a stent into the main artery.

I was informed that there was a risk of nicking the artery during the procedure, which would eliminate his only chance for a stent and possibly kill him. But the alternative—not taking that risk—meant that Alan was unlikely to survive more than a few months.

Dr. Wong was confident.

We rolled the dice.

Thankfully, the procedure went well.

Alan was always stressed around doctors. He took the approach that he just didn't want to know. The white coat stress led to a condition in the hospital setting which caused hallucinations.

Alan was convinced that there was an underground poker game going on in his hospital wing. But they had to move it to different rooms to avoid his detection. When I arrived in the mornings, he recounted in detail the comings and goings of the players. There was a combination of regular high rollers and some hospital staff doubled as security for the players.

And for about six hours one night, he was also convinced I was Catherine Deneuve, which I took as a great compliment.

Given the extreme degree of congestive heart failure, Alan's cardiology team was surprised by Alan's energy and vitality. One doctor remarked that he had a very strong life force. They were shocked that Alan didn't exhibit any signs of congestive heart failure since his heart was pumping at about 10 percent of the norm.

Over the previous few years, Alan became more slow moving. It was attributed to the bad arthritis in his knees, which seemed to be his only health issue beyond the high blood pressure, which was being managed by medication.

By age sixty, when Dante was born, Alan had limited his smoking to two to three cigarettes at night in the studio or the pub. He always said he enjoyed it too much to quit entirely and was willing to make the health trade-off. Yet, the stroke/heart attack was a severe wake-up call. He never smoked again after May 16, 2012.

***

When Alan returned home from the hospital, he resumed most of his work.

His cardiologist told him no drinking, and he had to take nine pills daily for the rest of his life. It would be a couple of years before he got the green light to resume drinking, and then only an occasional glass of wine, unless he was performing.

But something had shifted. It started after Alan's seventieth birthday celebration when he realized: "Holy shit, I'm seventy, not sixty." He had lost his mom when she was only fifty-eight and his brother at age fifty-nine. He felt physically vulnerable. Time started to haunt him.

Over the next few years, he wrote and made drawings like a madman on a mission.

***

In 2009, Alan had met filmmaker Marie Losier at the Lincoln Center screening of the film *Sombre*. They had an illuminating, exciting discussion about Marie's fascinations with Suicide and Alan's work. Alan invited her to come by the loft and continue their colorful talk.

Alan and Marie Losier, 2013. *Photo by Liz Lamere*

Marie ended up connecting with Alan, Liz, and Dante and filming them for one of her short documentaries. Marie had been making short film documentaries since the early 2000s of avant-garde directors, artists, and musicians. She spent close to two years following Alan and his family—some time before his stroke but mostly after his stroke.

The result was a sixteen-minute film titled *Just a Million Dreams* where Alan:

> [E]njoys the friendship of filmmaker Losier, while also loving, fighting and living with his family (Liz Lamere, his wife and collaborator, and their son Dante, young replica of Alan)*

***

---

* See https://letterboxd.com/film/alan-vega-just-a-million-dreams/.

Marie Losier
Filmmaker
2023

The first time I saw Alan from up-close was at the Knitting Factory in downtown Manhattan, for a Suicide concert. I was lucky to be close to the stage. He and Martin Rev were so alive—Alan talking, screaming, and touching his body while singing, groaning, and making the greatest faces, so scary and so tender: A real punk, a free spirit, so alive and so beautiful. It was the best concert I have ever felt and seen and that I keep as a treasure in my memory.

Strange enough, that night I met Genesis P-Orridge, who was reciting poems onstage after Alan's concert. I had no idea who she was yet but she took me on tour a week later and I spent the next seven years making what became my first feature film, *The Ballad of Genesis and Lady Jaye*. It was also extraordinary that I had no idea then that years later I would meet and become friends with Mr. Alan Vega—for the circle to be completed.

In 2009, I was at the cinema at Lincoln Center and the film screened was a movie for which Alan had made the music—*Sombre*—and, to my surprise, Alan and his sweet family—his wife Liz and his son Dante, appeared at the end of the screening. The audience in the cinema had a warm talk with them. That night—I have no idea why exactly—but after our conversation, Alan said to me, "come visit, call and come."

This is how I ended up at the door of the Alan in Wonderland! When he opened the door, his hat and hair were hiding half of his face. A giant smile was there facing me, "Come in baby!"

We spent a couple of hours talking and laughing a lot. He showed me the drawings and paintings he was working on. I loved seeing his artwork. It was the part of his life I had never seen or known much about. It was really wonderful to see his work so close and understand how and where he was creating. I knew about his music but not much about his art, yet it was the main focus of his every day at home. His art was very much like art brut—direct, collaged, clumsy, and mysterious. I loved how direct and pure the gesture of creating was coming to us.

Often, when Liz and Dante would come back from school and work, they would all three work together on some music, with Alan saying "No rehearsal, I don't want to do it! Fuck this!" Dante was doing all the tech and recording with Liz playing the keyboards. Alan was so direct and abrupt, no bullshit. I loved that part of him, and it really gave me comfort in the belief of "Just do it" and "Fuck them!" My favorite!

If he didn't want to do something, he would not do it. Free style, free spirit. He had his way, his rhythm, his rituals. No bullshit. Not interested in selling himself. He really was, for me, part of the best of the underground!

What he loved doing most was watching and listening to Dante's trombone lessons in the living room. It was always very touching to watch them silently. It was so natural to spend time with him on a regular basis. I could not help asking them if it was possible to bring my Bolex and film some part of their life for a film portrait of Alan. Having a camera and filming is my way of communicating and playing together. Alan really played with me and the film. It was always a creative time. His loving family, Liz and Dante, were so similar in spirit and heart and part of the game! I remember being part of the family for two years with deep care, heart, and much laughter, all together.

My first impression of his music was pure joy and electricity! I jumped a million times in the air in love when I heard "Jukebox Baby" and still do this to this day . . . so when you hear and see Alan sing it live, it is heaven on earth! He had the beat and screams that really changed people's ears and music for all the generations after him.

His melodies are so tender and loving while also breaking the air with no concession. He was such a free spirit and so pure in his music and being. The expression, "he is a punk" is really made for Alan, a real New York Punk—in spirit and soul! DIY and free, not caring what others think and might think—stubborn to the core, illuminated, surrealist, always ready for a laugh, and with a beautiful body language of his own. There was an enchanted dance traveling through his body. He made no compromises and lived life with his passion and with much love toward his family.

When he showed me his drawings, there were portraits of people he would meet and remember and then draw from the feelings that they left in him. But strangely, many of them looked like a portrait of himself, over and over, and this was very touching to me. The lines were like his music, intense, raw, nervous, and often the characters were alone on the page, electric and in solitude. It was dark, lonely, and somehow a part of himself that he kept deeply inside.

His impact on me: for once, I was the cool kid on the block. He really laughed with me, enjoyed so much to play and share creative time together. His health was fragile after his stroke, yet he was so solid, a real clown, and happy to scream and say what came to him when he wished. He was dedicated to his art and his family. I had filmed many intense artists, but none had a family that I filmed, and it gave me real tenderness for this electric bomb of Alan!!!

Life and art were one for him and that is precious to me today and every day.

I wanted to shoot a scene in the cleaning room in the building where they lived—an old-style NYC laundry room with washing machines and dryers and a great feel to it. I asked Alan if we could film there and as I turned around to prepare my camera, he had already gone there with his family and a chair, and he

© *Marie Losier, NYC, Courtesy Saturn Strip, Ltd.*

was reading aloud a book on Suicide for me to film. He knew what was good to film and record and he had a sense of rhythm and situation that was perfect for the film.

Once, I filmed him in stop motion down his hallway with him sitting on his large comfy chair and the chair seemed to move forward down the hall alone, by magic like a magic carpet. Of course, a friend of mine was behind the chair hiding and pushing the chair one step at a time for me to film, image by image, and that took a long time. Alan had a blast playing that game down the hallway with Joana pushing him slowly while people were coming in and out of the elevator looking at us like crazies. He loved it and this feeling traveled with us through every experience of the film.

Once in Paris, when Alan did a show with Dante and Liz, they were all in the flat that was rented for their stay, but the door would not lock, plus the elevator stopped working. It was so hilarious, as we had to carry Alan like a prince in our arms down the five floors of the building to go to a car for his concert! Alan was laughing so much at the situation while the family had to carry this beautiful clown down the steps without falling while thirty minutes later Alan was the king onstage, furiously singing with his cane, side by side with Liz and Dante. ∎

***

Over the next few years, Alan was not going into the recording studio very much when Jared Artaud from the Vacant Lots reached out to Liz. His band had done a cover version of "No More Christmas Blues." Liz played it for Alan, and he immediately wanted to meet them. They invited the band over for brunch and Alan struck up an instant connection, especially with Jared, who upon moving to Brooklyn, started visiting Alan on a regular basis. The two would spend hours talking and talking and talking.

***

Jared Artaud
Musician, Producer
The Vacant Lots
September 2021, April 2023
The First Time I Met Alan

The Vacant Lots were invited to be part of a Christmas compilation album back in 2013, which included Iggy Pop, Psychic Ills, and others. When searching for a song to cover Brian (MacFadyen of the Vacant Lots) and I discovered Ze Records' *A Christmas Record* from 1981 that had the most beautifully depressing "No More Christmas Blues" on it by Alan Vega. When the record came out, I sent the MP3 to Liz along with a message expressing how much we admired Alan, that Suicide is like the Beatles to us, and I really hope Alan doesn't think we butchered his track.

Later that night, she wrote back saying how much she and Alan loved the version we did and that Alan wanted to meet us.

Not too long after that we were on tour with Dean Wareham in the USA and went over to meet Alan at his downtown Manhattan studio/apartment before soundcheck at the Bowery Ballroom.

I remember being in the elevator thinking Alan was going to come to the door with a fucking axe or chainsaw. Instead, he greeted us like we were family, and I felt this instant connection with him.

We really hit it off and over the next two years I frequently took the one subway stop from my apartment in Brooklyn Heights over to his place. That led to a couple of years of a very intense and deep connection—he was more than a mentor to me.

I remember saying, "Hey Alan, what are you doing right now? Can I come over?" And twenty minutes later after crossing the East River where Albert Ayler died, I would be at fucking Alan Vega's apartment. It was surreal.

One of my favorite memories was sitting on the couch in his living room and asking Alan what he had been working on. He said, "hold on," and went into the other room, grabbed a fat stack of writings and drawings and dropped them on my lap. "Here," he said. "Look at this shit." I was honored and in shock to be that up close to his process and work, seeing firsthand the electricity and intensity in his writings and drawings. Moments like that would happen a lot with Alan and they were a game changer for me. It's hard to explain, but the first time I met him I felt like I'd known him forever.

Iggy Pop's Influence

We immediately bonded over discovering Iggy Pop and how that led to changing directions in life—Alan as a visual artist turned performer/musician and for me from playing basketball in high school then switching over to music. I know Alan liked the Stooges, but I think it was more than Iggy's music that did it for Alan. I think the fearless stage presence and no-fucks-given attitude that Iggy embodied, like Elvis too, inspired Alan in finding his own original style as a performer.

The Vacant Lots "Suicide Note"—Possibly the Last Recording Session and Collaboration with Alan Vega

The Vacant Lots opened for Suicide at Webster Hall in NYC at the second-to-last show they ever played. I remember seeing Alan onstage and thinking he never lost his edge with age. Shortly after that I went over to Alan's and he gave me some wisdom. He looked at me, paused and said: "Never quit."

"Never quit what, Alan?" I asked.

"Music," he said. "It took people thirty years to come around to Suicide. You should never quit."

Right before he died, we were making plans to go in the studio with Alan to record "Suicide Note" for the Vacant Lots' second album. We were two weeks away from going into the studio when he ended up in the hospital. That would have probably been the last recording session he ever did. When he died, as an homage to him, we went back into the Vega Vault and found a Vega vocal track that worked with the instrumental we had. This is what started Liz and me collaborating on working on Alan's music together. We both felt like we were channeling Alan. It's very hard to explain this feeling but it's closer to a kind of spiritual intuition and instinct that really inspires this process.

Thoughts on Alan's Process, Art, Vision

Alan was an architect of sound and visionary genius. He was a master of minimalism and innovation, not just in music but art and fashion too.

He relentlessly challenged himself to always break new ground, in whatever medium he explored.

His work was driven by an uncompromising perspective.

He was such a proponent of the underdog and wanting to change people's lives. Like no other, Alan lived and breathed art.

Alan remixing "6 AM" by The Vacant Lots, 2014. *Photo by Liz Lamere*

I realized Alan didn't record demos. Life was his rehearsal, and the studio was the recording zone where he could experiment continually in order to create original sounds. He was more like a sculptor in sound than a traditional musician.

If you handed Alan a synth, he would give you a new sound.

I think coming into music as an autodidact freed him up a lot and was a major factor in the originality of his sound and the work he produced.

And Suicide—they were one of the most innovative bands of all time because it wasn't just the fact they had laid the groundwork for punk and the subsequent genres that came out of that but they were one of the first to merge rock 'n' roll and disco. Punk rebelled against disco, and they were like, fuck that and did both.

The Last Time I Saw Alan and Continuing His Legacy

When I went over the last time to see Alan—it was a few weeks before he went into the hospital—I went over there with a portable speaker and an iPod so he could listen to the track and work on lyric ideas before we went into the studio. We ended up listening to the new Vacant Lots album a few times as well as Pharaoh Sanders, Cecil Taylor, Albert Ayler, and Coltrane.

So, my last interaction with him was just listening to the finished mixes of our second album.

He said to me, "I'm not going to be here much longer. . . . I'm ending, you're beginning, I'm passing down the torch to you."

Hours later, he walked me out to the street. It was there, before I left to go to the subway, where we made a pact—something I will never forget and that has stayed with me forever. It's something that I live up to this day in carrying his legacy forward.

As I walked away from Alan down the street—far enough away where I felt like he couldn't see me distinctly—I turned around and he was still there, watching me.

That's when I got the feeling that that may be the last time I would see Alan. I fucking lost it, and I got on the subway home.

Alan died in 2016. I was one of the first few people to get the call from Liz that night.

I remember sitting on the floor of the hotel bathroom I was in for a few hours in total silence.

In his absence, Liz and I have been on a mission, dedicating endless time and energy over the years since his death to keep Alan's legacy alive.

From releasing his posthumous final album *IT* and most recently the lost album, *Mutator*, we continue to coproduce and mix material from the Vega Vault together. Alan left behind an immensity of work, songs, art, notebooks, drawings, music finished and unfinished, which we now call the "Vega Vault."

Original ADAT tapes of *Mutator*, 2019. *Photo by Jared Artaud*

From the Vega Vault. *Photo by Jared Artaud*

Alan and Jared, 2014. *Photo courtesy of Hillary Archer*

I've gotten to collaborate on art direction and produce and mix Alan's and Suicide's music with an amazing crew, primarily, Michael Handis, Ted Young, and Josh Bonati.

Most recently we designed Suicide's *Surrender* and *A Way of Life: Rarities* albums.

Liz and I are currently working on another album of Alan's lost recordings called *Insurrection*, which will be the follow-up to *Mutator*. We also have a live album in the pipeline, among other releases. I'm grateful I got to spend time just hanging out and talking for hours in Alan's zone with him. It's an incredible honor to now be part of continuing his legacy. I learned a lot from being around Alan, not just in music but in life too.

In these fucked-up times, his music and art are needed more than ever. ∎

***

Everything I've done has always been associated with
death, because that's all there is, death. It really gets
to me, because sooner or later we all die.*
—Alan

***

Death left its old tragic heaven and became the lyrical
core of man: his invisible truth, his visible secret.†
—Michel Foucault

---

* Alexandre Breton, *Alan Vega: Conversation with an Indian* (Le Texte Vivant, 2017), Kindle.
† Michel Foucault, *The Birth of the Clinic: An Archaeology of Medical Perception* (New York: Vintage, 1994).

24 Sincere

2015 . . .

Do not fear death so much but rather the inadequate life.*
—Bertolt Brecht

By 2015, Alan was finding it more difficult to get around. For decades, his main source of exercise was walking—nightly excursions around the downtown streets. But those outings had slowed way down. Now, even short walks in the neighborhood were fraught with potential injury.

But he still enjoyed his daily jaunts—buying lottery tickets, replenishing his medication, and stopping into local delis and restaurants for his favorite foods.

Having lived on Hanover Square for decades with his distinctive look, Alan was a recognizable local figure. Neighbors set their clock by his daily routine. Everyone he encountered along the way—from the staff at his co-op building to the local vendors and store owners—treated him like family. Alan regarded everyone with the same care and concern regardless of their so-called station in life. He often went home loaded up with extra goodies that all his buddies had given to him.

***

When Alan and Liz first met in the late '80s, they regularly went to the Limelight nightclub on Friday and Saturday nights. Kuch and his girlfriend, Debbie, would pick them up at the Gramercy about midnight and they'd hang out in the library/ VIP room there until after 2:00 a.m.—sometimes until after 4:00 a.m., and when they emerged, the sun was rising.

---

* Bertolt Brecht, *Jewish Wife and Other Short Plays: Includes: In Search of Justice; Informer; Elephant Calf; Measures Taken; Exception and the Rule; Salzburg Dance of Death*, trans. Eric Bentley (New York: Grove Press, 1994).

"Vision," 2016, from the collection of Michael Handis. *Courtesy Galerie Laurent Godin*

They never paid for admission or drinks, thanks to Claire O'Connor, who was in charge of PR for the club and ever-present in the chapel library, where she spent many a night trading jokes with Alan. Claire was a razor-sharp force of nature and Alan thought the world of her. She later served on the board of directors of HOWL Arts Collective. Alan was saddened to learn of her passing in 2011.

> She booked bands, threw parties, held events and created concepts. She did it until the Limelight was a place to "see and be seen," and a virtual "celebrity magnet."*

Many bands passing through NYC to play gigs were either pulled in by Claire or knew that if they swung by the Limelight they were bound to meet up with Alan. On some of the more memorable nights at the chapel in the Limelight, Alan and Liz hung out with Billy Idol and Steve Stephens, Bobby Belenchia, Joey and Johnny Ramone, New York Jets defensive end Mark Gastineaux, the actors William Hurt and Marlee Matlin, John Lee Hooker, with whom Alan had a great long talk about his favorite blues song "Tupelo Blues," BB King, Robin Zander from Cheap Trick and Kevin Rowland from Dexys Midnight Runners. Lemmy from Motorhead visited Alan at the Gramercy as well as Johnny Thunders—who shot up heroin in the bathroom, which pissed Alan off especially since Liz was there and he didn't want her exposed to a potential heroin overdose situation.

By the '90s, Liz stopped joining those late-night excursions. Alan and Kuch continued and hung out at the second-floor bar talking and meeting up with photographer Bob Gruen and various musicians. Jesse Malin joined them on some of those nights.

***

Jesse Malin
Musician, Club Owner
April 2023
As a kid growing up in Queens, getting into punk rock at an early age, I started to come into the city and I'd see bands like the Ramones and the Dead Boys and groups that had guitars and drums and were really aggressive. This would be around 1980. I started to play at Max's when I was around twelve and thirteen. Our older brothers turned us on to the three basic groups of punk—in my mind—the Sex Pistols, the Clash, and the Ramones. And then you go deeper—the Heartbreakers with Johnny Thunders—and eventually it led me back to Iggy Pop and the Dolls.

At that point, in 1980, a lot of the punk bands were trying to have hits and go funk and disco and power pop. And so, I got into more aggressive music—hardcore. I spent time in the city at a studio where I rehearsed on Avenue B. And these older

---

* See https://www.howlarts.org/archived/in-memory-of-claire-oconnor/.

guys in this group—the False Prophets—shared the studio with us. They were about five, six years older and they were very aggressive.

People would talk about Suicide, and I saw this guy in the New York Rocker with Johnny Thunders—Alan Vega and his cool jackets and headbands and hair.

I checked out Suicide. The name was so intense and great. As I listened, I couldn't understand where the drums were, where's the guitars? It kind of scared me. I was like—I don't know what this is. I didn't know how to digest it. It didn't seem like the kind of sound that punk was to me. My mind wasn't open enough yet.

A few years later, around the mid-1980s, after hardcore seemed to really burst into the whole country and became a phenomenon, it started to come to me—we're too metal and too macho. So, I dropped out of that and I formed another band called Hope. And we were playing one night at the Cat Club, and Marty Thau comes backstage and says, "I wanna work with you."

Next thing you know, he offers us a big gig. He says, "You guys are young, you'll open up for Suicide at CBGBs." And you know, we were this five-piece guitar, rock and roll band. And we get on this bill—it's August, and it's hot as hell. And CB's is sold out. Marty Thau comes in with his little briefcase and he starts to mix Suicide.

And it's the loudest thing I've seen at CBGBs. The place was shaking. And there's Alan dressed kind of like Elvis. It is so loud and so hot, and Alan's sweating like crazy. And he's just shouting and screaming. It was so aggressive, the way it was mixed and it started to kind of get to me, but I was still a little scared. And then after the set, Alan came right back into our dressing room—still so hot, you couldn't breathe—there was no air in the place.

And he was so friendly to us, but he was very quiet. Suicide still seemed like something I couldn't really get my head around.

A few years later, I'm at the Limelight and I see this Sunday night show with Ric Ocasek on guitar and Suicide with Alan pacing—and they do "Cheree" and "Dream Baby Dream," and some new songs. And the way Martin Rev is standing and the way he turns and spins around, and it finally hit me. I got it. I got the minimalism, the connection to fifties rock and roll. It was from another planet and light years ahead. And it had this aggressive primal grunting like the Stooges and Iggy—I just noticed, wow, this works on a caveman level and it works on a completely advanced, intellectual, art level where they're in this other realm of pushing the boundaries. And the way Alan paced around—he was free-forming it. It had this tension that Black Flag had and bands like that used to create in a room—a mood that anything could happen. And that happened at CBGBs that August when we opened for Suicide.

And maybe around that same year, me and my buddies would go Sunday nights to Limelight and Rock 'n' Roll Church. And we didn't really relate to the LA Hairband thing. We'd go to talk to girls, and it was sometimes an open bar and sometimes somebody cool like Jane's Addiction would play. We would kind of laugh and walk around the whole Limelight, and there, in the sidebar by the balcony would be Alan, standing—every Sunday, smoking, drinking with a buddy of his.

We were welcomed into his conversation with his friend, who was this tall guy with a satin jacket that said, "Max's Kansas City" on the back. And Alan would just go into things so passionately and talk about theories when there's a Democratic president and things that happen when there's a Republican president—and everything from sports to philosophy, to how the country or the world is affected. And as I spoke to him, I was thinking—this guy is so New York. He's like somebody in my neighborhood we grew up with. He was just so approachable and down to earth, yet created these discussions that were way above my head.

We were just so impressed. There was no snobbery. It was a warmth and a sweetness and the way he smoked his cigarette and looked at you and the way he drank from his drink and the way he was with his friend—he was just there holding court, and this is what he did. There was no agenda.

Flash forward—I'm starting to become a fan. I buy all the records—I'm buying all kinds of stuff of Suicide. I'm starting to understand it. I go to gigs watching them play. I noticed how Alan is up there pacing and free-forming and building the energy in the room and working whatever was going on—and walking back and forth with his cigarettes.

So, in the middle of the '90s, I had a band called D-Generation and we were making a record with Ric Ocasek at Electric Lady studio, and we just start talking about the records Ric had made with Alan, and he says, "Well, Alan's my friend, you know, if you want him to come by, I can call him." Alan comes by the next night and he's sitting on the couch and just talking to us.

And, and you know, certain people, it's very rare, but as they're there for a couple minutes, you start to feel like you know them—like they're one of the guys that you grew up with—you don't think of him as—this is Alan Vega from Suicide that toured with the Clash.

Then, Ric says, "Would you want him to sing on something?" And I said, "Oh my God, that that would be amazing." And Alan's was like, "Yeah, sure. I'll do whatever you like."

So, uh, I had a song called "Frankie," which was like a Frankenstein—about a misunderstood person. It was about a friend of mine, a heterosexual guy that used to like to dress up in drag and go out.

So, Alan walks into the tracking room, to the booth with, with a cigarette. And he says, "Take all the guitars out. Take everything out except Jesse's voice, the kick drum and the bass guitar, and that's all I want."

And he goes in and suddenly free-forms all this stuff, he starts moaning and screaming and groaning. It was a ton of great stuff and then he just walked out of the booth—one take it was down. He gave us gold.

And over the years after that, you know, the record came out and the band started to change then break up. Eventually I would see Alan at different shows. Ric would be there. I had a club called Coney Island High, and Alan and Liz would come and play Alan's solo stuff, which was just so great.

This guy who was so scary and intense onstage. But was really totally mellow and sweet.

He was this guy who was so New York—into doo-wop in the fifties and sports and New York food on the street and had a very Brooklyn—real New Yorker thing. A guy who could drink at the Blarney Stone with regular New Yorkers and working-class people, but yet they're still trying to catch up with him in art museums and in galleries—everything he's done is like light years ahead. That combination is something that I've just seen a few times and really impressed me. I think the Ramones had that too—where they were just these guys from Queens that liked pop songs on the radio and girl groups and would give you a punch in the nose if you said something wrong. But at the same time, they reinvented rock and roll.

Alan's heart was so great. Every time I saw him, he would light up.

I started to get to know Bruce Springsteen a little bit and realized that he was such a fan of Alan and Suicide—and how *Nebraska*, his minimalist record, was supposedly inspired by Suicide. The cover of the record reminds me of Suicide record covers. And I started to see at some of the Suicide gigs, Alan would occasionally riff into a Springsteen line from "Born in the U.S.A."

Bruce and I would hang out here and there and we'd talk music, and wow, this guy loves Suicide, and also loves Alan Vega. Bruce knew all the solo stuff. So, he started to play "Dream Baby Dream."

So, I called up Liz and said, "You know, Bruce is doing this. Does Alan wanna maybe come up and see it?" So, we drove up to this arena in Connecticut, and we got there at sound check and they took us right backstage, and after Bruce finished soundcheck we were sitting in his dressing room. And he comes in and Bruce and Alan start talking about their kids and talking about when they briefly met in the '70s.

And Bruce is just so into talking to Alan, and he says—if Elvis was born again, he'd be Alan Vega. I'm just sitting there watching these two guys talk—and I realize those were two people that I just love—the way they sing and do their work and their music.

So, we go out to our seats—it's time for the show to happen, and they're playing preshow music and there's stuff from *Dujang Prang* on it.

Alan turned to me and said, "This is really cool. Do you know who this is?" And I said, "This is you. This is your solo record." He really liked it.

In an interview in *Mojo* magazine, Springsteen listed "Dujang Prang" as one of the top ten songs he listens to.

It's this big mainstream show with Bruce then this edgy, cool stuff is playing and its Alan's—we can't believe it! We're in the front row. The show is great. It's real stripped down, really dark. Bruce gives Alan a shout out and he does "Dream Baby Dream" on this organ. We go backstage again and hang out some more, and then take the ride back downtown.

I could tell Alan, who'd probably seen it all and lived through so many great things and tours—I could feel that he was beaming. He had this little smile going on as we drove home.

Then a funny thing happened, I got a call from Bruce's assistant and well, Bruce wanted Alan's phone number. He wanted to call him and tell him something. Not only did Bruce play "Dream Baby Dream" at his gig, and that would be on the whole tour for *Devils and Dust*, but he had a new record coming out and he recorded "Dream Baby Dream" and it's on that album—*High Hopes*.

Bruce rarely did covers. He's such a songwriter writer.

Of course, we had to inform Bruce that Alan had a stroke, so he was going to sound different on the phone.

When Alan passed away, people all over the Lower East Side started spray painting his name really big on all kinds of walls: "Alan Vega's God," or just "Alan Vega." They needed to put his name on a wall.

If it was anything weird or different in the late seventies, early eighties—then Alan just standing there alone with nothing, no band, just him and Marty, and Alan as this small guy who wasn't like some fighter, but brave as hell taking on like 15,000 people. Wow. And I know what that's like as an artist who has opened for bigger acts, especially back in the day when they hated anything.

And to watch him and Ric speak with each other, the way they talked to each other with so much affection and so familiar. It was like such a sweetness the way they interacted and laughed and smiled—two basic loving dudes.

One day I was on tour and I was pretty drunk. I was in Dublin, Ireland, and after the show, I wanted to go out and hear a DJ or do something in a rock and roll bar. And I was in this club, Whelan's, and there's a girl, like in her twenties, just a DJing hipster kid. And then suddenly I'm hearing "Jukebox Baby" and I'm in Ireland, maybe my third time there—I feel like I'm a million miles away from a New York club. Wow. Wow. And hearing "Jukebox Baby,"—I've listened to this record for so many years. Sonically, musically, it's like the best mix of everything.

There is a connection with his music and his art—it plays with the darkness and the beaten-down parts in life for people, the struggles. But there's light in it. There's a love of humanity. A name like Suicide for a band which was all about being *alive* in the moment. ∎

***

Alan could talk in-depth about anything from sports, physics, astronomy, philosophy, jazz musicians, to world affairs. He was fascinated by all of this, and his creations were often informed by his observations of the world he was living in. He had zero intertest in "making the scene." If someone wanted to talk about early Suicide or anything reliving his past, it would make him uncomfortable. He also found it ridiculous when people would ask, are you still making music or art. His response was always: "Am I still breathing?"

Being an artist was life—a calling—not a career. Alan loved talking about the present and future but not about his past. And he could engage in-depth on almost any subject. ∎

Liz: Long before Netflix and the abundant content on streaming apps, Alan surfed the TV for documentaries and films that imparted knowledge about anything and everything. I was always amazed when I watched Jeopardy *and* Wheel of Fortune *with him—he watched both religiously. He knew about 95 percent of the answers and could solve the word puzzles with very few letters on the board.*

Dante became an amazing Wheel of Fortune *player too. I remember him eating dinner in his highchair, watching with Alan and calling out "big money, big money" as the wheel spun.*

Alan was by nature very empathetic and caring. He made me feel very safe and loved and he adored Dante. While he gave Dante solid guidance and was very protective of him in many ways, he also gave him the respect and space to follow his own path. Although Dante was always a strong learner and the teachers loved his contributions to the class, he sometimes ran into problems for not following the rules—especially if he felt they weren't necessary for him—something he may have picked up on intuitively from being raised by Alan.

I remember an early instance in school where Dante was called to the principal's office. While I was concerned, Alan was happy and relieved to hear that he wasn't a "follower." Throughout middle school and high school Dante excelled in the classroom and a constant theme from his teachers was how much value he added to discussions and how often he helped others. He led his chem lab group to straight As on every lab assignment, but when it came time to write up the lab report at home, he refused to do it.

"The teacher knows I know the material," he said.

He was willing to take an F for the incomplete labs, bring his grade way down for not completing written homework. The teachers let him get away with it because he proved to them he knew and understood all the material and could use it to problem solve.

He is so much like Alan.

***

By the time Dante was born, Alan had little interest in hanging out in nightclubs. Instead, his local pub became the site of his nightly wind down after Dante and Liz were asleep—usually between 12:00 a.m. and 1:30. And for Sunday afternoon sports, he wandered over to Blarney Stone by Bowling Green or the Killarney Rose on Pearl Street.

They were Alan's favorite places to relax, talk with the regulars and write or draw in his notebooks.

Alan first dropped into the Killarney in 1988. At that time the area was populated by financial industry workers. Sitting by himself at the end of the bar with his beret, sunglasses, and leather motorcycle jacket writing in his notebook, Alan was a bit of an anomaly.

But as he developed a nice rapport with the bartenders, the regulars could tell he wasn't intimidating. Soon the curious started sitting closer to him and striking up conversations. The floodgates opened as they found out how well-versed Alan was on pretty much any topic, especially sports.

By 2015, Alan had been walking with a cane for a few years since his stroke, and his balance was unsteady, even with help. One day, after leaving Duane Reade, as he stepped off the sidewalk to cross Water Street, he fell, narrowly missing a moving car. He suffered a black eye and a broken finger.

So, he started spending more time at home. As he did, he created several portraits every day and wrote endlessly in his notebooks. He always went through periods where his focus was on music and then he'd shift his focus to his visual art. With his mobility issues, he was very much into his visual art.

Liz started to notice that the portraits Alan was creating didn't have faces. They looked like spirits. When she mentioned this to him, he just nodded. It seemed this wasn't a conscious decision on his part.

In front of the Killarney Rose. © *Bob Gruen/www .bobgruen.com*

Liz: I believe he and I both knew his spirit guides were reaching out to him.

Even though Alan had studied painting during college and switched over to sculpting in the '70s, he continued doing some painting over the years, but it was exclusively abstract works. He liked to experiment with blending colors and often talked about how the earliest masters and Native Americans made pigment for the paint from plants and bugs, especially beetles.

***

Liz: The first one of these portraits was on a small 8 x 11 canvas. When it was finished it was almost as if he was possessed. He sent me out to buy several large canvases. Every night, he set up all his paints in the kitchen and put the canvas on the built-in bench nook and proceeded to spend most of the night painting. I often woke up several times and when I came downstairs and dropped into the kitchen, it seemed like he was in a trance. Prior to this period, whenever I woke up, Alan would engage me in conversation, but not during this time. I knew not to disturb his focus. Like the drawings, the figures in these paintings didn't have any facial features.

In the past, when we talked about creating something, Alan would describe the process as initially having a general idea of what he was creating, but then, at a certain point, the piece of art or music took on a life of its own. It began dictating to him what it would become.

This is very much how this final series of faceless paintings and drawings evolved. There was also a distinct sense of urgency in his energy like he was running out of time to get out as much as possible of what he had left inside.

The energy of Alan's art had always been quite electrifying.

He believed that there are no mistakes, which made the creative process so open and free. It was existentialism in practice. One of his favorite mantras was "Fuck 'em if they can't take a joke," which to him meant, don't let others' judgments limit you. He loved Michael Jordan's quote "I missed 100 percent of the shots I didn't take." Alan's attitude helped me get beyond my tendency toward perfectionism.

He often said he wasn't looking for accolades and never pursued opportunities beyond the opportunity to create. I used to joke with him that my main job as his manager was to "get us out of this thing"—whatever outside commitment, promotion, show he had agreed to, usually at my behest which took him away from working on his art.

It was uncanny how almost every professional opportunity came to him because of someone reaching out to him or me. And that started back in the '70s when he was busy inventing a new type of light sculpture with piles of found objects, electronics, wires, and lights on the ground back at the Project for Living Artists when Ivan Karp of OK Harris happened upon Alan's work and said: "How soon can you have a collection of these ready for a show?"

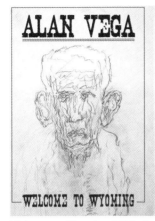

Welcome to Wyoming, 2015. *Courtesy INVISIBLE-EXPORTS*

From the time Dante was born, Alan became an avid coin collector, reading *Numismatic News* magazine and steadily investing in series of limited-edition mint-condition coins. He really enjoyed the selection process and put together an impressive array of coins that he left for Dante. He amassed a collection valued in the tens of thousands. His father had been a stamp collector and part of his interest in collecting coins may have stemmed from that.

In early 2015, Ben Tischer and Risa Needleman of Invisible-Exports gallery approached Alan about doing a solo show that would focus mostly on his drawings. They had represented Alan in the private sale of one of his light sculptures and Alan had great respect for Ben and Risa.

The show was titled *Welcome to Wyoming.*

Leading up to this period, Alan had become obsessed with the TV show *Longmire* and often said to me in his next life he'd be living on a ranch in Wyoming—hence the title. It was apropos that the spirit drawings were featured on one wall. Across from them and shedding red light in the room was a large cross light sculpture entitled *Jet.*

"Jet," Alan Vega, 2014. *Photo by Michael Alago*

***

Ben Tischer
Art Curator
April 2023
It was around 2013 when I met Alan when this collector named Javier Magri, who I had been working with, reached out and said that he would love to have an Alan Vega sculpture. And I knew that Marie Losier had been doing this video project with Alan. So, I reached out to her and she said, "Alan's the sweetest. He's so nice." So, then I went down to the apartment with Carol McCranie. Alan was a little bit stiff for all of sixty seconds. Then we started having a conversation and he turned into this complete ball of light.

He was so happy to share what he was making once he saw that we were genuinely interested. I have to admit that when I first went over to the apartment, I was not aware of Alan's visual art legacy. I knew him from Suicide, of course. I'd seen Suicide before and had the records and I knew that the sculptures existed, but I didn't realize the breadth of his work over all those years. I was completely floored.

The whole impetus for our visit was this collector reaching out and asking if we could score something. I assumed there were maybe two or three sculptures that were around. But then we go over there—this entire living room was full of treasure. Alan worked every night—there was so much material there—whether it was a drawing or a collage or a sculpture.

That's a rare thing to discover such a huge body of work that is not being displayed in any public manner. I know Jeffrey had done that huge show but there should be Alan Vega shows every year.

We immediately offered Alan a show, and I think it was pretty great. It was mostly drawings—new drawings we showed which were done to improve his motor skills after the stroke.

I remember Alan saying during the studio visit that different drawings had different personalities. He referred to a lot of them as just bums that he saw down on the Bowery. But then he also said, "Maybe every single drawing is me." But then I remember at the gallery, I was reiterating that to a potential collector while Alan was there and he said, "No, none of those drawings are me. I'm better looking than that."

The Spirit Paintings were incredible. That was the last thing we expected Alan to do. It kind of goes to show what kind of artist Alan was. The fact that he was able to switch to painting. And they very much have the same aesthetic as the drawings, but with vivid color. There's a couple of black and white ones, but it's really phenomenal. And he would also use graphite in them, which adds a very particular quality to the canvases. They're really gorgeous.

We framed them and put them all in a single row and they looked fantastic.

His work is controlled chaos. It's like an aestheticized chaos. And the fact of what he is doing with the sculptures—it's all assembled, everything is found materials. And the fact that there's also the light aspect—it is so uniquely Alan. There's not that many artists that do that stuff.

It's different for all Alan's bodies of work. The drawings were very much the "everyman" but also not every man. And as I understand it, in the early days Alan wandered around downtown often and found these characters that he would capture in his drawings. It's like this post-depression America that he captured in the seventies.

It was the chaos of New York at that moment in time. He really does capture those cultural moments in his objects. Every single one of those pieces reads as Alan—you had a little piece of Alan—you're collecting Alan more than you're collecting the object, and the object can also be incredibly beautiful.

Someone who came to Alan's show after seeing that one amazing work that Liz and Dante kind of reconstructed—the large body-shaped floor piece at the 2017 Deitch Retrospective—sensed there was a little bit of the smell of danger in it. Like you'd smell electricity. That was like a thing at the early shows—Alan's sculptures—you could always smell a little bit of danger.

It was always incredible how many visitors to the gallery—both artists and musicians—idolized Alan. He influenced so many people. ∎

***

Around the same time in 2015, Ben Vaughn reached out to invite Alan into the studio to record what would be his last collaboration. Ben invited musicians Palmyra Delran and Noelle Hover Felipe to join in at Steven Van Zandt's studio in the village in NYC.

Once again, in a one-night session an entire album was created. They called it *Alan Vega After Dark*.

Like the process he used with *Cubist Blues*, Alan freestyled almost all the vocals while the musicians played. The night of the recording, Liz dropped Alan off at the studio and later, when she circled back to pick him up, the session was nearly completed.

It was immediately clear from Alan's energy and enthusiasm that he had a blast working with Ben, Palmyra, and Noelle. He was blown away by their talent and spontaneity. R&B and blues were so close to his heart and the type of music he felt most comfortable singing. The solo experimental music Vega created was the most challenging for him when it came to performing his vocals, and he enjoyed setting up that challenge for himself, but he felt very free and inspired singing the blues.

Despite his ever-weakening state, Alan did two more significant Suicide concerts in 2015. The first was a sold-out show at Webster Hall on March 7, 2015,

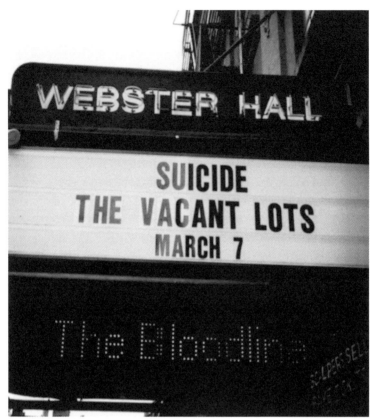

Photo by Jared Artaud

Webster Hall, 2015. © *GODLIS*

with the Vacant Lots opening.

That night was electrifying. Marty and Alan hadn't seen each other since they last performed together at a concert in front of Roman-style ruins on an island off the coast of Marseilles in France during the summer of 2014. A few days prior to the Webster Hall show, Marty called Alan and they had a quick conversation about the set list. On the night of the concert, the venue made a backstage area for Alan behind thick velvet curtains. It was on the same floor as the stage because the upstairs wasn't accessible to him.

He saw Marty for the first time that night when each walked out from separate sides and launched into the show. The audience in the packed hall was mesmerized throughout the set and Dante joined Alan in a duet for the encore of "Dream Baby Dream."

Webster Hall was filled with young fans, many of whom had never seen Suicide perform and certainly weren't around when their first album was released in '77. Liz had 300 T-shirts made of Suicide's first album cover and by the time they got there for the show, the T-shirts were sold out. It was the one and only time Suicide ever had merch at a show.

After their set, Alan sat behind the velvet curtain and what seemed like a hundred people stood in line to go backstage and sit with him and chat.

As always, whenever you were in front of Alan, he treated you like you were the only person in the universe and for most who sat with him that night, it would be for the last time.

Liz: I have since met quite a few people who told me they were at the show and how electrifying the energy was. It was clear to all that Alan had significant physical constraints, but it didn't dampen the intensity of his performance and that was incredibly inspiring.

Webster Hall wouldn't be the last Suicide show. On July 13, 2015, Suicide performed in London at the Barbican Centre in a concert billed as "Suicide: A Punk Music Mass." An entire wall of Moog synthesizers filled the back of the stage. The set combined a Martin Rev solo music performance complete with a backing choir, followed by a Vega solo music performance. Dante and Liz played synths and added vocals to songs that would eventually be released on Alan's final album, *IT*.

Then Henry Rollins took the stage to introduce Suicide. The Suicide set was capped with encores of "Ghost Rider" with Rollins singing a duet with Alan, then "Dream Baby Dream" with Jehnny from the Savages and Bobby Gillespie of Primal Scream joining Alan on vocals. It was an awe-inspiring night guaranteed to not be forgotten.

It was the last time Alan appeared onstage.

Paul Smith

"One the strangest concerts I have ever seen"—*The Telegraph*, British national newspaper headline, 2015.

Alan's health was getting poor, his mobility compromised by a bone spur on his foot and arthritic knees.

Suicide's first gig flyers back in 1970 bore the foreboding strapline of "A Punk Mass." So we decided to go out where they came in by headlining an evening curated to their joint and individual activities with some guest vocalists and major Vega fans—Henry Rollins and Bobby Gillespie.

The show was at the Barbican, London's largest arts center and was hosting American multimedia artist Doug Aitken's "30 day happening." A Suicide fan himself, it was the perfect cover to stage our likely last stand.

During the soundcheck, after some pleading on my behalf, Rev somewhat reluctantly ran through a version of "Ghost Rider" to help settle our understandably trepidatious guest singers. "Alan never wants a run-thru, so if they want the real Suicide experience, we just do it live!" Nor were there ever any set lists—whoever started first dictated the next number in the set.

I hired Vega a throne, which I think he rightfully deserved and from where he could deliver his vocal blasts while saving his depleted energies for the bill-topping Suicide set. Because we shielded Alan from the audience as he got himself settled, there was an audible gasp when the audience first saw him in the flesh.

Thirty seconds into the first track he's out of the throne and prowling the stage—snarling and shrieking in his classic style.

The four-song set had the audience reeling and as Alan hobbled off the stage, he said, "So we can go home now?" seemingly having forgotten he was yet to deliver the main Suicide set. Much yelling ensued from Liz and me: "No, no NO, you've another set to do!" while Alan sat, sipping his straight vodka with an evil grin on his face. Now, Henry Rollins is without question a top-flight, highly experienced aggressive performer who was clearly looking forward to a call and response vocal interaction with his hero, Vega.

Rollins delivers and then some. Alan just grins his head off. He does not sing his parts and leaves Henry to do all the heavy lifting for the song. Afterwards, Alan says "I thought he wanted to sing it, so I just waited to see how it went."

Girls invaded the stage to dance—bouncers chased them out and I chased around the bouncers trying to keep the dancers from being ejected.

In my experience, Alan and Marty were not known for being overly effusive in expressing their feelings on any of their performances—it is was it is, take it or leave it. They trusted their own gods to guide them wherever that may lead.

That night, the last gig—in the van, back to the hotel, Rev leaned over and quietly said to me, "You batted a thousand tonight, kid" and later, on arrival at the hotel, as Alan slid out of the van onto the street, he leaned back and gave me the most gentle peck on the lips then stood straight and tall and snapped a smart salute to me . . . job DONE. ■

***

Alan ended up doing seven of the "Spirit Paintings" and each seemed to be coming from a different era, starting with medieval times. This series would be his final paintings, his last works, and truly the culmination of his creations as a visual artist.

Alan had studied human anatomy drawings as his first art class at Brooklyn college. It evolved into intense surrealist drawings under the tutelage of Seligmann and abstract painting with Reinhardt. He had now come full circle with the aid of his spirit guides.

Painting is self-discovery.
Every good artist paints what he is.*
—Jackson Pollock

***

Liz: *Like the faces on his portraits, Alan seemed to be physically fading away. He was getting weaker and falling more. At one point I said: "You know, if you fall and break your hip, it's game over."*

On Friday May 21, 2016, I got a call at my office from Antonio, our co-op building superintendent. He was in the apartment with Alan, who had fallen in the kitchen, and it was clear that his hip was displaced and likely broken. Our cleaning person had alerted the front desk after Alan had tripped over the supplies left by the kitchen entrance. An ambulance was on the way, and I rushed to meet them at the Downtown Hospital, a few blocks from our home.

When I arrived, Antonio was there with Alan. His cardiologist was based in this hospital, and I immediately let him know what had happened. Alan had developed a close relationship with Dr. W, who wanted to make sure he got the best possible care given his heart condition. Dr. W reached out to the surgical team and lined up the head of anesthesiology department to personally administer the anesthesia during the surgery. The hip fracture could be fixed with a small part inserted in the joint and the surgery was scheduled for that Monday.

Meanwhile, Marc Hurtado was in the air flying to NYC to film Alan for clips to be shown during Christophe's upcoming tour.

On Saturday, Marc came into the hospital and Alan let him film him. Alan was heavily medicated for the pain but knowing Marc had just flown in from Paris to film him, he told him to go ahead. It is very difficult to watch that film, which was released a few years later.

---

* Elizabeth Frank, *Jackson Pollock* (New York: Abbeville, 1993).

Waiting for the surgery to be finished was grueling. It was getting to a point where I felt I could barely breathe. I'd been warned of the added risks Alan faced given his severe congestive heart failure. I went for a walk around the local park imploring the higher power to keep him with us. Begging.

Soon after, I went back into the waiting room and someone came out to tell me the surgery went well, and I could see him soon. The plan was to have Alan up and walking in a few days and transferred to a rehab facility in about a week. As it turned out, Alan had a very tough time trusting that he could stand up without falling and was an uncooperative physical therapy patient. Every morning, I arrived at the hospital before the doctors made their rounds, stayed a few hours, went to work for the afternoon and came back at dinnertime until 11:00 p.m. I made sure to coordinate my visits with the rehab team to help support their efforts. Over the years I would often say "Alan's bark is worse than his bite." That was an understatement. Alan's energy could be very intense and when he was nervous and you didn't know what a sweetheart he was, it could be extremely intimidating. He feared falling and some of the PT staff were very petite and tentative with him.

Once the team got to know Alan, they fell in love with him. Just as he was making a little progress, he developed an infection, and they couldn't transfer him to the rehabilitation facility until they figured out what it was and how to treat it. That took about two weeks and was very stressful. When the time came for him to go into rehab he had been in the hospital for several weeks and was very weak.

When he finally arrived at rehab in Fort Greene, we were starting from scratch to get Alan's strength back and get him up and walking. I was with him for a couple hours in the morning and again for several hours at night and I got to know his PT team well. I started working alongside them to get him comfortable with the exercises. It was a slow process to rebuild his strength and the weeks went by.

On June 23, Alan's seventy-eighth birthday, Toots flew in from Florida. She joined me, Dante, his girlfriend Allison, my niece Kelsey, her husband Adam, and Ramon (a fighter I managed who had become a close family friend) for a small celebration in Alan's room, which we had decorated with balloons and streamers. Alan was exhausted that night and stayed in bed while we sang happy birthday and had black forest cake and cheesecake from nearby Juniors, which Alan loved. Toots asked Dante and Allison to sing. They had sung together in the Trinity Wall Street Choristers for ten years. Their acapella rendering of the Gregorian chant Panis Angelicus was incredibly moving.

When they finished, Alan spontaneously started to softly sing "Dream Baby Dream." Just those three words over and over. I'm pretty sure there wasn't a dry eye in the room and I joined in with "forever."

By early July, Alan was making good progress and we were hopeful he'd be home in a week or so. His niece, Amie, and her wife, Vivi, came to visit and we all talked and laughed. Alan was in great spirits—so comforted and happy seeing Amie.

© Pierre René-Worms

The next night when I arrived, his nurse told me she had taken Alan down to the community room that afternoon. There had been a musician performing Elvis Presley songs. She told him Alan was a rock star and when he invited Alan to join him, she handed Alan the mic. He sang "Blue Suede Shoes" from the wheelchair. I didn't know then, but it would be his final performance. For weeks I'd been saying "We miss you so much at home Allie" and he'd say, "I want to come home—but one never knows."

Eight weeks after the accident, despite making progress walking and being only a week away from being released, one night—he didn't wake up.

***

No matter what happened in our world, I knew Alan had my back and I'm certain he felt the same way about me. He was one of the most genuinely loyal persons I have ever known. And I realize how fortunate we were to have found each other. We shared an amazing journey that also allowed each of us to fully actualize as individuals. A big part of that was because we had true unconditional love, trust, and respect for each other and no filter when sharing our feelings. Whatever we said to each other was sure to be exactly what we were thinking and feeling. The most significant gift he gave me was his unconditional honesty. That and the example he set by living fearlessly as a creative being.

To the day he passed, I never stopped getting butterflies whenever I was about to see Alan and no matter what was happening, good or bad, I knew we both were so happy to be together.

Liz

March 2023

I could live in a refrigerator box on the Bowery.

—Alan

LEGACY

Liz: *Toward the end of his life, Alan's desire to create intensified. This likely was fueled in part by his intention to leave an annuity for his family. In addition to the writings, drawings, paintings, and light sculptures, Alan left a vast amount of unreleased recorded music. In 2014, when we released the "Nike Soldier" split single with the Vacant Lots, Alan recognized how much unreleased music we had recorded.*

He took comfort in knowing that in addition to exploring my own musical evolution with solo records, I would be coproducing Vega music releases.

When the Vacant Lots asked us to do a split single with them in 2014, Alan suggested I go into the studio with Perkin to see what we could find amongst the unreleased material. By that time, Perkin had been digitally transferring the Vega recordings made from the period 1988–1993 before we had begun using Pro Tools. I was surprised to see the extensive inventory from the earlier period, as well as all of the Pro Tools sessions for each of the albums we had recorded between 1993 and 2015. For each released album there were countless sessions of prior iterations of soundtracks and vocals, in many instances complete songs and fragments of songs. As we scrolled through track listings, the title "Nike Soldier" caught my eye, and I asked Perkin to pull up the tracks for that song. We spent the afternoon mixing the song and I brought it home to play for Alan.

It was a "Holy Shit" moment with Alan saying "Wow, that's incredible!" He hadn't remembered leaving that song behind but was very happy to hear how vital it sounded almost twenty years later. He said I did a great job mixing it. He'd be shocked at the amount of unreleased material there still exists. He dubbed it the "Vega Vault" and said, "After I'm gone you should go into the Vega Vault and release anything you think is good. I've always trusted your opinion on anything I've done. I know there's a lot of music we didn't release because I was always moving on to the next thing."

Although Alan's focus was on creating without conscious regard for commercial success, that didn't mean he didn't want his art and music seen or heard. And he was always humbled and appreciative when his work was acknowledged—especially as an influence on other artists to pursue a creative calling.

Over the years, the sphere of influence seemed to widen and expand beyond the groundbreaking music of Suicide to Vega's solo music—from the early rockabilly and Elektra era records to his later eight experimental albums—as well as into the art and fashion worlds.

Alan was grateful to see the increasing appreciation of his contributions in the last two decades before he passed. And from the time I met him he often said, "Just wait till I'm gone, then my work will be more widely recognized and understood." He was well versed in the long list of artists who didn't gain a place in history until after they had passed away. I believe he inherently knew he too would have a historical impact.

Alan was a seeker and a visionary. After he passed, two different psychics told me Alan wanted me to know that so many unimaginable things were revealed to him in a way he hadn't known possible in this realm. Hearing that gave me tremendous joy. Alan spent his entire life exploring the unknown, always searching for the next sound, color, light, feeling he hadn't yet experienced. He was fascinated by the mystery of it all. The phrase he kept repeating in his final weeks was "one never knows."

Now he knows.

And my mission, and that of all those who have taken up the charge to bring Vega's works to light, will continue as we make sure his contributions to the cultural zeitgeist are shared with as many as possible.

Henry Rollins truly understood Alan as both an artist and a human being. He had also seen firsthand the mutually supportive relationship between Alan and me. After Alan passed, Henry said to me, knowing Alan's work—that doesn't happen without being able to run headfirst into a wall over and over again, and that I gave him the encouragement to maintain the strength to do that. Henry was dead on. I believed so completely in Alan and his unwavering commitment to his art and I knew I would carry that devotion forward.

Henry immediately stepped up to take on the daunting task of announcing Alan's passing on behalf of his family. The press response was widespread and beautiful. There was an outpouring of words of love from those whose lives he touched, and many impromptu tributes sprung up around the globe.

There was also a big uptick in the "Frankie Teardrop" challenges.

Alan never wanted a traditional funeral and burial. His body was cremated, and the ashes brought home to the place where he loved his family, raised his son, inspired his wife, and created his drawings, poetry, and sculptures. That space is still filled with his energy, many of his most personal effects and art, and it is now a recording studio where I am producing new Vega releases from the Vault such as Mutator *and* Insurrection *with Jared Artaud as coproducer, as well as my solo music with Dante as my sound engineer.*

***

Alan had to shuffle off his mortal coil; although he shed his body, his beautiful spirit has enveloped his loved ones. We internalized his values and we know and feel him as part of us. His insights and guidance are always with us—and there have been many profound moments of receiving uncanny direct messages from him.

The day Alan's ashes came home I had planned to go into our storage facility, which contained many of his sculptures, promo copies, and test pressings of music releases dating back to the earliest Suicide and Vega recordings. By that time, Michael Alago and I had sorted through his home studio and earmarked art materials that could be moved into storage for safekeeping. We also began to inventory notebooks, drawings, writings, and works on paper. I worked around the clock. I'd been going through his space, finding comfort in being surrounded by and delving into the images, lights, paper, and objects in which he had immersed himself.

On the day planned for the trip to the storage unit, my friend Ramon drove his car over to transport all the curated objects and art materials. When we opened the storage space, there was room at the front of the unit, yet I suddenly had an overwhelming urge to open a box at the very back of the space, along the far-left wall.

This plan required moving many boxes out of the unit. I couldn't explain why or what I was looking for, but Ramon could tell I wasn't leaving without opening that box. So, we both set about clearing out most of the space.

When I opened the box, sitting near the top was Alan's Bar Mitzvah pouch that Mariette had returned to Alan many years before. It was blue velvet with embroidered gold lettering in Yiddish. The rest of the box was filled with records. I had no recollection of putting this very personal item in storage.

Moments after I returned home with the Bar Mitzvah Tefillin pouch, the urn with Alan's ashes arrived. It suddenly made sense. I knew Alan wanted the pouch with him. I put it with his urn on the top shelf of a case that had long been home to his favorite classic books, classical music albums, personal memorabilia, and portrait drawings.

Alan and I had finished mixing his last studio album, IT *well before he passed, but we hadn't done anything about arranging a release. After we finished the work, Alan's focus had shifted very intently to visual art, although he agreed to do those last few Suicide shows.*

Alan had often said IT *would be his last studio album, his final music masterpiece, and he was very proud of the evolution of his music that led him to that point. Months after he passed, Kevin Patrick suggested I meet with Jon Cohen at Fader Records, and it was decided that Jon would release the album. I invited Jared Artaud into the studio to help me oversee the mastering of the album with Perkin Barnes.* IT *was released on Fader Records in June 2017.*

On July 16, 2017, the one-year anniversary of Alan's death, Jeffrey Deitch mounted a major retrospective of Alan Vega's fine art titled "Dream Baby Dream."

IT, 2017. *Courtesy Saturn Strip, Ltd.*

"Dream Baby Dream" exhibition, Deitch Projects, 2017. *Photo by Liz Lamere*

The opening was a memorial for Alan, and it was such a special night with over a hundred friends and family coming from all over the country and world to commemorate Alan, including Martin Rev, Ric Ocasek, Mathieu Copeland, Ben Tischer, Laurent Godin, Jesse Malin, Jim Jarmusch, Sara Driver, Cynthia Sley, Bobby Gillespie, and many other artists, musicians, and pro boxers. At one point, a few who knew him best, such as Perkin and Toots, spoke. It was very emotional.

On loan were the large wall light sculptures from the collections of Ric Ocasek and Julian Schnabel, as well as numerous other light sculptures spanning the decades from the late '70s through 2015.

There was a large '70s-style floor piece, hanging light pieces, portrait drawings from the '60s through 2016. There were also photographs of Alan, Suicide, and the rock scene through the years as well as Paul Tischler and Marc Hurtado's documentary films containing interviews with Alan discussing his creative process.

Ric Ocasek had given us Suicide concert footage for the archives and that was projected on the large wall at the back of the space facing the entrance. It contained hours of concert footage on a loop and could be heard throughout the large three-level space. The films were of the various concerts when Suicide opened for the Cars.

During that same week of the one-year anniversary, there were several events to commemorate and celebrate Alan's life.

Invisible-Exports mounted an exhibition of the Seven Spirit Paintings series—Alan's final work—together with several light sculptures and some of Vega's surreal drawings from the '60s. It was a sweltering July evening, and the opening was packed for hours. "Alan Vega" graffiti had started appearing on buildings throughout the downtown area.

The remembrances and recognitions continue around the anniversary of his passing.

As a result of the Invisible-Exports exhibition, the New York Times *published an article in the Sunday Arts section that week titled "Alan Vega Ignored the Art World. It Won't Return the Favor." Pictured were Dante and me at home with Alan's artwork, including the Spirit Paintings, one of which, "Duke's God Bar," was acquired by collector Beth Rudin DeWoody.*

After sorting through Alan's studio and the piles of materials he had curated for inclusion in his sculptures, we had earmarked a substantial quantity of works on paper. There were over fifty notebooks filled with writings, drawings, collages, and a variety of ephemera. I reached out to Johan Kugelberg at Boo-Hooray. He was very interested in working with the Alan Vega archives. Johan is a historian well versed in counterculture, including punk and hip-hop. He had the resources and connections to ensure Alan's works on paper were properly inventoried, stored, and eventually placed in a major institution. Dante did an internship at Boo-Hooray and was part of the team that inventoried the material.

In June of 2019, Johan held an exhibition of a representative sampling of the works at his space in Chinatown as well as in Montauk. Mike Sniper from Captured Tracks came and that sparked his interest in publishing a book on the art of Alan Vega, which is slated to be published in 2024.

Several days after the opening at Boo-Hooray, Ric Ocasek came to see the exhibition. Dante and I joined him, and he spent the afternoon with us sharing memories of Alan. Ric was also very excited about his own visual art, which would be exhibited later in the year. He seemed so happy to be with us amongst Alan's work and talking about his art. Two months later, on September 15, Ric passed away and I'm deeply grateful that Dante and I had that time with him reminiscing about Alan. They have reunited.

***

In January 2018 and February 2019, Jesse Mailin and Diane Gentile organized Suicide tribute concerts at the Bowery Electric with "Mr. Pharmacist" aka Gregg Foreman, as musical director. Gregg had collaborated with Alan a few years prior on the song "You Pay/Too Many Teardrops."

***

Mr. Pharmacist aka
Gregg Foreman
Musician
May 2023

There's a saying: "Don't meet your heroes"—but my heroes have always been the underdogs, outsiders, antiheros and outliers of the underground's textured sonic underbelly.

The music of Suicide and Alan Vega have always represented and personified the true soul and spirit of the authentic punk rebel revolutionary.

In 2013, I started a podcast called "The Pharmacy." The concept was to have one musician speaking to another, letting these iconic legends of the underground tell their stories in their own unique voices.

To me, it was essential that I speak with the king of the outliers first—Alan Vega. He was the outsider icon and the vocalist of my favorite band, Suicide.

For almost two and half hours, I had this incredible connective conversation with this vibrant, brilliant, charming, absolutely hilarious king of the underground. During this chat we talked about how he likened the music of Suicide to the trash heaps of New York and described their music as "New York Blues."

The interview solidified us as fast friends. Alan then extended an invitation to visit his home when I was in New York.

That day came while on tour with Cat Power when I was able to make it to Casa Vega. We talked for a while about music and art and I got up and he grabbed my arm and said; "I like the way you look. . . . I couldn't help see the resemblance of current me to late '70s Vega/Rev!"

Just before leaving, after this larger-than-life meeting, I asked if he'd ever consider doing some music with me. In classic Vega style he said, "Mmm—if I like it I'll do it, if I don't like it, I'm not gonna do it."

So, I rushed back to the hotel and put together a track of some analog drum machine loops, Moog synth bass, gospel choir and '60s surf guitars. I brought it over the next afternoon, and he agreed that he would do it!

Fast forward a few years, I would stop in and spend some time with Alan when I was in New York.

He eventually did some vocal takes for the song, later he titled, "You Pay/Too Many Teardrops." There was talk of different labels putting it out, but it would not see the light of day until after Alan's passing in 2016.

Posthumously, I was invited to do the music of Suicide at the Desert Daze festival in California with a cast of notable musicians doing the vocals. After this, Jesse Malin (of D Generation) agreed to put out "Too Many Teardrops" on his label and celebrate the music and life of Suicide and Alan Vega with a series of concerts in New York City.

The concerts brought out the absolute honest and pure love for Vega and Suicide. While I provided the music, different singers interpreted the iconic Vega vocals. Some of those singers were Ric Ocasek, Kid Congo, Lydia Lunch, Liz Lamere, Eugene Hutz (Gogol Bordello), Jim Sclavunos and Jim Thirlwell—both of whom would produce the "You Pay" record—and, of course Martin Rev.

I could go on for an eternity about how vital and important the music of Alan and Suicide are, but I really just would rather share the absolute love and gratitude I have for knowing an absolute musical underground icon and someone who I can call friend. Alan Vega forever. Keep those dreams Burning. ∎

***

Liz: *Gregg did an amazing job re-creating Suicide and Vega songs for the array of guest vocalists to perform over the next few years. That first year, Jared, Perkin, Dante, and I performed two tracks from* IT. *Ric Ocasek and Martin Rev sang "Dream Baby Dream," Ben Vaughn did a rousing rendition of "Jukebox Babe," Jesse Malin went full*

Liz, Dante, Perkin, and Jared performing at Vega Tribute concert, Bowery Electric, 2018. © *Bob Gruen/www.bobgruen.com*

Dante performing at Vega Tribute concert, Bowery Electric, 2019. *Photo: Johan Vipper, johanvipper .com*

Gregg Foreman, Marty and Ric, Vega Tribute concert, Bowery Electric, 2018. © *Bob Gruen/www* *.bobgruen.com*

throttle on "Frankie Teardrop" and many other singers, including Kid Congo, Lydia Lunch, Eugene Hutz, Jim Sclavunos, Jim Thirlwell, Chuck Bones, Luke Jenner, and Johnny Scuotto channeled the intensity and spirit of Alan Vega. The second year I sang "Wild in Blue," a song Alan had told me was inspired by me.

For the following year's celebration, Dante, true to his dad's form, learned the lyrics to "Misery Train" in the taxi on the way to the venue and gave the most beautiful and unique jazz-infused performance of the night. Alan would've been so proud—especially as it was such a special song that Alan had written about his brother Robbie after he passed away.

***

On June 23, 2018, Marc Hurtado and promoter Alain Lahana organized a special event in Paris to celebrate Alan's eightieth birthday. There were over twenty special guests, including Marc, Christophe, Rachid Taha, Jac Berrocal, Christophe Van Huffel, Pascal Comelade, and Jesse Malin. There were also film screenings of Hugues Perret's Movimento *documentary about Alan Vega and Marie Losier's* Just a Million Dreams *film, and a panel discussion with radio host, critic, and writer Alexandre Breton, art curator Mathieu Copeland, Marc, Dante, and me. It was such a special event filled with so much love for Alan from everyone.*

The Godin Gallery in Paris mounted an exhibition of Alan's light sculptures and Spirit Paintings to coincide, and the opening was the next night.

On June 23, 2023, Trinity Boxing Club owner Martin Snow hosted a celebration organized by Samantha Sutcliffe/Uncensored New York to honor Alan's eighty-fifth

Liz performing at Alan's eighty-fifth Birthday, 2023. *Photo by Lauren Massie*

birthday, attended by an eclectic group of Alan's family, friends, and admirers. Jenni Hensler opened the night DJing Vega songs. The live performances in the boxing ring included Gavin (Dot Audio Arts) and Liz performing Keep it Alive.

At the end of the night, Johnny Scuotto (Death Dance Music) and Eric Ordaz performed a Suicide Set culminating in "Frankie Teardrop" which cleared the house.

Alan would've loved it.

Johnny Scuotto performing at Alan's eighty-fifth Birthday, 2023. *Photo by Lauren Massie*

***

By 2019, I had been working with Jared to organize the music archives and he was amazed that neither Alan Vega nor Suicide had established any social media presence. Alan rarely used a cell phone or computer other than overseeing Perkin engineering on Pro Tools in the studio. He kept in touch with the outside world via newspapers and cable TV. When not reading the paper, or watching films and documentaries, he spent his time creating his art and music, not surfing the ever-growing internet. He would have been blown away by how much of a game changer having a digital online presence is today, and the level of accessibility it provides in building his legacy.

Around 2018, Jared introduced me to Michael Handis, who was a marketing direc-
tor for an Italian fashion brand and an Alan Vega and Suicide aficionado. Michael
was well steeped in fashion and style and had a great eye as a photographer. I had been
approached by Herve DePlasse, formerly of Musidisc and Double T Records, labels
that had released Vega solo albums in the past—to reissue the six Vega solo records from
Deuce Avenue *through* Station. *His company,* GM Editions, *would be distributed*
through Sony and that would give new exposure to these underexposed albums.

***

Michael Handis
Creative Director
The Vega Vault Project
May 2023

It has been an incredibly rewarding challenge to take part in the current chapter
of Alan Vega. Especially in a time, culturally, where everyone wants to believe that
everything is acceptable (when it isn't) and that we've heard everything (when we
haven't)—the world still doesn't know what shoebox to store Alan in.

The strange thing about Alan's music is that it felt both familiar and alien to
me, at the same time. Music from a previous life? Possibly. It's music that makes
you dream of slow dancing, music that makes you see burning city blocks.

Within the duality of tenderness and terror lies a magical place for the artist;
this is the space Alan existed in and the space we continue to explore in this next
chapter of his legacy.

Legacy and posthumous work is very hard, both creatively and emotionally. It's
a real challenge to the artist in modern society to keep the outsider on the outside
and the original insiders on the inside. The world wants it all. But the moment
you engage too much, you are a grave robber. Here's the thing: Alan's war orders
are actually quite clear. We are simply conduits of his mission guided by those
who knew him best—at his worst and at his best.

The industry has built the lore of Alan Vega with blood and rusty chains,
but in reality Alan was heart and notebook paper. If you want to cut through
this media-engineered fog, study those photos of him smiling. You immediately
realize that all the performance confrontation was simply that—performance. Art
came first and always did.

I often think to myself "Most of you didn't like him back then so who the fuck
are you to say anything now?" Sit back and feel the fire. ■

***

Liz: *We wanted to provide new artwork for these six Vega solo album reissues, and*
Michael and Jared agreed to help with the project on a tight timeline. Over the course
of one night, Jared, Michael, and I pulled out an array of photographs—either of
Alan or taken by Alan—and arranged them in six collections on the living room floor.

Michael photographed them as collage artwork and then he and Jared designed all elements of the new packaging for all six releases. It was an exhilarating and inspiring collaboration that led to us establishing Alan Vega social media together in 2019.

Later that year, Jared and I began working with Ted Young, a Grammy Award–winning audio engineer, to help organize the Vega Vault.

Years before Alan passed, Perkin Barnes transferred, digitized, and organized the studio recordings dating back to the late '80s early analog tapes through the ADAT recordings and Pro Tools sessions from the '90s to 2015. It was a massive project, given all the recordings we'd done over almost thirty years and proved a daunting task that Perkin had been unable to complete.

Ted had worked on the Rolling Stones' archives. With him on board, I decided the best way forward was to inventory all of the physical recorded materials from 6/8 Studios. By this time, I had also unearthed several boxes' worth of live recordings and studio sessions from as far back as 1975.

We set about the arduous process of archiving and creating an inventory of the recordings.

Ted, Jared, Dante, and I set up camp in Dujang Prang Studio, the recording studio Dante and I built in Alan's space where he created his light sculptures, writings, and drawings. Enveloped in Alan's energy, we went through the Vega Vault together. Shortly thereafter Henry reached out to ask if there were any unreleased songs in the Vega Vault that we could use for a limited edition seven-inch for Record Store Day. He and Larry Hardy of In the Red Records would release it. Jared and I found a track titled "Murder One." The title grabbed our attention and the vocal and soundtracks matched its intensity. It was a nine-minute sonic assault. We mixed it and sent it to Henry, who agreed it was killer.

In Alan's photography archive, I found photos he had taken of statues of a bishop. These were used for the back cover art. The RSD limited edition seven-inch immediately sold out. Jared and I got so many requests online from people who hadn't been able to purchase it that Jared joked: "I'm giving them Henry's beeper number!"

Soon we were back to organizing 6/8 recordings in the Vega Vault. Scanning through track titles, I immediately saw there were songs Alan had intended for an album titled Mutator. The original ADATs of these recordings were in the 6/8 Studios box.

Our first major Vega Vault project was now dawning. Ted put the Mutator tracks into Pro Tools sessions. Jared and I mixed the tracks while Dante observed Ted's engineering process. Everything was filtered through the Vega lens with the mantra "what would Alan want?" Having played the machines on most of the tracks and witnessing Alan's sonic choices over the decades, I intuitively knew. I also knew he would tell me there are no mistakes or expectations—just open yourself to let the sound move through you—as the vessel.

He strongly believed you couldn't create something the same way today as you had yesterday. We completed these songs in a different time and place. Jared also instinctively knew Alan's aesthetic.

Jared Artaud

The moment Liz and I discovered the original ADAT tapes of *Mutator*, we knew we had found something special. The tape transfers revealed the original recording sessions from twenty-five years ago. The songs were in a raw and unmixed state, but Alan's vision was permanently embedded in those recordings. His performances and sounds were truly powerful, singular, and rife with intention. The better part of the last couple years leading up to the release of *Mutator* was spent producing and mixing the album. Liz and I wanted to make sure we kept Alan's vision intact, but also wanted the record to be a cohesive release that honored the past yet also brought the material into today. The themes Alan was exploring lyrically twenty-five years ago are still relevant now.

For me, the album's archetypal sonic framework is about balancing intensity with calm. Music you can do yoga to or blast during a riot. Vega's lyrics inspire strength for the individual to rise up and destroy those destroying us. *Mutator*'s mantra is blistering poetic truths that balance a dark vision with hope.

Working on this album, I was blown away by the sheer intensity and raw power of Alan's ability to transform sound and deliver inimitable one-take vocal performances. "Nike Soldier" is a supreme example of Alan's unparalleled instincts.

At the heart of it all, Alan was a poet. His lyrics always hit hard, and he was always pushing forward, trailblazing onto the next idea of his vision. ∎

***

Liz: Alan was quoted in interviews saying as he evolved as an artist he learned not to focus on what other people thought about his work with the exception of Liz, Ric, and a few others, including Henry. After spending many hours talking with Jared in the short but deep time they had together, Alan saw a kindred spirit and said he was "passing the torch" to Jared. We were confident Alan would stand by the choices we made.

Our mission was to stay true to Vega's vision while bringing Mutator *into the here and now for release. We referred to the record as the "lost album" as it had, in effect, been lost in the Vault at the time I had taken a hiatus from the studio in 1997. After we finished recording these songs, Alan moved ahead to work on the tracks that became the next studio album release, 2007.*

When thinking about releasing Mutator, *the Sacred Bones label—home to Jim Jarmusch, David Lynch, and John Carpenter—sprung to mind as synergistic with Vega. Alan's music was cinematic, creating soundscapes and mood—the auditory counterpart to his visual art. Label owner Caleb Braaten's initial reaction was that many of the artists on his label were making music due in part to the influence of Alan Vega. Upon hearing* Mutator *he was keen to align with us for its release.*

***

With a team in place working closely in alignment with a label that shared our vision and mission, we were well positioned to get Mutator *seen and heard. The Vega Vault team, including Michael Handis as creative director of marketing, designed the packaging and coordinated efforts on the campaign with the great Sacred Bones team. The brilliant film director Jacqueline Castel was tapped by Sacred Bones to create a video for the single "Nike Soldier," starring Alan Vega and Kris Esfandiari, and featuring Alan's trademark style and both* Jet *and* Holy Ghost *light sculptures. Michael and Jared reached out to Douglas Hart of the Jesus and Mary Chain to do a visualizer for "Muscles," creating a collage of images curated by Handis.*

Mutator *was released in the spring of 2021 and the reception was powerful. The press included a feature article in the* New York Times—*"Alan Vega Left a Robust Vault. The Excavation Begins with a New Album"—focusing on the vast amount of music Alan had left behind. Jared and I were interviewed for the article and described our mission to build Alan's legacy, including bringing his unreleased sound recordings to the public.*

Shortly after Mutator *came the release of* Alan Vega After Dark *on In the Red Records. This album, recorded in 2015, captured a one-night rockabilly blues–infused session with Ben Vaughn, Barb Dwyer, and Palmyra Delran (all members of Pink Slip Daddy) and it was time to unleash it. Ben made a video for the track entitled "Nothing Left."*

***

It took a while after Alan's passing to find the right time to record and release my first solo album, Keep it Alive.

During the Covid pandemic, Dante and I were in lockdown together, living through unprecedented times with no end in sight. For a few years, I'd been keeping journals of my thoughts and observations. Over the years, Alan often said I should make solo records. A key roadblock had been not knowing if I had something meaningful enough to say. Yet I'd learned from Alan that what mattered most was that my words and feelings were genuine.

And then two profound things happened early in the pandemic that rocked my core. In March of 2020, my father passed away after a short non-Covid illness. At ninety-four, he'd lived a long and robust life. For many years, we'd still enjoyed regular Sunday chats—his insights and advice were razor sharp. He'd always had a hardy constitution and was rarely sick, so it was still a shock to lose him so suddenly. And because of the pandemic we were not able to visit him or have any type of memorial service after he died. Then within weeks, my brother Kent was diagnosed with glioblastoma, an aggressive form of brain cancer. He was sixty-four and still playing ice hockey on

Friday nights during the New England winters—the picture of health. It was gut-wrenchingly hard to accept how unfair it was that he had to face such a brutal battle destined to take him out way too early.

The fleeting and unpredictable nature of life was smacking me in the face. The certainty of uncertainty. It was time to create my debut album.

By then, Dante had been engineering recording sessions with hip-hop artists at home in Dujang Prang Studios. Covid brought that to a halt—so, now I had a captive engineer with time on his hands!

Dante expressed some initial hesitation saying, "It's not my genre," to which I replied, "I'm making my own genre."

He soon realized, like his dad placing no limits or labels on his creations, he could help me "execute my vision," regardless of where that might take us.

It was an incredible process and we learned so much from each other. Dante has great technical skill and knowledge of music theory. He has an exceptionally strong ear—it had long ago been determined he has perfect pitch. And he appreciated my intuitive creative process. He remarked that we were both fortunate to have grown up relying on our ears, unlike many of his peer engineers and producers who have only worked in the digital world. We eschewed preprogrammed patterns and autocorrect.

When the songs were fundamentally complete, I sent the tracks to Jared, who did a great job remotely coproducing the arrangements to bring my album over the finish line. Michael Handis designed the artwork.

My goal for Keep It Alive was to take adversity and uncertainty and turn it into a message of resilience and empowerment. This meant I had to be brave enough to play it for others! On the short list was Henry Rollins. True to form, he listened and got back to me right away. He told me he loved every track, and if I didn't yet have release plans he'd like to send it to Larry Hardy at In the Red Records. He knew Larry was aware of the collaborations I had done with Alan over the years, and thought he'd like this album.

I was so grateful for the suggestion and gave Henry the green light. The next week Larry called me to discuss releasing it. I was blown away. Larry was incredibly supportive in all aspects of ensuring a great debut release including videos for several tracks, directed by the ultra-talented Jenni Hensler. Alan would love Larry Hardy. He is the real deal. And I know Vega is proud of my creative evolution. I can feel him cheering me on.

I was so inspired—I didn't stop recording music. Dante and I had locked into a great flow working together. I composed music for eight more songs that would be the foundation for a collaboration with hip-hop artist Slykat, who was a friend of one of the boxers I managed. We'd met ringside at a fight in 2019. Together with Dante engineering and coproducing, we made an album titled Unwitnessed Protection (UP). One of the tracks is an homage to Alan's "Cheap Soul Crash" off the album 2007. It's called *"Crash Cheap Soul"* and contains a sound track and alternate Vega vocal from the original song's early recording sessions found in the Vega Vault. It's the first example of what the Vega Vault team is planning for many further collaborations, as we intend to invite other musicians to create songs in collaboration with Vega's vocals and sounds.

***

In November of 2022, Dante, Allison, and I went to France and London to perform concerts of the Keep It Alive *album. I had never performed my solo music live and didn't have a track record for solo touring.*

Marc Hurtado invited me to open for his ongoing concert series with Lydia Lunch, combining songs from the Vega/Hurtado Sniper collaboration and classic Suicide songs. Lydia brings her own magic and poetry to the mix, and it is a very dynamic and powerful show. I knew it would be a strong fit with my solo music to open the night.

By then, I had recorded several songs for my next solo album. The first new song I wrote was dedicated to Alan and titled *"King City Ghost: King of the Bums."* For each of the seven shows, I started my set with this song, followed by the seven tracks on Keep It Alive *and ended by playing "Crash Cheap Soul" from* Unwitnessed Protection. Alan's was the last voice on the song and the perfect transition to Lydia and Marc's show.

Although Dante had never done live sound, he worked alongside the house sound person at each venue and learned a lot. Allison added to the stage show with backup singing and dancing as well as being a great help with the logistics of the tour. I'm deeply grateful for the very positive reception from the wonderful people who came to the shows. I've since done a few solo performances in NYC and aspire to continue evolving as a performer and recording artist.

My second solo album One Never Knows, *is slated for a 2024 release on In the* Red Records.

***

By the end of 2021, BMG UK *had decided to release the first Suicide compilation album. I reached out to Henry, Jared, and Michael to get their input. Jared and Henry weighed in with Martin Rev on song choices. Michael Handis and Jared designed the packaging, which turned out to be iconic white on white with a stunning silver gatefold containing portraits of Alan and Marty. They also suggested the title* Surrender.

> *Surrender* is provocative for the Suicide visual catalog because it fully commits itself to serenity and elegance. The world expected black and red, but we gave them white and chrome—a total palette cleanser. We believed it was important to show zero allegiance to any specific era of Suicide iconography, more so fetishizing minimalism, hypnosis, and severity—timeless codes of the band's sound.*
>
> —Michael Handis

---

* Interview Michael Handis, May 2023.

Liz: The Vega Vault team went into the archives for bonus tracks and found the original studio version of "Frankie Teardrop." Alan had initially recorded the song with lyrics about a detective and an alien, and this version had never been released. Michael and Jared reached out again to Douglas Hart to create a twelve-minute film for "Frankie Teardrop." The result was hypnotic and mesmerizing.

Surrender *was followed up with the reissue of Suicide's* A Way of Life *in the spring of 2023.*

Shortly after, Sacred Bones launched back-to-back releases of a Record Store Day seven-inch edition of "Jukebox Babe" and then a twelve-inch of "Invasion" b/w "Murder One."

✳✳✳

When Alan's last studio album, IT, *was released in 2017, I made the decision to leave the last song, "Invasion" off the album. Alan had taken almost all vocals off the track. For the release of this song, Jared and I decided to put Vega's vocal back in. "Invasion" became the transition to the next Vega lost album release.*

Jared and I had moved on to the next group of songs in the Vega Vault. "Murder One" was part of this collection and we thought "Invasion"—having been recorded twenty years later but still fitting seamlessly into these songs—was a great bridge to the past. We titled this next album Insurrection *and it's slated for a 2024 release on In the Red Records.*

✳✳✳

Alan Vega is becoming recognized as a fashion icon. Some of the styles he created out of necessity were popularized by more mainstream artists. When Michael and Jared began posting curated Vega images on social media, the uniqueness of his style, as well as its evolution over the years, became a key focal point of his followers.

> Alan Vega is one of the least credited fashion icons in the history of punk and electronic music. Each and every designer who has ever attempted to catch the lightning-in-a-bottle energy of the so-called punk aesthetic is deeply indebted to Alan's personal style and nuance. His devotion to Elvis and doo-wop clearly informed his iconic use of leather and Western wear. However, his art-haus twist on performance, mutilation, and public crucifixion pushed these dress codes into uncharted territories.*
> —Michael Handis

✳✳✳

Liz: Starting in 2019 Marc Jacobs licensed Suicide's "Dream Baby Dream" for their Daisy perfume commercial and a few years later started licensing "Cheree" which is an ongoing staple of their Daisy campaign. In 2019, Shane Gonzales of Midnight

---

* Interview Michael Handis, May 2023.

Studios reached out to us suggesting a collaboration with Vega. This resulted in a capsule collection titled "American Dreamer" utilizing Alan's lyrics, cross art from the cover of Righteous Lite, *and the Ric Ocasek portraits of Alan's face circa 1995. The collection included high-quality jerseys and hoodies with Alan's face and his artwork as well his titles such as "Goodbye Darling." Midnight Studios has steadily grown as a highly respected brand and counts many professional athletes and musicians amongst its ardent devotees. Alan would have enjoyed seeing his larger-than-life face on the jerseys worn for the ad campaign by* NFL *star Marquis Christian and rapper Playboi Carti.*

Iconic and beloved French fashion designer Agnes b has long loved Suicide and Vega's music and art. For the Sacred Bones release of the twelve-inch "Invasion" b/w "Murder One," Agnes b did a limited edition run of top-quality long-sleeved T-shirts emblazoned with Vega's titles on the sleeves.

In 2021, highly regarded Belgian designer Dries Van Noten chose "Dream Baby Dream" for their runway/ad campaign and to use the lyrics on several pieces in the men's AW *2022/23 collection. The title was emblazoned on sweaters and a beautiful satin bomber jacket—all of which immediately sold out.*

At the beginning of 2023, we were contacted by Celine's creative team. Hedi Slimane was interested in using Suicide's song "Girl" for the runway/ad campaign for the FW *23/24 collection inspired by Hedi's club era. Jared worked with Hedi to create an extended version of the song to play throughout the runway show. The music and Vega's seductive voice set the mood for the models, embodying young Alan and Marty swagger in the black leather and glamour-infused collection. At Michael and Jared's suggestion, Hedi decided to license Vega art collages for use in the collection. Celine invited the Vega Vault team to Paris to attend the runway show and incredible after party at Le Palace. It was an unforgettable night and we felt Alan's presence throughout.*

Currently, there are a number of Alan Vega multimedia art exhibitions in the works, highlighting the intersection of art, music, and fashion.

This reality echoes what Jeffrey Deitch said about the sphere of Vega's influence when he reconnected with

© GODLIS

Alan to mount the Collision Drive exhibition at Deitch Projects in 2002. It's all come full circle.

Vega's two vital symbols were the cross and infinity—the lines of the cross meet in Infinity—where Alan lives. As Henry Rollins says—Alan Vega is forever.

***

In the early '70s, Alan was sitting in a café in the east village, deeply embedded in the jumble of small round tables. He had chosen to sit at the back of the crowded room. He was drinking his coffee and writing in his notebook when he felt a presence and looked up from the page. Standing in the open doorway, at the opposite end of the room, was a figure lit from behind like an apparition. Alan couldn't see his features, but saw the outline of his long coat, gray hair, and beard. He couldn't take his eyes off this man. Somehow, Alan knew he was coming to him. He wove his way through the tables, stopping directly in front of Alan. In a loud and clear voice, he stated: "I am the king of the bums! And when I die, you will be the king of the bums!"

Alan took that to heart. He never forgot that prophecy.

© Photo - Mats Bäcker

"We're all Frankies."

INDEX

Page numbers in italics refer to figures. Page numbers beginning with p refer to figures in photospreads.